"Thom Rainer has gone through the correct source to find out what is wrong with the church—that is, those who were formerly the unchurched. As he has surveyed them, he has collected valuable data to tell us why we are not reaching the unsaved, what we must do to reach them, and how to go about doing it. Rainer provides insight that we have not previously known or heard. Reading this book will help you rethink your approach to evangelism."

—Elmer L. Towns, Dean
School of Religion, Liberty University

"Thom Rainer, one of the foremost church consultants in America, always gets to the heart of an issue, and it's nowhere more apparent than in this book. What he says here breaks new ground in church growth research. For pastors and others aspiring to lead God's people, this is must reading."

—Robert E. Coleman
Director of the School of World Mission
and Evangelism
Trinity International University

"Thom Rainer has written a book that validates what we believed all along—God is at work building his kingdom! In that kingdom there is much diversity of method and means, but only one King. This book has *Surprising Insights* that remind us God works through churches,who follow the Leader—to seek and to save those who are lost."

—Nancy Grisham
Assistant Director
Billy Graham Institute of Evangelism
Wheaton College

"Church leaders—especially ministers—will find this book an invaluable resource for developing a congregation that is effectual in carrying out its evangelistic mission. It garners, affirms, and illustrates some things you may already know about how to help unchurched people to become disciples. It may also cause you to rethink some things you have assumed to be true. And it will introduce factors you may not have thought of yet. The solid statistical findings are fleshed out by examples, making it refreshingly readable and easy to apply."

—Joe Ellis
Distinguished Professor of Practical Ministries
Cincinnati Bible Seminary

"Thom Rainer does an outstanding job helping pastors fulfill Christ's mission 'to seek and save that which was lost.' This book is full of relevant information that inspires us to go against the grain of popular thinking. This book will stimulate creative ideas and help your church develop new, productive methods of evangelism."

—Bob Russell
Senior Minister, Southeast Christian Church
Louisville, Kentucky

"This book is an absolute must read for every pastor and layperson interested in reaching the unchurched. It provides reliable and practical information to equip today's churches for ministry to the lost."

—Beverly LaHaye, Chairman
Concerned Women for America

"No one knows church growth and evangelism like Thom Rainer. He combines solid research with keen analysis—and comes to some surprising conclusions. The greatest evangelistic task facing the churches of North America today is reaching a generation of the unchurched with the Gospel, then guiding new believers to faithful discipleship. Every honest pastor knows this already. Thom Rainer now offers us a view into the mind of the unchurched. Every concerned Christian should read this book—and then go after the unchurched American."

—R. Albert Mohler Jr., President
The Southern Baptist Theological Seminary
Louisville, Kentucky

"This book is packed with 'surprising insights' based on careful research and important anecdotal perspectives that will provide a wealth of information and powerful applications for church leaders across denominational lines. If every pastor and church leader would read this book and implement the purposeful and intentional strategies and findings that Thom Rainer has brought to light, the church's impact in the secularized society of the twenty-first century could be greatly enhanced."

—David S. Dockery
President, Union University

"An excellent resource with fresh insight. Several convictions were reinforced, new ideas were generated, and some surprises surfaced. You will be challenged by what Thom has surfaced, and your church can gain many practical insights for Great Commandment and Great Commission health."

—Dann Spader
Executive Director, Sonlife Ministries

"I love Thom Rainer's opinions because they are based on solid fact. Here is a book like none other on how you can make the kind of adjustments in your church in order to maximize the harvest of the unchurched in your community. No action-oriented church leader can afford to miss this book!"

—C. Peter Wagner, Chancellor
Wagner Leadership Institute

"During the past decade Thom Rainer has become known as one of the most creative thinkers and evangelism strategists in the evangelical church. This is a path-breaking book: It explodes myths and stretches stereotypes about reaching unchurched people for Christ. Those who have quit preaching and thrown out doctrine need to take another look and another read!"

—Timothy George
Dean of Beeson Divinity School
of Samford University

"Rather than speculating or theorizing about what *might* reach people for Christ, Thom Rainer and team actually talked to those who *have* been reached, as well as the pastors and churches reaching them. This book is a fascinating compilation of what he learned—and worth its weight in gold for any Christian leader who is serious about fulfilling the Great Commission."

—Mark Mittelberg
Author of *Building a Contagious Church*

"Thom Rainer has been a valued and trusted friend over the years. This survey of the formerly unchurched provides a wealth of insight and guidance for church leaders to consider. Ministers and laymen alike would do well to consider this information."

—T. W. Wilson
Billy Graham Evangelistic Association

SURPRISING INSIGHTS
FROM THE UNCHURCHED

and Proven Ways to Reach Them

SURPRISING INSIGHTS
FROM THE UNCHURCHED

and Proven Ways to Reach Them

Thom S. Rainer

Dean of the Billy Graham
School of Missions, Evangelism and Church Growth

ZONDERVAN™

GRAND RAPIDS, MICHIGAN 49530

ZONDERVAN™

Surprising Insights from the Unchurched and Proven Ways to Reach Them
Copyright © 2001 by Thom Rainer

Requests for information should be addressed to:

Zondervan, *Grand Rapids, Michigan 49530*

Library of Congress Cataloging-in-Publication Data

Rainer, Thom S.
  Surprising insights from the unchurched and proven ways to reach them /
Thom S. Rainer.
     p. cm.
  Includes bibliographical references and index.
  ISBN 0-310-23648-7 (hardcover : alk. paper)
  1. Non church-affiliated people—United States. 2. Evangelistic work—
United States. I. Title.
  BR526 .R35 2001
  269'.2—dc21   2001026152
                                                      CIP

This edition printed on acid-free paper.

Interior design by Nancy Wilson

Printed in the United States of America

01 02 03 04 05 06 07 08 / ❖ DC / 10 9 8 7 6 5 4 3 2 1

To
John Emfinger
No better friend
has any man known

and always to
Nellie Jo
my wife, my joy, my love

Contents

PART ONE

Listening to the
Formerly Unchurched

PART TWO

Leaders of Churches
That Reach the Unchurched

List of Figures

Acknowledgments

W hat if?" I asked. "What if we asked new Christians and new church members what led them to the Savior and to the church they chose?" That simple question became a pursuit of passion for me. Over a period of nearly two years my research team and I interviewed over 350 of these new Christians, a group we called "the formerly unchurched." Their responses and insights became an inspirational and eye-opening experience for those of us involved in this project.

As in all of my projects that ultimately became books, an entire team of talented individuals are involved in the research and production of this work. Special thanks go to Sherrie Drake, Karis Ward, Cheryl Smartt, Susan Barnes, Todd Randolph, Gary Chronister, Chris Spradley, and Ahkeem Abdul Morella. Their efficient and diligent work and their own excitement about this project were a joy to observe. A special thanks goes to Brad Morrow, who led the research team and who was always available to go the extra mile with a great attitude.

I am especially grateful to the 353 "formerly unchurched" who gave our team thousands of hours of their valuable time. I am convinced that their sacrificial attitude will make a difference for God's kingdom. Though their names are omitted so that they might have complete freedom to share their experience, I hope most of them will see in this book the importance of their contributions.

More than 100 pastors of effective evangelistic churches were also interviewed for this book as well as 350 longer-term Christians (whom we called the "transfer churched"). My thanks for their time and patience as we compared their insights to those of the formerly unchurched.

Throughout the book I move back and forth from the first-person singular to the first-person plural. Much of the hard work was done by my research team (the "we" passages), yet at times I did my own follow-up interviews and research (the "I" passages).

The ministry staff of the churches in this study included men and women. Because it is often cumbersome to refer to both genders continually, I often use generic pronouns in the book. I am grateful to all the men and women who shared their insights with me.

This book is my first effort with Zondervan, and it has been a joy. I have been impressed with this group of fine Christians from my first day of involvement with them. Thank you especially to editor Paul Engle. Paul, your professionalism and Christian commitment made this work a labor of joy.

This project represents my twelfth authored or coauthored book. In every case, I stand amazed at the patience, commitment, and love of my family. I no longer have three boys; I have three sons who are fine young men. To Sam Rainer, Art Rainer, and Jess Rainer, thank you, guys, for always encouraging me and always loving me. God blessed me immeasurably with each of you.

Finally, I thank my Lord for my wife, Nellie Jo Rainer. No man has ever been so blessed with a wife so special. Nellie Jo, in your beauty and contagious smile, I see love for me, for our family, and for the God we serve together. This book never could have been written without your support and love. Thank you always, doll. May the next twenty-four years of marriage be as great as the first!

INTRODUCTION

Meet Donna and Joe

Yeah, I've tried church a few times.
One of the deadest places I've ever been.

—"LAGirl1" in the Jesus Only
Internet Chat Room

Donna C. was happy with her life. She met Brian at college in the late 1980s, and they were married in 1991. She felt even more blessed with the birth of two daughters.

"I guess I was really beginning to fit the soccer mom role," Donna told us. "Kari, our oldest daughter, was very involved in the peewee soccer league, dance lessons, and kindergarten. I decided to quit my job and devote full time to the kids. Brian was very supportive."

Donna and Brian's home was not the typical starter house of a young couple. Brian had landed a job with a fairly new high-tech company in the Detroit area, and the quick success of the company translated into higher salaries and bonuses for him. The couple built their dream home in a Detroit suburb before they turned thirty.

Donna and Brian's religious background could be described easily: nonexistent. Indeed, the couple represented a growing segment in the profile of religious affiliations in America; they were a second-generation unchurched family. Their parents did not attend church, nor did they encourage their children in any religious direction. Brian had some religious influence from his grandparents, but it was minimal.

17

After Melissa, their second child, was born, Donna suggested to Brian that the children might benefit from some kind of religious training at their young ages. Brian did not object, but soccer, sleep, and apathy usually had priority over any attempts at church attendance. In the past year the family had attended church twice.

Nevertheless, Donna told us she was happy. "I had a great family. Brian was making good money. We lived in a great neighborhood. Life seemed good," she reflected. Then the bomb dropped.

Brian arrived at home after 9:00 P.M. one Tuesday. His work hours had become longer, which concerned Donna. She tried not to complain, because she knew Brian was working hard to provide an upscale standard of living. Nevertheless, she was worried that Brian was becoming more distant from her and the girls. She was right. But Donna underestimated how distant Brian had become.

"I remember his words so clearly," Donna said slowly. "He told me he loved Susan, and that he was leaving me to be with her." The interview paused while Donna regained her composure.

"Susan was a coworker. She had an outgoing personality. I liked her. I knew she and Brian were spending a lot of time together at work, but I did not think. . . . I guess I was too naïve," Donna said quietly.

The bomb that dropped devastated Donna's life. The divorce was quick. Brian agreed to give Donna most of the couple's assets, mainly furniture and household items. They had little savings. Neither of them could keep the house, because it was almost fully mortgaged. Donna kept the girls.

"I never considered I would be a single mom. I guess I was fortunate that my parents lived across town. Even with the money coming from Brian, I could not afford a house," she said matter-of-factly. Donna and the girls moved in with her parents for seven months.

"There is one big blessing that came out of this tragedy," Donna said. "I had noticed that Mom had changed a good bit over the past seven months. She seemed happier and more at peace than I had ever known." While living with her parents, Donna learned that her mother had been attending a Bible study with a group of ladies from a growing Presbyterian church about ten miles from her home. Donna's mother soon became a Christian and joined the church.

The decision was simple. So much of Donna's happiness was connected to things that were now gone: her husband, her home, and her upper-middle-class lifestyle. What could fill the void? She decided to give church a try. The natural choice was her mother's church.

The friendliness of the Presbyterian church members impressed Donna. The worship service seemed joyous and relaxed. The style was a bit more contemporary than churches she had visited with Brian.

One major factor attracted Donna back to the church: the pastor and his preaching. "I never realized before that the Bible had anything to do with my life. Pastor Frank's messages are so relevant. Yet he explains the Bible in its historical background. His preaching helps me to understand the Bible, which makes me desire to study it even more."

Donna's difficulties had a happy ending. She became a Christian and joined the church. Nine months later she met Ted in a single-again Sunday school class. They recently announced their engagement.

Donna C. and the Formerly Unchurched

Donna C. is one of several million people in America whom we call "the formerly unchurched." By our definition, a formerly unchurched person is one who has not been in church, except sporadically, for at least ten years (most for a lifetime) but has recently become active in a church. All of the formerly unchurched have also recently become Christians, not merely church attenders.

What did we learn from Donna and others like her? This book will explore those issues, but note some of the factors directly related to Donna:

- Two major factors prompted her to "try" a church: a crisis in her life and a relationship with someone who was active in a church. But Donna and many others shared with us that the relationship was more of a factor than the crisis.
- Relationships with churched family members or relatives were vitally important.
- For Donna, the church name was hardly a factor in her decision to attend. The fact that her mother attended was the key issue.
- Donna, like most of the formerly unchurched we interviewed, was not totally ignorant about church or religious issues.
- Donna also displayed a common characteristic of other formerly unchurched. She did not ignore churches altogether when she was

unchurched, but her attendance was very sporadic, perhaps once or twice a year.

- So why did Donna stay with the church she eventually joined? From a human perspective, the pastor and his preaching were key. More on this issue later.

The Formerly Unchurched Project

I am very grateful for the years of research on the unchurched by out-standing Christian leaders and even some secular writers. This book does not attempt to diminish the value of their contributions. Indeed, some of their findings are used in the context of this book. My concern, however, is that we need to focus some of our questions and research on a group that has been largely ignored—the formerly unchurched. Most research of recent years has asked questions of those not attending church, that is, the unchurched. A possible problem with this approach is that as many as 80 to 90 percent of this group may never attend church.[1] In other words, we could be developing strategies to reach a sector of the population, which, despite our best efforts, will never attend church.

> We could be developing strategies to reach a sector of the population, which, despite our best efforts, will never attend church.

Why not ask questions of those who did make the transition from the unchurched to the churched? Why not ask what influenced them to come to church and perhaps to become Christians? Since they were the receptive and responsive people, perhaps the principles we learn from reaching the formerly unchurched can be applied to reaching the presently unchurched.

> Perhaps the principles we learn from reaching the formerly unchurched can be applied to reaching the presently unchurched.

For example, we learned from Donna C. that she chose the church that she eventually joined because of a crisis in her life, because her mother was active in the church, because the church was friendly, and because she liked the pastor and his preaching. When we look closely at all of the formerly unchurched responses to this issue, the insights are fascinating. Indeed, we will analyze the chart in figure I.1 more fully in chapter 2.

Figure I.1

What Factors Led You to Choose This Church?

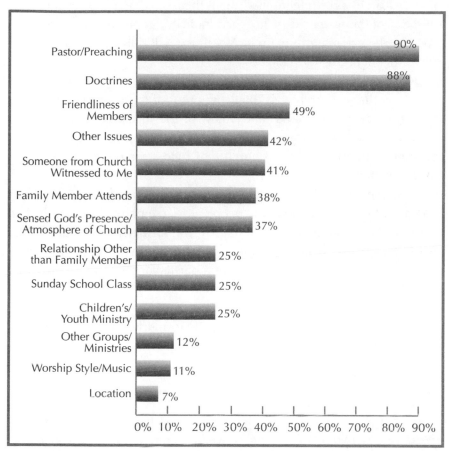

This simple graph (figure I.1) alone could speak volumes to a strategy for reaching the unchurched. Almost all of the formerly unchurched, for example, told us that they used to come to a church on a very sporadic basis. They were not totally boycotting churches. So if they did indeed make that occasional visit, what factors would encourage them to return?

The graph shows us that issues related to the pastor and his preaching were overwhelming reasons that the formerly unchurched came back for another visit. The issues of the pastor and the pastor's preaching and leadership were so critical in our study that the second portion of this book examines these fascinating issues. I'll have more on this item later.

Another major factor that led the formerly unchurched to a particular church was the personal witness of a church member. We hear very little in the research of the unchurched about the issue of personal evangelism. Yet many of the formerly unchurched indicated to us that it was a major factor in their coming to church. Again, we will delve into this issue in greater detail in the next chapter.

Does doctrine matter to the unchurched? Although we sometimes stereotype the unchurched as totally ignorant of biblical teachings, such an assumption is not always valid. Many of the formerly unchurched in our study did know basic doctrinal issues before they became Christians, and they were attracted to a church that held strong convictions about biblical matters.

Other recent research on the church seems to complement our study. One study looked at reasons why people attend a particular church. The study surveyed church attenders, not just the formerly unchurched. The formerly unchurched, however, would be included in the totals. The number one reason given for the choice of a particular church was the theological beliefs and doctrine of that church.[2]

These are a few samples of the issues we will be addressing as we further investigate the fascinating world of the formerly unchurched. Before we proceed, I want to introduce you to the process we used to get our data through a series of questions and answers.

- Who are the formerly unchurched?

The formerly unchurched are people who have recently (typically within the past two years) become active in a church. For all or a large portion of their lives they were not in church. Some of the formerly unchurched considered themselves Christians even when they did not attend a church. Most were not Christians before they found a church home. We interviewed 353 of these persons.

- Why are you studying the formerly unchurched instead of the unchurched?

The study of either group is valuable in helping us understand better how to reach the lost population of our nation. We chose the formerly unchurched for two reasons. First, very little research has been conducted on this group. Second, when they tell us why they chose a church, we have an actual case study of someone moving from the ranks of the unchurched to the churched. When the unchurched tell us what *might* attract them to a church, we do not know for certain if they will respond as they indicated.

- Where did you find these people you called the formerly unchurched?

Over the past six years our research teams have studied more than two thousand effective evangelistic churches.[3] We asked some of these churches for the names, addresses, and telephone numbers of the formerly unchurched who now attend their churches. These people represent seven denominations, independent Christian churches, independent Baptist churches, community churches, and other nondenominational churches.

Figure I.2

Formerly Unchurched Were Represented by Different Denominations

- Assembly of God
- Evangelical Free Church of America
- Nazarene Church
- Presbyterian Church of America
- Southern Baptist Convention
- United Methodist Church
- Wesleyan Church
- Thirty-seven churches represented independent Christian churches, independent Baptist churches, community churches, and other nondenominational groups.

- What do you mean by an "effective evangelistic church"?

We defined an effective evangelistic church to be a church that has at least twenty-six conversions per year and a conversion ratio (membership/annual conversion) of less than 20:1. (The conversion ratio attempts to discern how many church members it takes to reach one person for Christ in a year. The national norm for churches in America is 85:1.) Less than 4 percent of churches in America meet both criteria.

- How did you conduct the survey?

Our research team conducted most of the interviews over the telephone. A few were done in person. We asked "cluster questions," that is, questions that often led to other issues. Appendix 1 is a list of the cluster questions asked by our interviewers.

- Are all the stories in this book factual?

Yes, with an explanation. We promised the formerly unchurched and the leaders of the churches anonymity in the surveys and interviews. Most of the personal names and church names are fictitious. On some occasions we combined the stories of a few formerly unchurched into a single story to avoid a fragmented illustration. The stories themselves are factual.

- Where do these formerly unchurched whom you studied live?

Every major geographic region of the United States was represented in our study. The formerly unchurched in our study live in thirty-seven states (shown in white) and represent a variety of demographic regions, from rural communities to urban areas to suburban communities.

- Did you interview anyone other than the formerly unchurched?

Yes. When we discovered the vitally important role the pastor plays in reaching the unchurched, we conducted an extensive survey and interview with the leaders of effective evangelistic churches. The entire second section of this book looks at these issues.

We also interviewed a group we called the "transfer churched." These are 350 Christians who have moved from one church to another. We were interested in learning the similarities and differences between the unchurched and the churched in looking for a church home. For example, the doctrinal beliefs of a church were important to both the formerly unchurched and the transfer churched.

Figure I.3a and I.3b

Were the Beliefs of the Church Important in Your Decision to Come to Your Church?

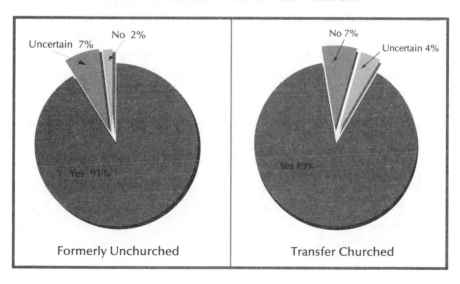

Formerly Unchurched | Transfer Churched

We found that many churches have developed strategies that reach Christians from other churches rather than reaching non-Christians and the unchurched. By comparing the two groups, we can perhaps help churches adjust their strategies more specifically for the unchurched.

A final group we surveyed were 101 pastors of "comparison churches." A comparison church did not meet our criteria to be an effective evangelistic church. We found that by comparing the pastors of the two groups we could discern why one group is more successful than the other in reaching the unchurched.

- Do the churches of the formerly unchurched represent different denominations?

Yes. The formerly unchurched represent churches of seven different major denominations plus numerous independent and nondenominational churches.

- Are there any biases in your study?

Undoubtedly. No study, including our own, is bias-free. From the development of the survey questions, to the interview process itself, to the interpretation of the data, biases may influence the study. We have done our best to maintain objectivity, including asking several "outsiders" to evaluate the objectivity of our approach and interpretation.[4] We also cannot claim that our study of hundreds of persons is a perfect statistical representation of the population of the United States. Interview-based studies tend to have more depth than breadth. Nevertheless, we feel confident that the information gleaned from our study is a good portrayal of the formerly unchurched in America.

- Most studies on the unchurched seem to focus on churches that reach Anglo, middle-to-upper-class people. Does your study go in that direction?

No. Though the "suburban" model for reaching the unchurched described about one-half of those in our study, another 50 percent represent different socioeconomic and ethnic or racial groups. As a conclusion to this introductory chapter, I will introduce you to one such example.

Joe M.: Not Your Stereotypical Unchurched Person

Joe M., by his own admission, graduated from high school with "a little luck, a little cheating, a little work, and a lot of grace." Joe lives in a small town in eastern Kentucky. The town is poor, and Joe's high school diploma represents more education than that possessed by 30 percent of the town's adult residents.

Still Joe does okay for himself. He learned automobile mechanics from his father. He had a decent job at the local Ford dealership at age sixteen. He would have dropped out of school, but his mother successfully pleaded with him to stay.

"I always enjoyed partying," he confessed to us. "I wouldn't get dead drunk, but I had my share of the liquor." Joe M. was one of the swinging bachelors in his rural eastern Kentucky town.

Unlike Donna C., Joe had connections to the church. He was a regular Easter and Christmas visitor to Antioch Baptist Church ("I stayed away from First Baptist Church—bunch of snobs I always thought"). One time he even volunteered to be Joseph in the Christmas play.

Joe's parents had taken him to church on occasion until he turned seven years old. For reasons he cannot recall, the entire family stopped even their irregular attendance. Other than the special occasion visits, Joe was never in church. And even in his first seven years of life, his family's church attendance was sporadic at best.

Joe continued to enjoy the life of a bachelor through his twenty-second birthday. Then something happened that would change his life forever. "When I saw Stacijo, my jaws dropped wide open," he said with a mischievous grin. "I mean, she was a knockout. I remembered her from school, but she was three years younger than me, just a silly kid. I never paid any attention to her."

That is, until Stacijo became the new secretary at the Ford dealership. Joe almost tripped over his feet in his attempt to speak to her the first time. "I thought I was pretty smooth with women, you know," he told us. "But I couldn't even talk straight around Stacijo."

Joe made four futile attempts to ask Stacijo for a date. Finally, he pleaded with her to explain the continuous rejections. Simply stated, she said she only dated Christians. Stacijo would consider going out with Joe, however, if he agreed to talk to three men from Antioch Baptist Church. Anything for a chance for a date, Joe declared.

The three men who showed up at Joe's home on Tuesday night were training in Evangelism Explosion, a personal evangelism program originated by D. James Kennedy of the Coral Ridge Presbyterian Church in Ft. Lauderdale, Florida.

Joe's clear purpose in allowing the men to come over was to date Stacijo. But, as the men began to explain how Joe could become a Christian, "I forgot all about Stacijo," Joe declared. "God really got a hold of me that night. It's the greatest thing that ever happened to me."

Joe married Stacijo within six months of that fateful night. They are both very active at Antioch Baptist Church.

Joe M. and the Formerly Unchurched

Like Donna C., Joe M. is another of the several million people we call the formerly unchurched. But there are major cultural differences between the two. Sometimes we have a tendency to see the unchurched in stereotypical terms such as Anglo, suburban, and upper middle-class. Joe is Anglo, rural, and lower middle-class.

What did we learn from Joe M.? These and other significant issues will be addressed throughout our book:

- Joe M. considered himself religious and Baptist even though he was an unchurched non-Christian. Not all of the unchurched are turned off by religious language and structures.
- The name of the church, Baptist, *did* affect Joe's decision to join the church eventually. It was a name that, although he had only vague ideas about Baptist doctrine, gave him a level of comfort due to familiarity.
- Joe entered the ranks of the formerly unchurched and became a Christian when three men personally evangelized him.
- By far, the greatest influence on Joe's decision to become a Christian and to join a church was his wife-to-be. We heard of the influence of a wife dozens of times in our study.
- The friendliness of the people at the church influenced Joe. He specifically compared the friendly people at Antioch with the "cold fish at First Baptist."

Interestingly, although Donna C. and Joe M. mentioned favorably the friendliness of the church members, the formerly unchurched in our study did not hold friendliness to be as important as the transfer churched did. Figure I.4 shows that 41 percent of the formerly unchurched view friendliness as a major factor in joining a church, compared to 61 percent of the transfer churched.

Figure I.4a and I.4b

Was the Friendliness of the Church a Major Factor in Your Decision to Join That Church?

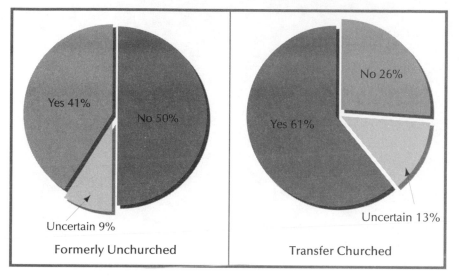

Formerly Unchurched — Yes 41%, No 50%, Uncertain 9%

Transfer Churched — No 26%, Yes 61%, Uncertain 13%

When the Unchurched Become Churched

Over 350 persons representing a diversity of locations, incomes, races, denominations, and backgrounds have provided us with a wealth of information. They have told us their stories of becoming Christians, of moving into the world of church membership. They have shared with us key reasons and key influences in this life-changing process. Our research team has listened carefully, and we have learned much.

Welcome to the world of the formerly unchurched. It is my prayer that you will have the same excitement and encouragement that I experienced in leading this study. And may that excitement motivate us all to reach an increasingly secular culture with the gospel of Jesus Christ, for the glory of God.

PART ONE

Listening to the Formerly Unchurched

In this first section we listen to specific issues from interviews with the formerly unchurched. Their insights and perspectives are nothing less than amazing, sometimes challenging conventional wisdom. Remember, as you listen to each formerly unchurched person, that each of them has been a Christian less than two years, most a year or less. You are thus hearing from people who have just left the world of the non-Christian unchurched and entered the world of the Christian churched. Their comments may surprise you.

CHAPTER 1

Shattering Myths about the Unchurched

You Christians really need help.

—"PM23" in the U4Christ
Internet Chat Room

Perhaps the reasons for writing this book are obvious. Perhaps if one wonders why we need research on the unchurched, the answer is easy: because we need to reach these people with the gospel of Jesus Christ.

Yet in my role as a church consultant, I find a lot of confusion about the lost and unchurched population. Many Christians do not realize how unevangelized and unchurched America has become.

Our Changing Country

Only 41 percent of Americans attend church services on a typical weekend.[1] Each new generation becomes increasingly unchurched. Slightly over one-half (51%) of the builder generation (born before 1946) attends church in a typical weekend. But only 41 percent of the boomers (born 1946 to 1964) and 34 percent of the busters (born 1965 to 1976) attend church on a given weekend.[2]

Our recent research on the younger generation, the bridgers (born 1977 to 1994), indicates that only 4 percent of the teenagers understand the gospel and have accepted Christ, even if they attend church.[3] Of the entire bridger generation, less than 30 percent attend church. America is

33

clearly becoming less Christian, less evangelized, and less churched. Yet too many of those in our churches seem oblivious to this reality. The primary concern for some is status quo for comfort's sake.

Figure 1.1

Who Attends Church in America Each Weekend?

Generation	Birth Years	Percentage Attending Church
Builders	Before 1946	51%
Boomers	1946 to 1964	41%
Busters	1965 to 1976	34%
Bridgers	1977 to 1994	29%

The growing ranks of the unchurched are not due to problems limited to certain geographical areas. For certain there are areas like Yolo County, California, in which only 28 percent of residents are claimed by any church, probably because of the influence of New Age and other alternative religions and the presence of the University of California–Davis.[4] While we shake our heads knowingly that Yolo County is 72 percent unchurched, do we realize that areas like Menifee County, Kentucky (population 5,200), are 87 percent unchurched?[5]

Nevertheless, religion and religious values remain vital to people. Over 80 percent of American adults said that "religious faith is very important in [their lives]."[6] Even groups that are often perceived to be less overtly religious affirmed the preceding statement, including residents of the Northeast (77%), single adults (79%), baby busters (81%), and liberals (74%) (see figure 1.2).[7]

> "At the same time that in America a multitude of new churches are being launched, and the mass media continue to report on the impact of megachurches, the number of unchurched adults is also on the rise."

Yet with religion being so important in the lives of the vast majority of Americans, church attendance and church affiliation have shown no improvement. The percentage of adults attending church on a given weekend in 1999 was the same level as it was in 1986.[8]

Despite a plethora of resources on reaching those who do not attend church, the population of the unchurched in America continues to

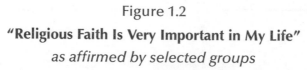

Figure 1.2

"Religious Faith Is Very Important in My Life"

as affirmed by selected groups

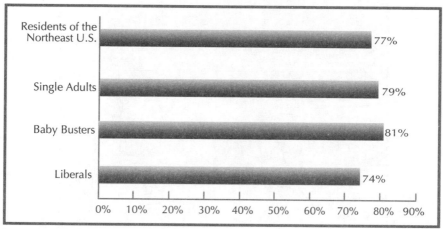

increase. Noted one Christian researcher, "At the same time that in America a multitude of new churches are being launched, and the mass media continue to report on the impact of megachurches, the number of unchurched adults is also on the rise."[9]

Our research team has come to similar conclusions. Less than 1 percent of churches in America meet our criteria to be an effective evangelistic church (see the definition in the introduction). And as noted earlier, only one person is reached for Christ for every 85 church members in America.

Paradigm Shifts in Methodologies But Not Principles

Once when my oldest son, Sam, was four years old, he started running a high fever. At first my wife and I were not too concerned, since young children often have fevers with viruses and infections. We calmly rationalized that his doctor could remedy the situation quickly.

The physician came to no conclusive diagnosis, and the fever did not break. We soon found ourselves in an emergency room with Sam, as numerous attendants tried again and again to get his fever to break. At one point the worried doctor looked at us and said, "Pray that we can find the problem. All we are doing now is treating the symptoms."

Only one person is reached for Christ for every
85 church members in America.

To this day I remember asking people to pray for his healing and to pray that the doctors would diagnose the problem. Thankfully, Sam is now a healthy young man completing college. The doctors never discovered the cause of Sam's illness. The fever broken without explanation.

Like that worried doctor, too many churches in America today have come to a diagnosis regarding the unchurched and are trying to treat symptoms. Only a small percentage of churches have recognized the problems of a growing lost and unchurched population in America. They have made intentional and successful efforts to reach the unchurched. They have been the "success stories" of evangelism that our research team has reported over the past decade.[10] Many churches, however, have been addressing only the symptoms. A certain worship style, the latest small group, a new church vernacular, or the "right" church name is seen as a panacea to the problem of not reaching the unchurched. Please understand my comments. Many times these "symptoms" need serious work. The church may need to change its worship style or rethink its name. Yet the real "treatment" must be at a deeper and more profound level.

As I have reported different phases of our research across the nation, some people have told me of churches that are growing with methods different than our research indicates. Certainly we have found a few exceptions. Upon further research, however, we found that most of these growing churches were not reaching the unchurched population; most of their growth was from the transfer of active Christian church members from other churches.

The Formerly Unchurched Share the Reality of the Status of the Unchurched

Our motivation in researching the formerly unchurched was to discover the problem that needed addressing rather than treating the symptoms only. Over 350 men and women who gave us their time and shared their hearts taught us much. Indeed, the formerly unchurched themselves shattered some myths about reaching the unchurched population. In this chapter I share nine of those myths.

Myth #1: Most unchurched think and act like Anglo, middle-class suburbanites with no church background.

Most people who read this book will acknowledge that the unchurched come from a variety of backgrounds. Yet most church strategies for intentionally reaching the unchurched in a particular community seem to be cookie-cutter approaches originating in areas that may have little in common with the church's community.

William B. is a twenty-three-year-old African-American with little church background. His grandmother, when asked by William what she wanted for her birthday, said simply, "I want you to go to church with me next Sunday." Reluctantly and seemingly trapped, William agreed.

William was pleasantly surprised. The Memphis-area Baptist church was alive with the hearty singing of black gospel music. The pastor was a great communicator who seemed to know how to speak to the African-American male. He pulled no punches on issues of sin, responsibility, and commitment.

No one had to invite William back to church, although several did. He asked his grandmother questions about God, Christ, and the gospel, and she patiently explained to him how he could become a Christian. He then became involved in various church ministries and programs.

"I just didn't know what I was missing," said William. "I can't understand why Christians aren't beating down doors to share the gospel. Why didn't someone tell me about Jesus before I turned twenty-three?"

William B. is not the stereotypical unchurched person conveyed in books and at conferences. He prefers black gospel music. He is challenged by direct and confrontational preaching, and sermons of an hour in length do not bother him. In fact, many of the unchurched "rules" were broken by the Memphis church when William visited the first time. But he loved every minute of it, and he returned.

One of my favorite books on the unchurched is *Inside the Mind of Unchurched Harry and Mary* by Lee Strobel.[11] Strobel, a reporter for the *Chicago Tribune* with a law degree, was one of the newspaper's authorities on legal issues. He was also an atheist. But through the ministry of Willow Creek Community Church in a Chicago suburb, Strobel met Christ. He eventually became a teaching pastor at Willow Creek, where he stayed for many years before accepting a similar position at Saddleback Valley Community Church in Southern California (hereafter referred to as Saddleback Church). The book is a fascinating account of Strobel's conversion and how Willow Creek did many things well to reach him. His primary thesis is that the church must understand the context in which unchurched people live.

Unfortunately, numerous church leaders have decided that it is the methodological model of Willow Creek that reached Strobel rather than a philosophical commitment to reach the unchurched in their context. The methods used to reach Lee Strobel probably would have proven highly ineffective in the previous examples of Joe M. in Kentucky and William B. in Memphis. But they may have been effective with Donna C. in Detroit.

Our study has reminded us with no equivocation that the unchurched are not a monolithic group. The next myth is but one example of this reality.

Myth # 2: The unchurched are turned off by denominational names in the church name.

Perhaps one of the biggest surprises in our study was that the name of the church had very little influence on reaching the unchurched. For the most part, neither the presence nor the absence of a denominational name influenced the formerly unchurched's decision to join a church.

When we asked straightforwardly, "Did the name of the church influence your decision to join?" we often heard pauses, as if the interviewee was unclear about the question. The pause would often be followed with comments like, "I don't understand" or "What do you mean?" After we explained the questions again, the respondent would express surprise at the nature of the inquiry.

Mark R. is a thirty-nine-year-old formerly unchurched person from upstate New York. His response is representative of many of the interviews we conducted. "The name of the church never really entered my mind," Mark told us. "I didn't have a clue what a Wesleyan church was, but that's not what got me interested in the church." Mark's primary influence in coming to the church was his sister and her husband. "After all," Mark reflected, "I really don't choose a store because of its name. What does 'Wal-Mart' mean anyway?"

Figure 1.3a and 1.3b
Did the Name of the Church Influence Your Decision to Join?

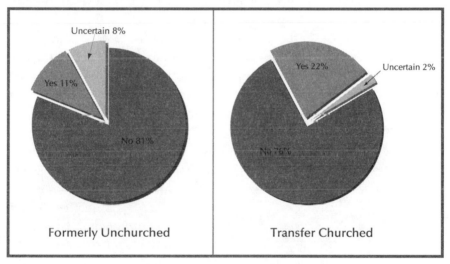

| Formerly Unchurched | Transfer Churched |

Over 80 percent of the formerly unchurched told us that the church name had little or no influence upon their joining a particular church. Seven of ten transfer churched said the same (see figure 1.3).

A further element of this surprise came when we asked follow-up questions of the formerly unchurched who said the church name did affect their decision-making process. Nearly two-thirds of those respondents indicated that the denominational name had a positive influence on their decision.

Jane L. from the Little Rock, Arkansas, area told us that "seeing Baptist in the name gave me some assurance that the church was not some wacko cult." Though Jane had rarely attended church in her forty-three years of life, she had several friends who were Baptists. Because they were "normal" people, she thought the church would be okay.

After we factor in the reasons for "yes" responses to our question, the results are perhaps even more amazing. Only 4 out of 100 formerly unchurched indicated that a denominational name had a negative influence on them as they sought a church home. The vast majority, 84 percent, hardly considered the church name in their deliberations. And one out of eight formerly unchurched told us that a denominational name actually influenced them positively.

Readers may ask regarding our findings, "What about the numerous surveys typically conducted by local churches that indicate certain denominational names were perceived negatively in the eyes of the unchurched?"

My first response to the anticipated question is, "I don't know." My second response is that our research and questions were asked of the formerly unchurched, not the unchurched. The thesis of this book is that the formerly unchurched provide us insights that we have not previously heard. A third response is that the formerly unchurched, once some person or event triggers within them a desire to go to church, focus on matters other than the church name. Evelyn F., for example, said that the name "Evangelical Free Church" might have engendered a negative response earlier in her life. But once certain crises in her life prompted her to seek a church home, "I could have cared less what the name of the church was. I was lonely and hurting and needed to find a community that cared."

Figure 1.4

Did the Name of the Church Influence Your Decision to Join?

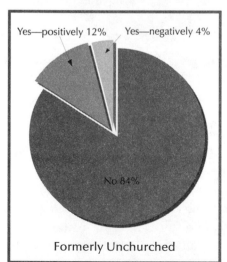

Yes—positively 12%   Yes—negatively 4%

No 84%

Formerly Unchurched

Myth #3: The Unchurched Never Attend Church

The word *unchurched* naturally implies that a person has no interest in a church and never attends a church. Our survey of the formerly unchurched indicates, however, that relatively few Americans *never* attend church.

Our information seems to have the support of other studies. George Barna's 1999 study of the unchurched found that 31 percent of the American adult population is unchurched. For his survey a

> The thesis of this book is that the formerly unchurched provide us insights that we have not previously heard.

person was classified as unchurched "if he or she had not attended a Christian church service during the past six months, other than a special event such as a wedding or funeral or holiday service."[12] Barna had to use a fairly tight definition to include as many as one-third of all adults in the definition of unchurched. He indicated that the unchurched person would not have been in church in the past six months only. Furthermore, the Barna study did not include attendance at a holiday service such as Christmas or Easter service as church attendance.

Such a narrow definition was necessary because most adults attend some type of church service in the course of a year. If we defined an unchurched person as one who never attends any kind of church service in a year, including holiday services, the population of the unchurched in America would be small.

Because some church leaders view the unchurched as people completely foreign to the church, they may also assume the unchurched are

> Our study of the formerly unchurched found that the church was neither strange nor frightening to them when they visited.

totally ignorant about biblical or church matters. Our study of the formerly unchurched, however, found that the church was neither strange nor frightening to them when they visited.

"I had attended some Easter services and a few 'regular' services over the past four or five years," Paul Y. of California told us. "I might not have been as familiar with the church as the regular members were, but I wasn't totally ignorant either."

When we asked a portion of the formerly unchurched in our study how often they visited a church a year prior to joining a church, none said zero

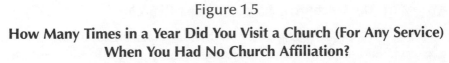

Figure 1.5

How Many Times in a Year Did You Visit a Church (For Any Service) When You Had No Church Affiliation?

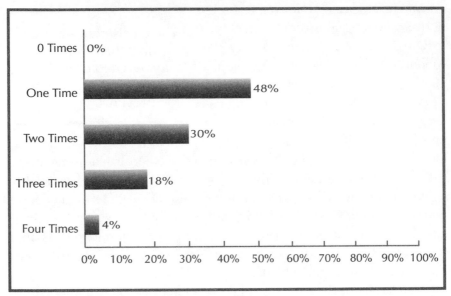

times. Some of the formerly unchurched attended as much as once a quarter even though they had no church affiliation in the past.

Church leaders should realize that the unchurched are not as unfamiliar with the church as we sometimes believe them to be. Indeed, many of our formerly unchurched respondents found some efforts to make the church seeker-friendly a bit amusing. Pam W. of Oregon noted that although she had not attended church ever with any regularity, she certainly understood the basic concept of sin, a word one preacher she heard avoided awkwardly.

> On Easter Sunday in 1999, 12 percent of atheists and agnostics attended a Christian church service, nearly a million adults.

The unchurched, for the most part, do have some familiarity with the church. On Easter Sunday in 1999, 12 percent of atheists and agnostics attended a Christian church service, nearly a million adults.[13]

If one out of eight atheists and agnostics attend at least one service a year, we can presume that the vast majority of the unchurched, who hold to some theistic belief, will show up at least once a year. Will the church be ready for them?

Myth #4: The Unchurched Cannot Be Reached by Direct Personal Evangelism

Mark W. lives in a medium-sized town about sixty miles from St. Louis. He was one of the several million unchurched who attended church the previous Easter Sunday. "I typically attended church on Easter," Mark told us. "There was no particular reason for my once-a-year church habit. No major crisis, no guilt trip. It was just something I did."

Mark gladly filled out the guest cards as requested in the service. He did not mind hearing from the pastor by letter and receiving information on the church. In 1999, however, he received a telephone call from someone at the church requesting an opportunity to visit him. Mark agreed to receive the two men from the church.

"The two guys got right to the point," Mark commented. "They explained to me how I could become a Christian. I received Christ and have been in church ever since."

The seeker-sensitive movement has been a needed wake-up call for dead, inwardly focused churches. The movement has rightly reminded churches to be aware of or sensitive to the presence of lost persons in a worship service. Some churches, however, experience a decline in personal evangelistic efforts when the church focus is on seeker sensitivity. This decline is due to an attitude that sees the seeker-sensitive worship service as *the only* evangelistic methodology.

The formerly unchurched in our study left little doubt as to the importance of personal evangelism in reaching the unchurched. Over one-half indicated that someone from the church they joined shared Christ with them. Another 12 percent told

Figure 1.6

Did Someone from the Church You Joined Share with You How to Become a Christian?

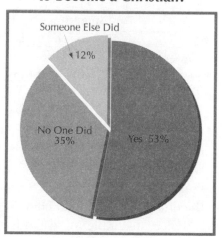

us that someone other than a member at the church they joined personally evangelized them. Only one-third of the formerly unchurched said that no one made an attempt to share Christ one-on-one (see figure 1.6 on the previous page).

The majority of the formerly unchurched who were personally evangelized also told us that someone made an effort to see them within a month of their visit to the church. While the building of relationships with the unchurched is critical, we heard repeatedly that an evangelistic visit, even by a stranger from the church, had an eternal impact.

Myth #5: The Pastor Must Be a Dynamic and Charismatic Leader for the Church to Reach the Unchurched.

Recently I spoke to a large audience in the Detroit area. John Maxwell preceded me and Josh McDowell followed me. In my imagination I could hear some of the audience saying, "I know John Maxwell, and I know Josh McDowell, but who is this Rainer guy?" I could have been intimidated to be sandwiched between two of the greatest communicators in America, but I decided to be myself. And I had a great time!

Do you ever go to a conference and hear a great communicator or charismatic leader and leave with a sense of frustration? Pastors often say, "I'm just not the leader that Rick Warren is." And laypersons often compare, unfairly, their pastors with many of these dynamic leaders.

Our research team interviewed the formerly unchurched about their pastors. For example, Joe M. of eastern Kentucky, mentioned earlier in this chapter, said of his pastor, "He's a great guy, but I've heard a lot of better preachers. And sometimes he doesn't seem to have the best organizational skills. But our church keeps growing and reaching lost people."

The pastors themselves often commented that they have to work hard when other leaders, perceived to be more dynamic, seem to have a natural ability to reach people. Micah L., a Nazarene pastor from Idaho, told us, "I have come to the conclusion that I can't be Bill Hybels or John Maxwell. I can, however, be faithful with the gifts God has given me. And God is blessing our church."

What then are some characteristics of these pastors whose churches are reaching the unchurched? Because the pastors played such a key role in the effectiveness of their churches, I have devoted several chapters in this book to that topic. We will return to the critical role of pastors later.

44

Myth #6: We Must Be Careful in Our Teaching and Preaching So That We Do Not Communicate Deep and Complex Biblical Truths That Will Confuse the Unchurched.

"You know what frustrated me the most when I started visiting churches?" Susan M. asked us. Susan was a lifelong unchurched person living in the Cleveland area until a life crisis prompted her to seek God. She tried to find him and his truth in the churches she visited. "What really frustrated me was that I had a deep desire to understand the Bible, to hear in-depth preaching and teaching," she continued. "But most of the preaching was so watered-down that it was insulting to my intelligence. I went to one church where the message was on fear. I was eager to hear what the Bible had to say about a subject that described my state of mind."

But Susan was sorely disappointed with what she heard. "It was more of a pop-psychology message. The biblical view was never explained. Bible texts were hardly mentioned," she lamented.

One important lesson we learned from the formerly unchurched is that we should never dilute biblical teachings for the sake of the unchurched. Jennifer K., a Minnesota resident, expressed similar sentiments: "You know, I have watched CNBC [a business cable network] for years, since I follow my investments closely," she said. "I remember the first time I watched the program. They used a language that contained some strange phrases, like stock splits, P/E ratio, and NASDAQ. Sometimes they explained them, and other times I had to go to the dictionary or the Internet to learn, but I enjoyed the learning experience."

Jennifer continued, "Now that I am a Christian and an active church member, I have been telling the pastor and the church staff that meaty teaching and preaching attracts the unchurched. I think they're listening."

Similar comments to Jennifer's were repeated by many of the formerly unchurched. When we asked if doctrine, or beliefs, of the church they eventually joined was important, the responses were surprising and over-whelming. Ninety-one percent of the formerly unchurched indicated that doctrine was an important factor that attracted them to the church (figure 1.7 on the following page)

Perhaps equally surprising was the fact that the unchurched were more concerned about doctrine than Christians who had transferred from another church. Almost all of the formerly unchurched responded that

Figure 1.7a and 1.7b

Was Doctrine (the Beliefs of the Church) an Important Factor in Your Choosing This Church?

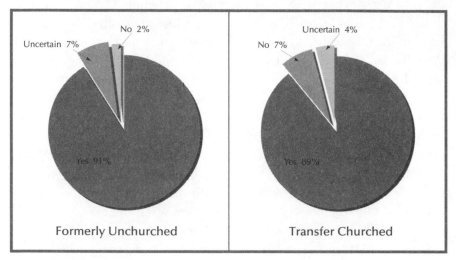

doctrine was important. Nine out of ten of the transfer churched responded likewise.

The implications of these findings could be significant in our attempts to reach the unchurched. How would our strategies change if we considered the teaching of doctrine to be a major issue in reaching the unchurched?

Myth #7: The Sunday School and Other Small Groups Are Ineffective in Attracting the Unchurched.

Over the past decade or so a worship revolution has begun to take place in many churches across America. The revolution is sorely needed. In thousands of churches, worship has become stale, ritualistic, and uninspiring.

This worship revolution includes the seeker-sensitive movement, a movement that reminds the church that what we say, sing, and do in worship is often confusing and irrelevant to the unchurched who may be visiting our churches. Again, many of the contributions of the seeker-sensitive movement were sorely needed.

Almost forgotten in these new emphases in worship was the two-hundred-year-old program called the Sunday school. I was among many church forecasters who thought that the Sunday school was a program that belonged in antiquity, a dinosaur headed for extinction.[14]

To many, Sunday school evokes mental images of a dimly lit room with old furniture, walls painted most recently in 1972, and an eighty-four-year-old teacher who sleeps through his or her own lessons. But our research has shown the resurgence of Sunday school in the more effective churches in America. Furthermore, we learned through this study that the formerly unchurched are positive about and attracted to Sunday school. In fact, the formerly unchurched were more likely to be active in Sunday school than the transfer churched. In a majority of our interviews, it was the formerly unchurched who indicated the greatest allegiance to Sunday school.

> The implications of these findings could be significant in our attempts to reach the unchurched. How would our strategies change if we considered the teaching of doctrine to be a major issue in reaching the unchurched?

We were amazed to find that nearly seven out of ten formerly unchurched were active in Sunday school at the point of our interview. Approximately six out of ten transfer churched were involved in Sunday school (figure 1.8 on the following page). Those in both groups were much more likely to be in Sunday school than any other small group.

Chris R., a formerly unchurched forty-two-year-old man from Oklahoma, expressed the views of many whom we interviewed: "Look, I'm a new Christian. I've got so much to learn. What better place to learn and to fellowship with other Christians than a Sunday school class?"

Interestingly, we did notice a slight transition from the nomenclature "Sunday school." Almost 20 percent of the churches in our study called their Sunday morning small group "Bible study." This shift was made because of the churches' perception of how the name "Sunday school" is received. No formerly unchurched expressed concerns about the name.

Myth #8: The Most Important Evangelistic Relationships Take Place in the Marketplace.

The marketplace most often refers to the place where we meet people who are not part of our family: workplaces, schools, neighborhoods, and places where we shop and do business. Many good studies and books

Figure 1.8

In Which Small Group, If Any, Are You Active Today?

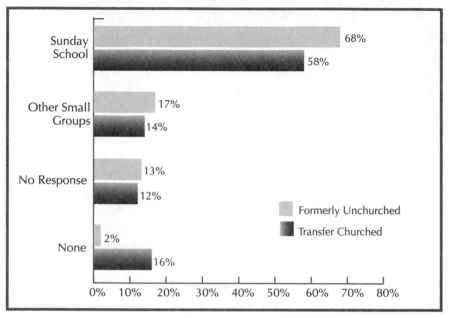

Figure 1.9

Which Person Was the Greatest Influence in Your Coming to Church?

(Note: Friends were included in the coworker,
neighbor, and other categories)

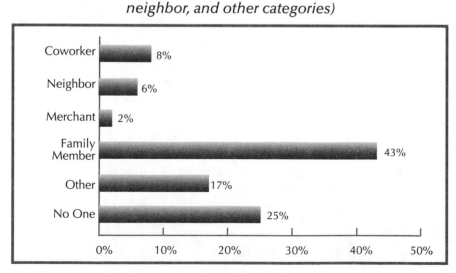

advocate the training of laity for marketplace evangelism or for the development of relationships with the unchurched in the marketplace.

While we would not diminish the importance of marketplace relationships for evangelism, our study of the formerly unchurched found that family member relationships were even more important. And of the different family members, wives were the ones most often mentioned as important in influencing the formerly unchurched to Christ and the church.

Figure 1.9 clearly depicts the importance of family members in leading persons to Christ and to the church. Art R., a Florida native, told us a common story: "The reason I'm in church today is because of my wife. When I saw the change in her life, I decided to try it out. Now I'm a Christian and hardly ever miss church."

Art not only told us that family members were the greatest influence in his coming to church, he told us specifically that his wife was the key person God used in the process. We cannot overstate the importance of wives in bringing formerly unchurched persons to Christ and to the church. We address this issue more fully in chapter 3.

Figure 1.10 depicts a breakdown of the 43 percent representing family members who influenced the formerly unchurched in their spiritual

Figure 1.10
Which Person Was the Greatest Influence in Your Coming to Church?

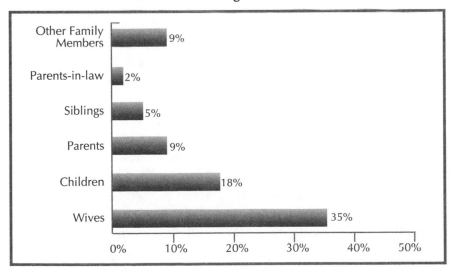

pilgrimage. More than one-third of this group indicated that their wives were the key influence, several times the number of the second-highest influence, children of the formerly unchurched.

Husbands of the formerly unchurched had a minimal influence. They ranked below wives, children, and parents in leading their loved ones to come to church.

Again we ask, Do most churches today have an intentional strategy to develop these relationships so that the unchurched may come to Christ and the church? Specifically, in those situations where wives are churched and their husbands are not, does the church provide resources and training for these women to reach their husbands for the kingdom? Perhaps the surprising aspect of this portion of the study is that the most receptive unchurched group is living in the homes of those already active in our churches.

Myth #9: The Unchurched Are Concerned Only about Their Own Needs.

The reasons the unchurched become churched are complex. In the course of our research we found no simple explanations to the process.

We have observed many strategies for reaching the unchurched that focus on meeting their needs. While there is much to commend this approach, an exclusive needs-meeting strategy neglects two major issues. First, as we will examine later, the unchurched often desire to be challenged. As Bobby J. of Pennsylvania told us, "I didn't want to be a part of a church that put everything on a silver platter. Even before I became a Christian, I sensed that I needed to be a part of something where I could help others."

Our study found that churches that expect much receive much, even from many of the unchurched. Perhaps an important lesson that we learned from the formerly unchurched is that churches should try to appeal to the unchurched person's altruistic motives. Bobby T. expressed it well: "I can tell you before I became a Christian, I knew I wanted to be in a place where I could make a difference. The church needs to hear the message not to dumb down the church or water down expectations."

A second major insight gleaned from the formerly unchurched was that the unchurched do not always seek a place of worship for their own needs. Almost one out of three of the formerly unchurched informed us that they came or returned to the church for their children.

Two major studies in the late 1990s affirmed that people are most receptive to the gospel before they turn twenty years old.[15] Many of the unchurched seem to know intuitively that "religious training" is necessary for their children, even though they cannot articulate specific reasons why.

Bobby T. explained: "I'm a single dad with almost year-round custody of two kids, ages nine and eleven. One of the reasons I wanted to find a church was for Robby and Kayla. Though I had never been a member of a church, I just knew that it would be good for them, that it would help me to raise better kids."

While the gospel of Christ clearly calls for believers to help meet the needs of others, the formerly unchurched told us that a church should not communicate an exclusively needs-based message. The unchurched do indeed have motives for seeking churches beyond their personal felt needs.

New Insights, New Strategy

More has been written on the unchurched in America in the past fifteen years than in any similar period in history. Yet with all the research and publications, the percentage of unchurched in our nation continues to increase. Is it possible we have been asking the wrong people the wrong questions? Are we involved in exercises in futility by researching a large group, most of whom will never attend church? Should we be talking to those who were unchurched but who now attend? It is this group, the formerly unchurched, from whom we have much to learn. And it is to that group that we now turn in an attempt to understand the mind-set of the unchurched. Perhaps in the process we can learn more about

> Is it possible we have been asking the wrong people the wrong questions?

reaching people who do not know Christ. And perhaps we can seek from God new strategies or revive old approaches that may still work.

The formerly unchurched have unique insights into our churches, its leaders, the worship services, and the ways we evangelize. They specifically have definite opinions about the pastors and their preaching in the churches they visited before they became Christians. We will look at this critical issue in the next chapter.

CHAPTER 2

Pastors and Preaching Are Critical

*We were hearing about moral failures
among pastors long before we heard
about moral failures among presidents.*

—"Born2Bwild" in the Born Again 3
Internet Chat Room

Cindy D. had been a Christian only four months at the time we interviewed her. She described the first thirty-four years of her life as "inconsistent, luke-warm, nominal Catholicism." A well-educated divorcée, Cindy had both a law degree and a Ph.D. in educational psychology. She recently joined Trinity Presbyterian Church in the Baltimore area after her conversion.

Several key issues moved Cindy to Christ and the church, including the crisis of her divorce, her desire to provide her four-year-old son with religious training, and her own "intellectual quest to discover religious meaning." A coworker at the school where she worked suggested that Cindy visit Trinity with her.

All of these factors were influential in Cindy's pilgrimage to faith in Christ and membership at Trinity. But "the clincher was Don," she told us. Don is the pastor of Trinity.

Her first exposure to Don was his preaching. "I am often perceived to be the brainy type, with all of my education and my six-figure salary," Cindy explained. "But the fact of the matter is that I was totally clueless about the Bible. My Catholic upbringing did little to help me. And when I would go hear a Protestant preacher, I would come away wondering if the guy had spent more than five minutes preparing his sermon," she pondered.

And already speaking in a postconversion vernacular, Cindy said, "I needed meat, and all I was getting was milk—that is, until I heard Don."

Proceeding with Caution

Though this chapter appears near the front of this book, it was not one of the first chapters I wrote. I had good reasons for not wanting to put in print this part of our study. The integrity of our research, however, demanded that this subject be given significant attention. The matter to which I refer is the critical importance of pastoral leadership and preaching in the church's success in reaching the unchurched. My hesitancy in reporting this information is twofold. First, in our research of over four thousand churches across America, we have seen clearly that many congregations are abandoning the biblical model of pastoral ministry. Instead of allowing pastors the necessary time and encouragement to spend time in prayer and the ministry of the Word (Acts 6:4), congregations are demanding time and energy from their pastors for tasks that have little biblical foundation. This reality will become obvious later in the book when we look at the weekly time charts of pastors.

I fear that as we begin to report the critical role of pastoral leadership in reaching the unchurched, new and unreasonable expectations will be placed on already overburdened pastors. Like the leaders of the Jerusalem church in Acts 6:1–7, if pastors have to meet all the perceived needs and demands of church members, they will have little time to give to their primary calling of preaching and the ministry of the Word.

A second reason for my hesitancy to report this information is an awareness that some congregations may use this chapter as "proof" that the reason their churches are not growing is an inadequate and inept pastor. Before I report the results of this part of the study, allow me the personal privilege of a short detour off the main topic. In the past several years since I left a pastoral ministry to become the dean at the Southern Baptist Theological Seminary, I have had the extraordinary opportunity of spending thousands of hours talking to and observing pastors of diverse backgrounds, locations, and denominations. I have come to a keen awareness that pastors are among the hardest working and yet least respected people in America today.

Just a few decades ago the position of pastor was a position of esteem and respect. Today many pastors receive little respect in the communities they serve. Not only has the office of pastor lost much of its respect in the community, but also some of the harshest and most unloving critics of pastors can be found within their own congregations.

I have a deep love and respect for pastors. I believe their calling to be the most awesome responsibility God can give. Yet I see these laborers of Christ pour out their hearts in work and sacrifice only to discover a new critic's own personal agenda was not satisfied. The only people who can survive in pastoral ministry are those with the unmistakable call of God in their lives. Therefore, I pray that the information in this chapter will not add yet another burden to faithful pastors. Nevertheless, I must say, if this study is to have any integrity, the evidence that pastors have an enormous role in reaching the unchurched is overwhelming.

The Formerly Unchurched Speak of the Influence of Pastors in Their Lives

As I prepared to write this chapter, I reread our written notes from our interviews with 353 formerly unchurched persons. The act of reading all the interviews at one time was fascinating, and it made me more aware of the vital role pastors played in the churches that reached the unchurched.

In our interviews with the formerly unchurched, we asked two questions that engendered significant responses about pastors. The first of the questions was a straightforward query directly about pastors that could be answered with a simple yes or no: "Did the pastor and his preaching play a part in your coming to the church?" Nearly all of the respondents (over 97 percent) answered in the affirmative. The second question required a more subjective response: "What factors led you to choose this church?"

Figure 2.1

Did the Pastor and His Preaching Play a Part in Your Coming to the Church?

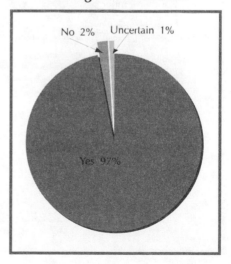

No 2%   Uncertain 1%

Yes 97%

> The formerly unchurched told us nine out of ten times that the pastor was key in their entering the ranks of the churched.

We acknowledge that the question is somewhat leading. Prior to asking this question, however, we asked the open-ended question, "What factors led you to choose this church?" The responses, noted in the previous chapter, show that facts related to the pastor and preaching were the most-often mentioned answers. Indeed, without any prompting from our interviewers, the formerly unchurched told us nine out of ten times that the pastor was key in their entering the ranks of the churched.

Figure 2.2

What Factors Led You to Choose This Church?

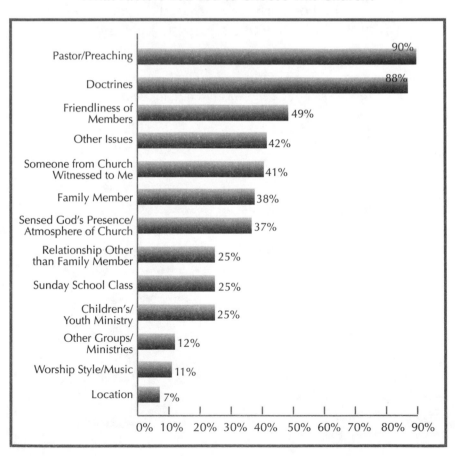

What then were the issues related to the pastor? What specifically did he say or do that so significantly influenced the unchurched? In most of the interviews, the respondents told us not only that the pastor influenced them, but they also shared how he influenced them. Eight particular issues were mentioned frequently. Figure 2.3 shows each of the eight factors related to pastors that influenced the formerly unchurched.

Figure 2.3

Factors Related to the Pastors That Influenced the Formerly Unchurched

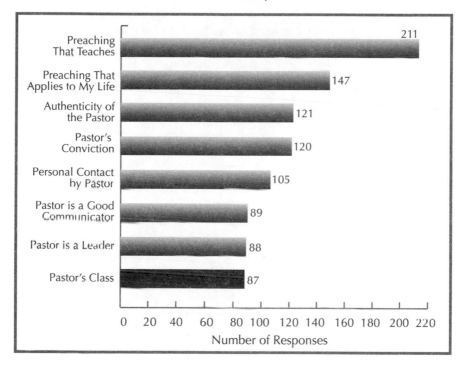

Issue #1: Preaching That Teaches the Bible

Vera M., like Cindy, is a former Roman Catholic by birth, although she never had much attachment to Catholicism as an adult. She never really thought of herself as unchurched, though she never attended any one church more than once or twice. "I always considered myself a religious person. I really didn't have any animosity against churches; I just never got into the habit of going regularly."

Vera's church habits included going to seven or eight churches ten or twelve times a year. "I was as active going to churches as my Baptist neighbor," she told us, "except I would go to different churches while she went to the same one."

Interestingly, a crisis was the impetus to Vera finding the Baptist church in a town near Charlotte, North Carolina, but the crisis was not in Vera's life. "Lindsay, my Baptist neighbor, found out that her husband was fooling around. It ended up in a messy divorce," Vera told us. "I went to church with her as a way of supporting her during her tough times."

But it was Vera's life that was changed. "I would go to several churches in the course of a year. All different kinds of churches. I guess it was my weird way of going to confession without talking to a priest," she explained.

"I was pretty satisfied with my life," Vera said. "No big crisis. No sense that something was missing in my life. Good family. I sure was caught off guard when I went to Lindsay's church."

Vera's intention was to offer Lindsay support by going with her to Thompson Memorial Baptist Church. But then she heard Mike Lovelett preach. "Mike preached in a way like I've never heard anybody," Vera gushed. She described his preaching as "line-by-line preaching," her way of describing verse-by-verse expository preaching.

Vera never had an interest in studying the Bible until she sat under the preaching ministry of Mike Lovelett. "Mike gave me 'meaty' preaching. He gave me a desire to study the Bible. It all happened so fast. The next thing I knew, I realized what the Bible taught about salvation. And I realized that I was as lost as lost could be."

Vera accepted Christ, and Lindsay started putting her life back together as she became a more devoted follower of Christ. Vera insists that the single issue that brought her to salvation was the strong teaching/preaching ministry of Mike Lovelett.

In a previous study,[1] we noted the high correlation between expository preaching and evangelistic effectiveness. Now we are hearing from the formerly unchurched that preaching that truly teaches the Bible in its original context is a major factor in reaching the unchurched. Indeed, this issue was mentioned by 211 of our 353 survey respondents. The formerly unchurched told us that they were attracted to strong biblical teaching and to understanding Christian doctrine. Pastors who understand this and who communicate doctrine clearly are among the leaders whose churches are reaching the unchurched.

Issue #2: "Preaching That Applies to My Life"

A challenge for pastors of evangelistic churches is to preach both expositionally and with life application. Yes, the unchurched are strongly desirous of learning deep biblical truths, but they also want to know how these truths can make a difference in their lives.

Craig L. is one of many formerly unchurched who makes his point cogently. I noted with laughter that the person on our research team who interviewed Craig wrote in the margin of his interview sheet, "This guy is really willing to talk and talk and talk." And the main issue Craig talked about was the influence of his pastor on his spiritual pilgrimage.

As we began to compile the different issues that impacted Craig, we noticed that many were related to the pastor of the church he joined:

- "The pastor was friendly and caring."
- "The pastor has a passion for new believers."
- "I was influenced by the humility of the pastor."
- "The pastor's preaching is incredible. He not only teaches the Bible well, he helps me understand how it applies to my life today."

We heard the latter issue repeated in over 40 percent of our interviews with the formerly unchurched. The topic of life application preaching was mentioned by 147 of the 353 respondents.

Craig had come a long way in his spiritual trek. "I was a successful forty-two-year-old attorney with all the trappings of success," he told us, "but I was really searching as well. I was particularly searching in Eastern religions. While my wife was reading the Bible, I was reading *The Tibetan Book of the Dead*."

Craig finally attended church with his wife. The friendly Wesleyan church north of Indianapolis surprised him, but the biggest surprise was the preaching. "For the first time in my life I heard someone explain the Bible in a way that made sense," Craig exclaimed. "The pastor didn't just teach the historical facts of the Bible, he explained how it applied to our lives."

Craig was one of many of the formerly unchurched who saw no dichotomy between deep expositional preaching and life application preaching. In fact, if a single unique feature surfaced related to preaching, it was the ability of pastors to combine what many see as two different approaches to preaching.

In part 2 of this book, we will hear from pastors whose churches are reaching the unchurched. But perhaps a brief preview is in order at this point. Listen to Doug Mulberry, Craig's pastor: "Preaching must first be biblical. We must understand what God was saying at the time the biblical text took place. But if preaching ends there, it is incomplete. Preaching must change the lives of the listeners as well. On a few occasions I was asked if I was an expository preacher or a life-application preacher. I enjoyed looking at the faces of those who asked the question when I gave the quick response, 'Yes.'"

Issue #3: "The Pastor Is a 'Real' Person"

The formerly unchurched spoke forcefully and clearly about one of the primary characteristics they desire in a pastor: authenticity. Many of these new Christians shared with us that inauthentic pastors were among the stumbling blocks that kept them away from the church.

Boston resident Larry M. said without hesitation, "I really thought most pastors were two-faced hypocrites with a holier-than-thou attitude." But Larry's opinion has changed dramatically; he now speaks of his pastor in a nondenominational church near Boston with warmth and admiration. "Pat is just a real guy," Larry notes. "He doesn't try to pretend to be somebody he's not."

Larry "discovered" Pat when he was best man at a wedding officiated by Pat. "I was really surprised to find this preacher kidding around with us and acting like a normal person," Larry said.

Indeed, humor was an often-mentioned characteristic of pastors whose churches reach the unchurched. The formerly unchurched are careful to note, however, that humor evident in these pastors is not a lightheartedness that fails to have reverence for God or take his church seriously. The 121 respondents who made some comment about pastors' authenticity often used the following words or phrases to describe pastors:

Down-to-earth
Friendly
Humorous
Willing to admit mistakes

Not holier-than-thou (described twelve times)
Real
Enthusiastic
Walked the talk
Relates well
Regular guy

The authenticity of the pastor was mentioned as the most positive character trait noticed by the formerly unchurched. And this characteristic was deemed third in importance overall, right after the two issues related to preaching.

Issue #4: A Person of Conviction

Frank and Shannon T. moved from upstate New York to southern Georgia. The Georgia town was about the same size as their former New York home, about ten thousand residents. "We felt like we would experience some culture shock," Shannon told us, "but we thought that since we were moving from a small town to a small town that the adjustment wouldn't be too bad. Boy was I wrong!"

Frank quickly jumped in: "It wasn't that the people of South Georgia were unfriendly. To the contrary, they were very friendly. It's just that it seemed like everybody already had their friends, and we 'Yankees' couldn't fit in."

The loneliness that Frank and Shannon experienced drove them to look for new relationships. They decided to visit a Southern Baptist church. "We were really desperate!" Shannon exclaimed.

"For us to visit any church, much less a Southern Baptist church, showed that we would try anything to make friends," Frank added with a knowing grin.

The excursion to a church in search of friends took an unexpected turn. "When John [the pastor] started preaching, we were mesmerized," said Shannon. "Frank and I didn't ever talk about seeking God; we were just seeking friends. But we never heard someone speak with such conviction," Shannon reflected.

The young couple did not realize how desirous they were for truth. "I guess we just expected relativity as the norm," Shannon said. "Our lack of religious upbringing meant that we didn't even know that anyone could know anything with certainty."

In chapter 5 we will look at the amazing attraction of doctrinal certitude to the unchurched. For many years the pundits of conventional wisdom told us that strong doctrinal preaching and teaching was a total turnoff to the unchurched. Not so, say the formerly unchurched. To the contrary, they are drawn to certitude and conviction.

Likewise, the formerly unchurched told us that preachers who taught and preached with conviction were a major factor in their coming into the ranks of the churched. Frank said cogently, "It's amazing that we found Christ by what we then called 'the confidence of the preacher.' Now we know that a better description would be 'the conviction of the preacher.'"

Shannon quickly added her insights: "We attended a lot of different churches for different reasons before we became Christians. I tell you, so many of the preachers spoke with little authority; they hardly ever dealt with tough issues of Scripture, and they soft-sold the other issues. Frank and I know now that we were hungry for the truth. Why can't preachers learn that shallow and superficial preaching doesn't help anybody, including people like us who weren't Christians?"

Figure 2.3 shows that a major attraction of the unchurched to preachers, and thus to the church, is preaching with certitude. By certitude we mean that the preacher really believes the truth of his messages and that he communicates that truth with clarity and obvious conviction. Of the 353 respondents, 120 indicated that the pastor's conviction in his preaching was a major factor in their coming to a particular church.

> "Why can't preachers learn that shallow and superficial preaching doesn't help anybody, including people like us who weren't Christians?"

Remember, these responses came from an open-ended question that asked the formerly unchurched to articulate the most influential factors in their choosing a church. Over one-third responded that conviction in the pastor's preaching was a major issue, an amazingly high response since we did not prompt or lead with an answer.

Issue #5: Personal Contact by the Pastor

Sue S. lived the first twenty-four years of her life knowing that something was missing. Although she attended different churches from time to time, Sue never made a habit of going to church. Sue was a second-generation unchurched person. Her parents, older members of the baby-boomer generation, still have no formal ties to a church.

An Assembly of God church in New Mexico provided a good experience for Sue. She called it "her quarterly church cleansing." Although she was an unchurched person all of her life, she confessed that she had occasional guilt pangs about not being in church. By Sue's estimate, she had probably attended nearly thirty different churches in her adolescence and young adulthood. Some were good experiences; some were not. First Assembly was definitely one of the good experiences. But then again no church had been such an outstanding experience that Sue felt compelled to return. Such was the case with First Assembly until Travis called.

Travis is the pastor of First Assembly, a position he has held since 1993. Sue said, "I was floored that the pastor would call me." She was even more surprised when Travis invited her to lunch with him and his wife.

The happy ending to this story is Sue's acceptance of Christ. She had been a new Christian for seven months when we interviewed her. The radiance and joy in her voice was obvious. "My only regret is that I didn't make the decision earlier. But, you know, Travis was the first person to tell me about Christ, even though I visited about thirty churches in the past. I was really impressed that the pastor himself would call on me."

Almost one-third of the respondents indicated that a personal contact from the pastor was instrumental in their acceptance of Christ and in choosing a church. Again, a one-third response is high for an open-ended question that has no multiple choice or yes/no options for answers.

Of the 105 respondents indicating that a personal contact from the pastor was important in their choosing a church, all of them said the type of contact was either a personal visit or a telephone call. No one mentioned a letter or e-mail. Obviously, the live voice or presence meant a lot to the formerly unchurched.

Issue #6: The Pastor Is a Good Communicator

Closely related to the various preaching issues is the importance of the pastor being a good communicator. We categorized it as a separate issue, since many of the respondents were not speaking specifically about preaching. Some of the formerly unchurched, however, were referring to preaching, but their idea of a good communicator was more than a teaching or life-application preacher.

Margaret D. of Little Rock, Arkansas, for example, spoke of her Baptist pastor as "a preacher who can be understood by adults and children alike." She told us that she "learns a lot from his preaching, but my eleven-year-old daughter understands him too."

> In our pursuit of the latest church-growth fad or desire to emulate other churches, perhaps we overlook the importance of communication skills in the pulpit and in interpersonal contexts.

Eighty-nine of the formerly unchurched told us in some fashion how their pastors communicated well in the pulpit and in other contexts. Anecdotally, I cannot recall a church with significant growth where the pastor is not an articulate communicator. In our pursuit of the latest church-growth fad or desire to emulate other churches, perhaps we overlook the importance of communication skills in the pulpit and in interpersonal contexts.

A number of the formerly unchurched also told us that their pastors were able to relate well to different generations. The ability to communicate across generations is a key component of successful vision casting.

Issue #7: The Pastor Is a Good Leader

Church leadership resources are plentiful, and one does not need to look far to discover that leadership is critical in growing churches. Our study does nothing to contradict this central thesis. What is somewhat surprising, however, is how quickly the unchurched recognized leadership skills in a pastor.

Meg P., for example, is an Indiana native who joined a Nazarene church seventy miles from Chicago. "I don't know if many lost people are like I was, but I knew I needed God," Meg told us. "I didn't know how to find God, so I started attending churches all over the place. I'm not exaggerating to say I probably went to thirty churches in one year. I probably attended church more regularly than a lot of church members. The only difference is that I went to a different church each time," she said laughingly.

The reason for Meg's extensive church search was her sense that most churches "didn't know what they were doing." When we probed to get her to explain, she said: "I'm a corporate vice president in a company that's almost large enough to be in the Fortune 500. I can tell when an organization knows what it's all about versus one that's just going through the motions. I'm sorry to say that most churches are just going through the motions."

When Meg visited First Nazarene, she found a church that knew its purpose, that understood where it was going. "Pastor Ricky is a leader," Meg said directly. "He understands that a church needs a leader to give it direction. Why is it that most churches have poor leaders?"

When Rick Warren wrote *The Purpose-Driven Church*[2] several years ago, the book quickly became a Christian nonfiction best-seller. The genius behind *The Purpose-Driven Church* is not its "baseball diamond" plan to bring people into greater obedience to Christ. It is not a particular style of worship. And it is not necessarily Rick Warren's understanding of the community context of the church. The true genius behind the book and Saddleback Church is the clear articulation that a church must have a purpose; it cannot wander aimlessly and hope to make a difference in the kingdom.

Not all Saddleback-type churches have succeeded. One of the main reasons for their lack of success is their failure to see the key issues at Saddleback: the church is purpose driven. Saddleback Church has been a tremendous success story for many reasons. Among the key reasons has been Rick Warren's leadership; he articulates with passion the vision that the church must be purpose driven. One Saddleback-model church that has succeeded is Hunter Street Baptist Church in Birmingham, Alabama. Hunter Street is a church that has grown in attendance from two hundred to about four thousand in a decade. Pastor Buddy Gray readily admits the influence of Rick Warren and Saddleback Church in his own ministry. Yet Hunter Street has retained "Baptist" in its name. Its worship style is more blended than contemporary. And it is one of the strongest Sunday school churches I know. What Buddy Gray gleaned from Saddleback is that a church must understand its purpose, and the pastor must lead the church to carry out that purpose.

> A church must have a purpose; it cannot wander aimlessly and hope to make a difference in the kingdom.

When we get to part 2 of this book, we will listen carefully to the insights of pastors of churches that reach the unchurched. For now, the insights of the formerly unchurched are telling: leadership is critical.

Figure 2.3 demonstrates the impact of leadership on reaching the unchurched. Eighty-eight of the respondents specifically articulated the pastor's leadership skills as a factor that influenced them to join a particular church. One issue that arose frequently was the interpersonal relationship skills of the pastor. I mention it here because it was often cited in the same context as leadership skills. For example, Randy D. of St. Paul, Minnesota, noted, "I knew the pastor was a strong leader the first time I attended church. He was clear in providing direction for the church, and he was very good in the way he related to everyone."

Issue #8: The Pastor's Class

Phillip R. began attending New Life Community Church near Kansas City, Kansas, after hearing the service on a radio broadcast. He and his family had just moved to the area, and Phillip was "ready for a new start, including finding God and a church."

> One issue that arose frequently was the interpersonal relationship skills of the pastor.

Phillip and his wife, Sharon, had a nine-year-old daughter who was immediately drawn to the church. Phillip noted: "New Life has a very good children's program. When we enrolled Denise in AWANA, she was hooked on the church. What attracted Sharon and me to the church was the pastor's Bible study. His teaching made the Bible clear. It was perfect timing. A month later we accepted Christ and joined the church," Phillip reflected.

Despite the negative publicity surrounding many well-known pastors the last several years, many unchurched still seem to have a high level of respect for pastors. By adding the factor of the pastor's class to the factor of personal contact by the pastor, we find that the formerly unchurched told us 192 times that they desire some type of personal interaction with the pastor.

As we will see in part 2, pastors tend to be intensely involved in a new members' class. The formerly unchurched indicated that they prefer a pastor's class, like a Sunday school class, as their introduction to the pastor. They strongly desire to see or hear the pastor in a setting where they can interact with him.

A "Superman Pastor" to Reach the Unchurched?

As I indicated at the beginning of this chapter, I was hesitant to write about the critical importance of pastors because of the tremendous pressures already placed on them. All they need is another "expert" telling the world that the church rises and falls on their leadership.

Nevertheless, the data is overwhelming. The formerly unchurched told us 968 times that some factor related to the pastor played an important role in bringing them to Christ and to the church! Remember, our interviews were conducted with 353 people, so something about the pastor was noted almost three times per interview.

> More than 90 percent of pastors in America spend only two hours per week in sermon preparation for each message preached.

Is it possible to reach the unchurched without having Superman as pastor? On the one hand, the expectations seem overwhelming. How can any one pastor be a great preacher, communicator, and dynamic personality while still being available to interact with the unchurched? On the other hand, the goals necessary to be an unchurched-reaching pastor are not unattainable. In a previous work, I noted that more than 90 percent of pastors in America spend only two hours per week in sermon preparation for each message preached.[3] Perhaps there is considerable room for improvement in the preaching and communication skills of many pastors. Perhaps the failure to connect with the unchurched is a reflection of some pastors' lack of time in the study of the Word or sermon preparation. Perhaps pastors could become better communicators if they spent more time on preaching than other matters.

> In today's pluralistic society, pastors must be equipped in the Bible, theology, apologetics, and church history.

The leaders of the early church in Jerusalem told the congregation that they would not wait on the tables of widows because they would be neglecting their primary calling of prayer and ministry of the Word (Acts 6:4). Perhaps today's pastors need to follow their example.

Regarding the issue of the unchurched desiring personal interaction, their demands are not really that great. A telephone call, an opportunity to be in a group the pastor leads, or a brief visit in almost any context is all the unchurched seek.

Another issue church leaders must address is the preparation of pastors for ministry. After hearing the formerly unchurched clearly articulate their desire to learn deep doctrinal truths, I am convinced that training in the classical disciplines is a clear requisite. In today's pluralistic society, pastors must be equipped in the Bible, theology, apologetics, and church history. Most evangelical seminaries and Bible colleges do at least an adequate job in training pastors in the classical disciplines. Where many institutions fall short, however, is in preparing ministers in preaching, leadership, and interpersonal skills. The equipping body of the twenty-first century must address these critical issues if pastors are to be adequately prepared in an increasingly pagan world.

CHAPTER 3

Relationships That Click

If you Christians would just stop talking to yourselves so much,
you might just learn something from the rest of the world.

—"Wobam," a self-proclaimed
"pagan" in the Glory2God
Internet Chat Room

The opportunity to interview Tim Z. was a treat. To this point, most of our interviews had been conducted over the telephone. My speaking visit to Southern California, however, afforded me the opportunity to have a long lunch, almost three hours, with Tim. The time passed quickly.

Tim's excitement was obvious when I told him the nature of my interview, that he was part of a large study of the formerly unchurched. "Man," he exclaimed, "that's exactly what I'm doing." My response was a dull-witted, "Huh?" Tim explained: "When I became a Christian several months ago, I got really fired up about reaching a lot of my friends who weren't Christians. But the first church I joined seemed oblivious about how to reach people like me."

Tim did not pause as he continued the description of his venture. "I began reading a lot of books about reaching people who were in the same boat as me," he said. "Many of the books were great, but I did notice something missing in a lot of them."

"What was that?" I inquired.

"They don't ask all of the right people the right questions," he responded. "You guys need to be talking to people like me, people who have just become Christians and gotten active in a church."

69

I leaned closer to him with my elbows propped impolitely on the table. I was really curious about where he was going with the conversation. My response was brief; I did not want to interrupt his train of thought. "Why?" I asked.

"Because my answers are different than they would have been if you had asked me before I became a Christian. And most of the books I read are about listening to the unchurched. How about me? Aren't you guys interested in what an ex-unchurched person has to say?"

"Tim," I interrupted.

"Huh?"

"That is what our project is all about—talking to formerly unchurched people like you."

"Oh, yeah," he deadpanned.

One Key Issue: Relationships with a Different Twist

If our study discovered anything, it is that conventional wisdom is not always affirmed by the formerly unchurched. Tim, for example, was one of many who told us a relationship was important in his pilgrimage to become a churched Christian. That observation does affirm the conventional wisdom of the reaching the unchurched literature.

But as my conversation with Tim progressed, I heard of issues that are not always addressed in the material on reaching the unchurched. For example, Tim explained that only one person with whom he had a relationship had much to do with his becoming a Christian: his wife. In *Inside the Mind of Unchurched Harry and Mary,* Lee Strobel notes the impact his wife had on his becoming a Christian. But few other books address the issue of a Christian spouse reaching an unbelieving spouse. Tim and his wife have organized a Sunday school class with the explicit purpose of equipping Christian wives to reach their non-Christian husbands. The results have been outstanding. In the first three months of the class, four husbands became Christians.

Going with the Grain, Going against the Grain

The purpose of our study was not to create a new paradigm that always goes against the grain of conventional wisdom. In fact, much of our data affirms the fine studies done by others. My research team and I studied over two thousand evangelistic churches (see the definition in the introduction) in America and almost the same number of "less evangelistic" churches. The reality is that some of our studies contradicted my presuppositions.

In an attempt to see the world of evangelistic churches in America more clearly, we asked questions not only of the formerly unchurched, but also of leaders in the churches that have reached them. These leaders gave us insights, many of which were neither anticipated nor sought. As we interviewed people in churches across America, we found among them true leaders and achievers who are willing, even eager, to defy the conventional wisdom of the day if it will enable them to

> If our study discovered anything, it is that conventional wisdom is not always affirmed by the formerly unchurched.

better evangelize and minister. These leaders do not ignore the musings of pundits, and they do not compromise biblical truths. They do, however, seek to discover the most effective ways to reach people regardless of experts' opinions.

Why Did You Choose This Church?

George Barna has for years provided excellent research related to the church. In 1999 he produced a study called "What People Say They Want From a Church."[1] Barna asked a nationwide sample of adult church-attenders to rate twenty-two different qualities of churches according to the ones they would look for if they were moving to another community and seeking a new church home. Frankly, I am surprised that Barna's study has not received greater attention, as it does seem to fly in the face of conventional wisdom.

Of the twenty-two factors offered, only nine were considered "extremely important" to the group Barna studied. Barna's study included people who were currently attending a church. They were essentially asked to identify the factors that attracted them to their churches. Interestingly, the factor of doctrine and theology was the highest-rated factor,[2] a result similar to our research on the formerly unchurched. In fact, only 6 percent of the respondents indicated that doctrine was unimportant.

Another issue that Barna uncovered in his study related to the pastor and his preaching. The third most important factor in church selection was the preaching; the eighth most important was whether the respondent

Figure 3.1

**What Factors Are Extremely Important to You
in Selecting a Church?**

(Asked of People Attending a Church)

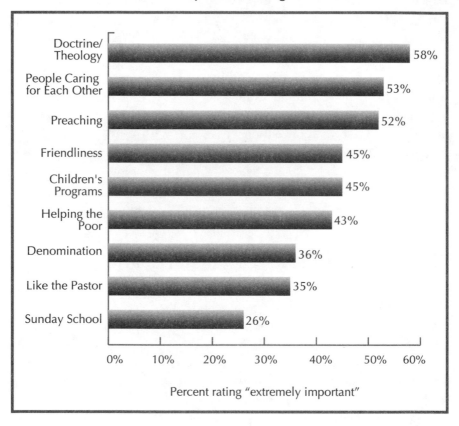

Percent rating "extremely important"

liked the pastor.[3] Again, Barna's numbers complement our study in emphasizing the importance of pastoral leadership in reaching people.

Note the issues that were not deemed important by Barna's group. Less than 20 percent of the respondents indicated that the following were extremely important in choosing a church home: variety of ministries and programs, convenience of worship times, music/worship style, quality of music, location of church, amount of music in service, comfort of the sanctuary or auditorium, length of sermons, small groups, emphasis on fundraising and money, friends in the church, easy access to parking, and the type of people who attend.[4]

Barna's study did not specifically ask the importance of relationships in choosing a church. He did ask, however, questions about friendliness and number of friends in the church.[5] Interestingly, only 12 percent said that the presence of good friends was extremely important in choosing a church.[6]

Our study differed from Barna's in two major aspects. First, our research group was the formerly unchurched. Second, we specifically asked questions about relationships. Still the common data were striking. Both studies indicated that the doctrine of the church and the leadership and preaching of the pastor were very important to respondents in choosing a church.

What about relationships? Again when we compare our results to conventional wisdom, we see not a contradiction but a difference in the levels of importance. Charles Arn has done excellent work on researching the unchurched for years. Note, for example, his results on why people come to church:[7]

Special need	1–2%
Walk-in	2–3%
Visitation	1–2%
Church program	2–3%
Mass evangelism	0–5%
Sunday school	4–5%
Pastor/staff	1–6%
Friend/relative	75–90%

Arn's research obviously focuses on the importance of relationships in reaching the unchurched. Indeed, his study shows that relationships are overwhelmingly the most important issue.

Our study of the formerly unchurched, however, indicated two significant differences. First, we found that the reasons the formerly unchurched chose a particular church were complex and could not be simplified into one or two major issues. Second, while we found that relationships were important in bringing the unchurched to the church, this single factor was not the overwhelming reason as most studies have indicated.

Before we examine more closely the issue of relationships, let us see once again the factors that led the formerly unchurched to choose a particular church. Remember, we asked the open-ended question: "What factors led you to choose this church?" The respondents, therefore, could give us multiple answers.

Figure 3.2

What Factors Led You to Choose This Church?

(Open-ended question, multiple responses possible)

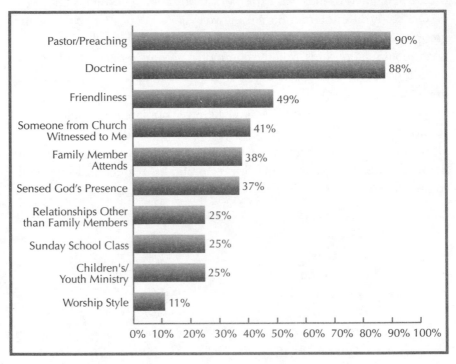

Figure 3.2 depicts once again the importance of the pastor and his preaching and the doctrine of the church. These responses are only slightly different than our surveys mentioned earlier, again because of the open-ended nature of our questions.

> We found that the reasons the formerly unchurched chose a particular church were complex and could not be simplified into one or two major issues.

And what about the issue of relationships? We can affirm the conclusions of other studies: relationships are important in reaching the unchurched. We do not, however, see the high level of importance indicated in the other studies. Almost four out of ten of the formerly unchurched indicated that family members were important in their choosing a church. Another one of four said that relationships other than family members brought them to church. If we assume that the responses are mutually exclusive (while they are not), then 73 percent (48 percent plus 25 percent) of those we interviewed told us about the importance of a relationship in their choosing a church. Although our study affirms how important relationships are in reaching the unchurched, it indicates that other factors as important or more important are at work.

A Living Example of "Relationships Plus"

Tammy D. is a fairly new Christian; she accepted Christ four months prior to our interview. She joined and was baptized in a nondenominational community church near Scottsdale, Arizona. Our time with Tammy was a delight. Our initial and follow-up interviews lasted over ten hours.

Tammy, a grandmother in her mid forties, dealt for nearly a year with bitterness because her only grandchild had been taken from her home by a social service agency. She blamed the child's other grandmother for much of her troubles. She said that she had the "weight of the world" on her shoulders. "I hated social services and I hated the other grandmother."

This crisis and her unbearable bitterness prompted Tammy to seek relief and answers. She started looking for a church even though she rarely had attended church in her lifetime. Like many unchurched people, Tammy chose Easter Sunday as her day of entry into the church.

The week after Easter another major crisis took place in Tammy's life. She came home from work to find her husband dead. That same evening the pastor and a woman from the church visited her, unaware that Tammy's husband had died earlier in the day.

"Their visit was like seeing two angels walk through the door," Tammy reflected. "I didn't have anyone to do the funeral, and they just showed up. The pastor agreed to do Bob's funeral," she told us.

Shortly after the funeral the same woman from the church asked Tammy to lunch. "Jodie told me how to be saved, how to accept Jesus," Tammy exclaimed. "I guess I was a pretty easy sell. I was looking for hope."

Tammy, though a new Christian, was hesitant to go to a church on a regular basis. She also was uncertain about baptism. "Look," she said, "I knew very little about church. It just wasn't the life I was used to."

That problem was solved when she discovered that a friend had started attending the church that she had visited on Easter Sunday. "I felt braver going with a friend," Tammy told us. They continued to attend as they found the church members to be extremely friendly.

The factor that sealed Tammy's decision to join the church was the pastor's preaching. "His sermons are deep but easy to understand. He is always able to hold my attention," she related.

We understand that Tammy's story is not typical, but then again, we rarely spoke to any of the formerly unchurched who had a "typical" story. That is our point. We cannot offer simple explanations to describe the pilgrimage of a person from the ranks of the unchurched to the churched.

How would you explain Tammy's decision? Among the possibilities you might include:

- The crisis of losing custody of her grandchild
- The crisis of the death of her husband
- The crisis of bitterness in her life
- The in-home visit of the pastor and a church member
- The big event of the Easter service
- The personal evangelistic witness of a church member
- The relationship of a friend
- The friendliness of the church member
- The preaching of the pastor

While we would certainly affirm that the relationship Tammy had with her friend was an important factor in choosing the church, many other factors were at work. Thus, it would seem unwise to devise a church strategy to reach the unchurched based on one factor alone. As we further examine the issue of the unchurched and relationships, we will do so with the understanding that many other factors are at work.

Focusing on Relationships

In addition to the open-ended question of what factors led to the formerly unchurched to the church, we asked the straightforward question:

> It would seem unwise to devise a church strategy to reach the unchurched based on one factor alone.

"Did relationships play a part in your choosing this church?" The responses were a simple yes or no. Over one-half of the formerly unchurched gave a positive response to this question (figure 3.3a).

Tim A. of Sacramento now attends a small Baptist church. His spiritual pilgrimage included both Buddhism and Mormonism before he became a Christian. "One of the reasons I started attending the church was the invitation of my stockbroker," Tim told us. "It seems like I've been searching for something all my life. Two big factors led me to Christ. First, I started seeing the truth of Christianity in my Sunday school class. Second, the preacher would share a clear gospel message in his sermons."

Figure 3.3a and 3.3b
Did Relationships Play a Part in Your Choosing This Church?

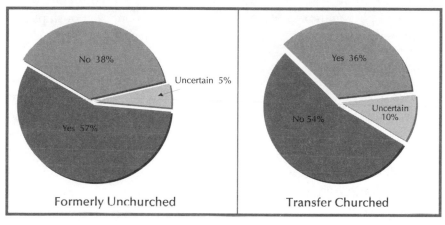

Tim is among the many formerly unchurched who indicated that relationships were among the factors leading him to Christ and to the church. The transfer churched, Christians moving from one church to another, were not as influenced by relationships in their choosing of a church home. Only 36 percent indicated that a relationship played a role in their decision to join a particular church (figure 3.3b).

Why were relationships less important to the transfer churched? We received two common responses. First, the transfer churched have been Christians for a while. Though they would like to have friends or family in the church they are joining, other issues are more important to them. The doctrine of the church, the quality of the Sunday school, the opportunity to get involved, and the availability of particular ministries and programs are among the issues that supersede relationships. And most of the transfer churched felt that they would have no problem getting to know other Christians in the church.

Second, many of the transfer churched told us that they had just moved to a new city or community. They therefore had no relationships established as they looked for a new church home.

Five Major Conclusions about Relationships and the Formerly Unchurched

Because the issue of relationships in reaching the unchurched is the most often mentioned issue in all of the unchurched studies we found, we were careful to establish its import in our study. In the remainder of this chapter, I examine our five major conclusions about relationships and the formerly unchurched.

Conclusion #1: Relationships Are Very Important

Our study complements other studies that concluded that relationships are key to reaching the unchurched. Though our findings diverge in some of the specifics related to this issue, we nevertheless affirm the validity of the basic thesis. Melody N., for example, visited an Evangelical Free church after a neighbor invited her. Her story is not unusual among the numerous interviews we conducted.

"Our kids play together in the neighborhood," Melody told us. "It was just a natural part of our conversation. I don't even remember how we got on the topic. The next thing I knew, she had invited me to church and I had agreed to come." Melody continued, "My husband wouldn't go, but he was okay with me going. Now that I'm a Christian I'm working on him."

We could recall hundreds of stories in which the formerly unchurched told us of the importance of relationships in their coming to Christ and to the church. But the issue of relationships is only a part of the story.

Conclusion #2: Rarely Do Relationships Alone Explain the Best Way to Reach the Unchurched

The story of Melody N. could leave one with the impression that her neighbor's invitation was the sole explanation for her visiting the church. But Melody told us that God was working in other ways as well. "If I had been invited to a church four years ago, I probably would not have accepted. But since I had a daughter, I felt a responsibility for her and me."

Church growth is complex. Reaching the unchurched cannot be accomplished by some quick-fix ministry or program. Myriad factors are at work. God is working through events, people, and life situations to bring people to himself. We in the church are to use our God-given wisdom to discern those issues. Such has been the focus of this project.

Conclusion #3: God Sometimes Works to Reach the Unchurched without Using Any Relationships

No matter how we asked the question, at least one-fourth to one-half of the formerly unchurched indicated that they came to a church without any established relationships. "I didn't know anybody," Mickey R. of West Virginia shared with us. He continued, "Three people from the church I ended up joining showed up at my house one evening. They told me how I could get saved. I accepted Christ that night, got baptized three weeks later, and I've been attending church ever since."

Martie is another person who gave us numerous reasons why she came to the church and became a Christian. She is representative of the nearly four in ten formerly unchurched who insist that a relationship was not a factor in leaving the ranks of the unchurched. "I can't explain my decision to try church other than I knew I wasn't living for God," Martie told us. Martie's first foray into church was a mid-size Southern Baptist congregation in the Dallas–Fort Worth metroplex. "The minute I entered the sanctuary, I knew I was in God's presence,"

> Church growth is complex. Reaching the unchurched cannot be accomplished by some quick-fix ministry or program.

she exclaimed. Even though Martie has been a Christian less than a year, she has already begun to speak like a churched Christian: "The Holy Spirit convicted me the moment I heard the preaching. God's Word pierced my heart."

Martie continued her story: "The people at Davis Baptist Church are so friendly. I bet I was greeted by ten people before I left church that day." And by Monday evening Martie had received a visit from three people from the church. They were part of the FAITH ministry, she discovered. FAITH is a Southern Baptist evangelistic ministry that seeks to integrate all of its activities through the Sunday school. We found that 8 percent of our respondents had received a FAITH evangelistic visit. Of course, the percentage was higher among Southern Baptist churches.

"Jodie was the one who told me about becoming a Christian," Martie reflected. "I wanted to accept Christ right then, but I was confused and felt pressured. She backed off, and the three people from the church left me on good terms."

Martie did not hear from anyone from Davis Baptist Church for a few days. But on Saturday evening she received a telephone call. "It was Jodie." Martie shared with us. "She blew me away with what she said. She asked if I would go to church and Sunday school with her the next day. It seemed like the right thing to do. She even took me to lunch after church."

Martie offered a straightforward assessment of the preaching, which she was hearing for a second time: "That sermon was great. There were two things about it. He taught the Bible first, and second, he applied it to my life. I was hooked."

The pastor offered an evangelistic invitation, and Martie prayed to receive Christ during the service. A few weeks later she presented herself to the church for baptism and membership.

Martie listed for us the most important factors that led her to Christ and to the church:

- *Holy Spirit conviction:* Martie told us: "I was looking before anyone ever came to talk to me. I didn't know it at the time, but God was getting my attention. I probably would have accepted Christ by hearing a television preacher. The people at Davis Baptist just showed up at the right time."

- *Direct evangelism:* Despite the detractors who claim that a one-on-one sharing of the gospel is ineffective, Martie was one of many we interviewed who was personally evangelized.

- *Friendliness of the church:* Martie "fell in love with the people of the church." "What if," we asked, "you had walked into Davis Baptist, and the people had not been friendly?" "That is a question that scares me to death," she told us. "It really scares me that friendliness has eternal implications."

- *Preaching:* Once again we heard from the formerly unchurched that preaching was a major factor in their decision-making process. And once again we heard two key words to describe the preaching: *biblical* and *relevant*.

80

Conclusion #4: Family Relationships Are the Most Important

Marion W. of Indianapolis was different than most of those we interviewed. She was a senior adult (seventy years old) when she became a Christian. Rarely did we speak to a formerly unchurched person over fifty years old.

While many of the people described thus far named multiple factors that led them to Christ and to the church, Marion's explanation was simple: her niece invited her to an Easter presentation at a Presbyterian church. The gospel was presented, and she accepted Christ, joined the church, and is very active in the church two years later at age seventy-two.

> "No one ever invited me to church before. Why is that?"

When we asked Marion what she liked about her church, Marion listed numerous factors. "The worship services are so exciting, the pastor is a great preacher, and the people are so friendly," she gushed. But when we asked her why she went to church in the first place, her answer was simple, "My niece invited me." Then she followed with a simple but profound question: "No one ever invited me to church before. Why is that?"

Even in Marion's straightforward answer, we have at least three possibilities to explain her pilgrimage from the world of the unchurched to the church. First, someone invited her. Our research team heard from many of the formerly unchurched how few times they received invitations to attend church.

I remember, as a child, that we would turn in offering envelopes during the Sunday school hour. On the offering envelopes was a place for us to indicate if we read our Bible daily, if we studied our Sunday school lesson, and how many people we invited to church during the week. While the offering envelope check-off system may not be practical today, it does raise a question. How do we engender accountability from our members to invite people?

A second reason for Marion's entry into the world of the churched was the big event, the Easter drama/musical at the Presbyterian church. Our previous studies indicated that the big event alone is not sufficient for churches to reach the unchurched.[8] Yet the big event, if highly intentional for outreach and combined with some other factors, can be effective in reaching the unchurched. The "other factor" in Marion's case was the invitation by a

Figure 3.4

What Person Was the Greatest Influence in Your Coming to Church?

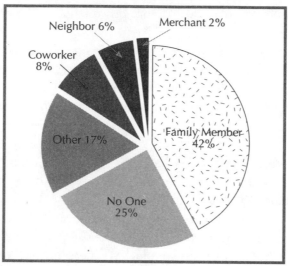

relative. Would Marion have attended the Easter event if someone other than her niece had invited her? "I honestly can't say," she responded. "But I do know how much I love my niece, and that had to affect me."

In chapter 1 we previewed the importance of a family member in reaching the unchurched. Far more than any other person, the family member was influential in persuading an unchurched person to come to church. Just less than one-half of the respondents indicated the importance of this relationship.

> If family members are indeed the most important relationships in reaching the unchurched, should churches not provide resources and strategies for reaching people through these relationships?

If family members are indeed the most important relationships in reaching the unchurched, should churches not provide resources and strategies for reaching people through these relationships? Though the work of the research team provided me new insights personally, this issue was among the most profound. It indeed seemed to call for more research and greater intentionality in reaching the unchurched through family members.

Conclusion #5: The Wife Is the Most Important Relationship in Reaching the Unchurched

We noted briefly in chapter 1 the importance of wives reaching husbands. It is worth noting how important this relationship is.

Figure 3.5

If a Family Member Influenced You to Come to Church, Which Person Was Most Influential?

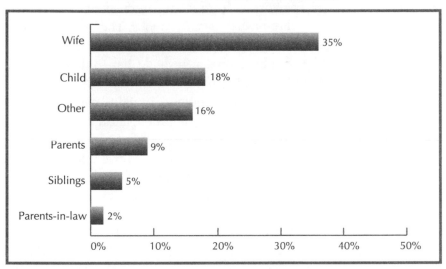

Wives were most influential in reaching the unchurched. When we asked those who were influenced by a relationship to come to church who influenced them the most, over one-third responded that it was their wives. The implications of this response are noteworthy.

Men seem to be more likely to be reached by relationships than women. Women were more likely to visit a church without an invitation from a friend, acquaintance, relative, or coworker. Men, on the other hand, were more reluctant to go to a church where they knew no one.

The paradigm of effective youth and children's ministry seems to be changing. Ten years ago the paradigm of youth ministry was "reach the parents to reach the children." Today the paradigm is "reach the children to reach the parents." Almost one out of five of the formerly unchurched who were influenced by some relationship indicated that their children were the most important of these relationships.

Most churches indicated that their members included a significant number of churched wives who were married to unchurched husbands. The implication of this issue may be profound. We may have within our churches today a group that could be the most effective in reaching unchurched America.

Relationships That Click

Liz Z. from Ohio has been a Christian for thirty years. Liz was one of our interviewees in the category of the transfer churched. She had moved from Iowa to Ohio when her husband changed jobs. The question about relationships seemed to trigger some painful emotions in Liz. Instead of talking to us about the relationships that brought her to the Wesleyan church, she talked about her relationship with her husband.

"My pastor warned me about the problems I might have marrying a lost person," Liz told us. "But I was so young then, and I was head over heels over Roger. I thought I could change him."

The pause in our conversation allowed Liz to review mentally the events of the last two decades of her life. "Don't get me wrong," she insisted, "Roger is a great husband and a great father. It's just that we have a lot of different values."

Then Liz got to the heart of her concern. "My church really has a concern for the lost and unchurched people, she said. "But you know the main lost person I'm concerned about. Yet the church hasn't made any effort to reach out to Roger. Why don't churches reach out to those closest to us?"

Liz's question was rhetorical, but it deserves a response. Relationships are important, and many churches do a good job of emphasizing the need for their members to connect with the unchurched. But the most receptive unchurched people may be living in the homes of our church members.

> The most receptive unchurched people may be living in the homes of our church members.

One other issue related to unchurched family members is worth pursuing. In almost every case where we asked the question, we found that the unchurched family member attends church at least once a year. And when that person attends, he or she is profoundly impacted by "first" impressions. I use the word *first* loosely, because the person may have attended the church on previous occasions. But each new visit is like a first impression because of the time lapse between visits.

What do these unchurched family members (and other unchurched persons) see when they walk into the church? How do they perceive the people in the church? The music? The order of service? The facilities? All of these issues were important, the formerly unchurched told us. In the next chapter we will hear how much they really do matter.

CHAPTER 4

Impressed by First Impressions

*I've been to one church where I visited twice,
the only time I ever went back to a church. The only
reason I went back is because they had this really
cool preschool class for my two-year-old daughter.*

—"LAGirl1" in the Jesus Only
Internet Chat Room

I love churches. For many years I have been a consultant to churches—newer churches, older churches, traditional churches, contemporary churches, growing churches, declining churches.

Do you know what almost all of these churches have in common? They think they are friendly churches. I can walk into a worship service at one of these churches and no one will speak to me. Maybe someone will give me a perfunctory hello and a handshake, but he or she will not engage me in any meaningful conversation. Their greetings are more obligatory than expressions of care and concern.

A few weeks prior to writing this chapter, I provided a consultation for a church with about seven hundred in attendance. The church is located in a southern state and has a reputation of being a pretty good church in its region. A slight but steady decline in the church's attendance prompted a call to me. The leaders wondered, "What could be wrong with our church?"

The consultation included an observation of the morning worship service. I intentionally arrived about five minutes before the service was scheduled to begin. The most conspicuous parking lot was full, and there were no clear markers or signs for additional parking. I finally found a spot in a more distant lot. When I got out of the car, I noticed the parking lot had numerous cracks with grass growing in them. Two huge potholes were within ten feet of my parking space. And the striping in the lot was faded almost to the point of invisibility.

I made my way toward the sanctuary though no one was available to offer directions or greetings. Upon entering the foyer of the sanctuary, I was half-heartedly greeted by five men whose average age I estimated to be in the seventies. One of them pushed a church bulletin toward me without saying a word.

Upon entering the sanctuary, I immediately discovered that all of the back rows and middle rows were filled. The first available seating appeared to be on the fourth row from the front. I made my way uncomfortably toward the unoccupied seat, sensing that fourteen hundred eyes were watching my every move.

The church did have a greeting time for guests. The pastor informed us alien beings to remain seated while the rest of the real people stood and greeted us. To be fair, several people did at least acknowledge my presence. But the view I had while seated and others were standing was not the most scenic! When the time of greeting was over, the real people returned to be with their own kind while no one dared sit within six feet of me.

I finally took the time to observe the facility in which I worshiped. Circa 1974 would be my guess at the décor.

I have a tolerance for a wide range of music styles. I love many of the old hymns but enjoy most contemporary music as well. The music in this church, however, was too traditional to reach the younger families the demographics indicated. But the problem was not just that the music was too traditional; it was slow, dirge-like, bad-quality traditional music.

The sermon was pretty good, consisting of solid exposition of the text with a contemporary application. No complaints there.

At the end of the service I approached others to attempt conversation, but most of the individuals were already engaged in conversations with people they knew. *Oh well,* I thought, *it's time to leave.* So I made the trek to the distant parking lot without a word spoken to me.

Upon returning to my hotel, I reviewed my notes from the interviews conducted the day before with some fifteen church members. The most common remark given to me by those members? "We're the friendliest church in town!"

The Struggle with Consumerism

I wish I knew the perfect balance. The church I visited obviously needed work. The members seemed to have little awareness of visitors or guests in their midst. They did things the way they had always done them and wondered why they were not growing.

Some churches, on the other hand, have taken seeker friendliness to another extreme. Fearful that factual biblical teaching will offend the scripturally uninitiated, the message is compromised and the method becomes sovereign. Such churches have a consumer-driven mentality. A church that totally disregards the needs of the unchurched will reach few if any for the kingdom. But a church that makes most of its decisions based on the perceived needs of the same group is in danger of losing its biblical identity.

> A church that totally disregards the needs of the unchurched will reach few if any for the kingdom. But a church that makes most of its decisions based on the perceived needs of the same group is in danger of losing its biblical identity.

The problem has been accentuated with the rise of consumerism in America. Lyle Schaller notes, "Forty years of television have taught the younger generations that the producers of lectures, seminars and other forms of oral communication carry 100 percent of the responsibility for grabbing and holding the attention of the potential listener."[1]

The children born in the 1950s and '60s were raised in a culture that increasingly demanded more rights and privileges for the consumer. Now some of the businesses created by consumerism are recognizing that they must become more consumer-friendly in order to remain competitive.

McDonald's, for example, made a decision in 1998 to invest $200 million in redesigning the kitchens in their restaurants. For almost fifty years the company's philosophy had been to combine a consumer-driven fast-food menu with a producer-driven method of preparing the food. By 1995, however, Burger King had become a more threatening competitor after introducing the theme "Have It Your Way." Each sandwich should be prepared, not according to the producer's mass production, but individually according to the customer's desires. The new McDonald theme "Made for You" promises that sandwiches will be prepared one at a time to meet the demands of the consumer.[2] The new kitchens were designed specifically to prepare the sandwiches individually.

The McDonald's story is but one of thousands in which a consumer-driven society is changing the landscape and culture of an entire nation. The church is not exempt from this major cultural trend. Though we will expand on the issues later in this chapter, note some that were important to the formerly unchurched before they became Christians:

- Adequate parking
- Clean facilities
- Modern facilities
- High-quality preschool/nursery
- Variety of quality programs
- Relevant and quality music
- Clean bathrooms
- Friendly people
- Outgoing greeters
- Clearly marked and functional welcome center
- Good signage
- Comfortable pews/chairs
- Attention-holding preaching

For most of the generations born before 1950, church is a place where you serve, sacrifice, and give. For most of the generations born after 1950, the question is not "What can I do to serve the church?" but "What has the church done for me lately?"

The struggle with consumerism for church leaders is the need to know where to draw the line. Certainly the friendliness of church members is a "consumer-friendly" factor that any church should encourage. And basic cleanliness of facilities should not be an issue of debate. Even physical facility improvements that provide comfort to members and guests are not inherently wrong. Not many churchgoers in the South are debating the value of air conditioning. But how far should such comforts go? How much of a church's budget should be spent on comfort and aesthetics when it could otherwise be used directly for missions and evangelism? What level of capital commitment should be expended on a state-of-the-art preschool facility in order to attract young families?

Southeast Christian Church in Louisville, Kentucky, is one of the largest churches in the United States. When the church needed to relocate and build new facilities because of its rapid growth, it became the subject of fierce criticism. A pastor of another local church lamented the excessive capital expenditures of Southeast that could have been used for ministry. Yet when I calculated Southeast's per capita expenditures to reach a person for Christ, I discovered that Southeast was thirty times more efficient in its expenditures for outreach than the critic's church.

Since we do live in a consumer-driven nation, no church is immune from the harsh realities of dealing with a culture that views congregations from a consumer mind-set. What adjustments do we make to accommodate this culture? Where indeed do we draw the line?

At times it seemed as though our research raised more questions than provided answers. The formerly unchurched were very clear that certain issues of friendliness, cleanliness, and comfort did affect their decision-making process in choosing a church. And from their perspective, some of these issues had eternal consequences.

Gina M. and the Eternal Value of a Quality Nursery

"I am a thirty-two-year-old divorcée," Gina said. "Divorcée" hung in the air with uncertainty. You could tell that Gina was intensely uncomfortable using the word. "I was on the top of the world just two years ago. Mike and I finally had a child. The best days were ahead," she reflected.

Gina was immediately apologetic. She said she had no right sharing these matters with us. The quiver in her voice revealed her emotions. We assured her that we understood.

We asked her how she found Lakeview Community Church. Located less than two hours from Seattle, Lakeview is a beautiful nondenominational church with a breathtaking view of a large lake. Started just eight years ago, the average attendance is already over four hundred.

"The story is pretty simple," Gina responded. "After Mike left me, I started looking for a church. I asked a lot of people where I could find a church that would take care of Elizabeth. I wasn't about to put my two-year-old in an unsafe, unsanitary, and uncaring place. Lots of people told me to check out Lakeview."

Gina made the eight-mile journey to Lakeview with trepidation. "Elizabeth is my whole world now. I wanted her to be raised in a religious setting, but I was scared to death."

Her fears proved unfounded. "I was really impressed that they had designated parking for single moms. There were signs that pointed me right to the 'Wee Care' wing at the church. And the moment I entered the building, people were greeting us and helping us," she continued.

"You should see this place. It's cleaner than Disneyland! And it's every bit as attractive as Disneyland. Elizabeth was so excited she tried to run from me to get to one of the rooms with a bunch of toys. And I had thought she would scream when I left!" she said laughingly.

> "Do you think churches realize that good childcare may make an eternal difference in someone's life? Do they really understand?"

The safety concerns at the preschool ministry really impressed Gina. They required her to complete a form asking questions about Elizabeth's health, allergies, and personal preferences. "Then they gave me a personal pager. I really couldn't believe that I was in a church," she exclaimed.

The adults in the worship service were very friendly. The music was contemporary and upbeat. The pastor preached a biblical and relevant message. And when Gina picked up Elizabeth, she found a happy and content two-year-old.

"I was hooked. For the first time since the divorce I began to see a glimmer of hope," she told us.

When we asked Gina when she became a Christian, she remembered the specific moment she prayed to receive Christ in one of the worship services. "But there were so many other factors that moved me closer to accepting Christ. When I prayed to receive Christ, it was the culmination of many events."

Gina continued, "One of the first things I did after I joined the church was to volunteer to work one Sunday a month at Wee Care. You know, I now realize I was hell-bound until I came to Lakeview. And I never would have returned to Lakeview without the great ministry of Wee Care." She paused for a moment and then spoke with urgency, "Do you think churches realize that good childcare may make an eternal difference in someone's life? Do they really understand?"

Second Impressions and Wake-up Calls

I am amazed by how much this research has changed my perspective. Indeed, every time I have led a research team to investigate a facet of church life, I have experienced some degree of my own paradigm shift.

This study was no exception. Two issues related to the topic at hand were particularly surprising.

The first issue was that the formerly unchurched were more impacted by their second visit than their first visit. In a technical sense, then, the issue is second impressions rather than first impressions. But unchurched people like Gina may not have returned if the first visit had been negative.

Why did the formerly unchurched tell us that they really noticed the church on a second visit? They were overwhelmed on the first visit, and issues like cleanliness and even friendliness were not as noticeable because they were "on spiritual overload," as one formerly unchurched Alabama man told us. "God was dealing with me in so many ways," he said. "I couldn't even have told you if the church building was brick or wood that first time." The point of the difference between first and second impressions is interesting but does not alter the primary concern that the unchurched do notice their surroundings when they visit a church.

The second issue that surprised me was the intensity with which the formerly unchurched spoke of their first (or second) impressions of churches. One of our set questions was "What were your initial observations?" Ninety percent of the formerly unchurched indicated that some factor about the people or the facilities impacted their decision to return for another visit. Most of those indicated that their decision to return was made within a few minutes after they arrived at the church.

My bias does not want the issue of first impressions to be such a major factor in reaching the unchurched. I am concerned that the consumer mentality is already dominating some churches to the extent that many have moved from being consumer-friendly and seeker-friendly to becoming driven by consumerism. I confess that I certainly

Figure 4.1

Was Friendliness or Facilities a Major Factor in Your Decision to Return to the Church?

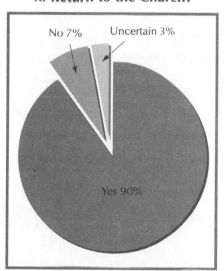

No 7%   Uncertain 3%

Yes 90%

do not know where to draw the line. No one will find me arguing against comfortable seating and clean facilities. Bob Russell, the senior minister of Southeast Christian Church in Louisville, is a stickler about first impressions. And lest you think that a story about one of the largest congregations in America does not relate to your church, he reminds us: "When I first came to Southeast Christian Church in 1966, people were meeting in the basement of a small house. But the basement was spic and span, the bulletin was printed without typos or grammatical errors, the people were friendly and the worship was well planned and orderly."[3]

When I begin to see the first impression issue as one of excellence more than pleasing an insatiable consumer appetite, my perspective changes. And when I hear stories like Gina's, whose eternity was impacted by excellence in facilities and childcare, I am almost convinced of the importance of first (or second) impressions.

Bob Russell says further about excellence: "Mediocrity breeds indifference, but quality attracts. . . . Imagine how much easier evangelism would be if your church services were done with so much excellence that they inspired people to the extent that they couldn't help but tell their friends about their experience."[4]

Pastor Russell is quick to state that the emphasis on excellence is a major part of the remarkable story of Southeast and the tens of thousands who have become Christians in his ministry there. "But why have our people been so bold in inviting their friends and so effective in getting them to come?" he asks rhetorically. "Because they are excited about what they've experienced and are confident that every week the grounds, the nursery, the greeting, the singing, and the preaching will be done with excellence."[5]

Okay, I am convinced! With testimonies such as the story of Southeast Christian and the dozens of stories told to us by the formerly unchurched, the evidence is overwhelming: excellence does matter. First impressions are important, because someone's eternity may be in the balance.

What Kind of First Impressions?

What specific factors are important to the unchurched when they finally choose to visit a church? Statistical graphs and charts do not paint an entirely accurate picture of the importance of each of the first impression issues. For example, the preschool/nursery/children's facility was deemed an important first impression in 36 percent of our interviews. At first glance the relative level of importance may be understated, since only about one-third of the respondents deemed preschool and children's facilities important. But if one takes into consideration that only about one-half of our respondents have young children, the responses of one out of three has a higher impact.

> The evidence is overwhelming: excellence does matter. First impressions are important, because someone's eternity may be in the balance.

Still one issue of first impression stands clearly above others in importance. The formerly unchurched told us that one of the key reasons for their returning to a particular church was the friendliness of the members.

First Impression #1: Friendliness

Leonard and Connie M. were truly frightened. When they first received word that a job relocation to Orlando was in the works, they had been very excited. Connie mused, "Orlando meant sunshine, Disney World, beaches close by, and a fun time!" But reality set in within a few days. Orlando was a long way from their small hometown in Wisconsin where they had lived all their lives.

"From dairy farms to Disney World," Leonard contributed. "Yeah, it seemed great at first. But when we got to Orlando we realized how big this place is. People are so busy too. It was just hard to make friends. We made the effort to introduce ourselves to our neighbors. They were friendly, but everybody was too busy to get involved with others."

The couple had had virtually no church involvement in Wisconsin. They really did not consider visiting churches until Connie discovered a lump in her breast. Connie began to consider, perhaps for the first time, her own mortality. "That was a wake-up call," said Connie. "For the first time we started thinking about a church."

The first church they visited was a Southern Baptist church near their home. By the number of cars they saw at the church, Leonard and Connie could tell much was taking place there.

"The people were incredibly friendly," Connie told us. "I felt love all around me the first time we walked in. The people seemed to really care."

Connie cannot remember how someone found out about her surgery. She does remember, however, that three women from the church showed up the day of her surgery.

"We've heard about churches where the people are cold and unfriendly. I'm sure glad that wasn't the case at our church," Connie said. "Not only am I okay physically now, but both Leonard and I met Christ at the church. It's amazing what a smile and a kind word did."

Figure 4.2
First Impression Issues Mentioned in Interviews: Friendliness

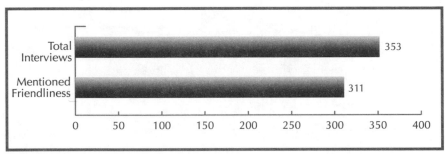

In our 353 interviews with the formerly unchurched, 88 percent of the respondents told us that the friendliness of the people was a major attraction to the particular church they joined. Yet friendliness is an intangible issue. A pastor or other church leader cannot simply tell or ask church members to be friendly and expect immediate results. In the course of our interviews, we found other factors at work, some of which were difficult to implement. Listen to some of the insights we gleaned from the formerly unchurched.

- Most church members believe they are friendly when in reality they are friendly only to others whom they already know.
- "Manufactured friendliness" is obvious. Notes Lela from Pennsylvania: "You could tell that they were trying to be friendly, like someone told them that they needed to be friendly. It was almost as bad as being unfriendly."
- Friendliness of members to non-Christians tends to be correlated to a church's evangelistic effectiveness. Members seem to be enthusiastic about new Christians, which engenders friendliness toward others who are not Christians.

- Friendly churches are likely to have friendly pastors. The pastor's modeling of friendliness is critical.
- A relationship is also apparent between the friendliness of a church and the members' willingness to accept change.

Lela was perhaps one of our most outspoken formerly unchurched on the issue of friendliness. "After visiting nearly a dozen churches, I am amazed how cold some of them are. I was looking for someone who cared enough about me to offer me a smile or a kind word. Thank God I finally found one church where the people acted like they were happy to be Christians."

First Impression #2: Nice Facilities/Adequate Space

One of Zig Ziglar's favorite expressions is: "Efficiency is getting the job done right. Effectiveness is getting the right job done. Excellence is getting the right job done well."[6] I expressed initial reticence in reporting that the formerly unchurched said that first impressions were important. I simply resisted the idea that a clean facility could make an eternal difference. But after listening to 353 formerly unchurched, and after six years of researching over two thousand effective evangelistic churches across America, I am the convinced skeptic.

Margaret T. of Spokane, Washington, noted of her conversion: "I have no doubt that God used the preaching of his Word and the witnessing of his people to bring me to Jesus. But I never would have heard the message if I had not been thoroughly impressed with the quality of their facilities. I showed up at the church one Sunday to be there for my nephew's baptism. One of the reasons I came back on my own was a sense that the church did everything with excellence, and it showed from the parking lot to the rest rooms."

Even with my former reluctance to acknowledge the importance of clean and neat facilities, I confess that I saw that importance in a church where I served as pastor. Every six months I would ask a woman to do a thorough examination of our grounds and buildings. (My apologies to men. I tried using men on a few occasions, but all of them were blind to obvious dirtiness and poor facilities.) The woman would be someone who had never been in our church. We would give her a notebook with a page for every room, hallway, foyer, and area of grounds. She would go from area to area taking notes and then report to our staff and key lay leader what she saw. It is amazing how she saw dirtiness, cracked windows, dead bushes, and a plethora of other items that we passed by everyday. We were happy to give her a stipend for her few hours of work.

Figure 4.3 shows that almost half of the formerly unchurched mentioned something about the grounds or facilities when we inquired about their first impressions of the church. And though some of them may have returned even with negative impressions, it is obvious that these issues were vitally important to many.

Figure 4.3

**First Impression Issues Mentioned in Interviews:
Nice Facilities/Adequate Space**

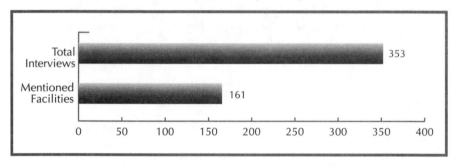

When we inquired about issues related to the physical facilities of the church, we gleaned a variety of insights from the formerly unchurched.

- Clean rest rooms are essential. We were surprised to hear unsolicited comments about dirty rest rooms.
- Adequate parking was mentioned as a need only if the person experienced problems finding a parking place or if the parking was too distant.
- Some basic comfort issues mentioned frequently were pew or chair comfort, indoor climate control, adequate seating space, and covered walkways and drop-off points.
- Sound systems engendered a few interesting comments, but only if there were problems. Apparently the best sound system is one that is unnoticed.
- We received several positive remarks about attractive and neat landscaping.

- The issue that generated the most intense comments was the cleanliness, neatness, and safety of nursery, preschool, and children's areas. We will look at this issue now as a separate item.

First Impression #3: The Nursery/Preschool/Children's Issue

Of the 161 formerly unchurched who told us that the condition of the facilities was clearly noticed by them, 63 percent volunteered their observations about children's facilities. Again, our questions were open-ended. No responses were prompted by our research team. The fact that almost one-third of the formerly unchurched volunteered their opinions is significant. While parents with young children were among the most vociferous about quality care for children at church, they were not alone. We heard similar comments from parents with older children, adult children, and no children. It seems that many unchurched people measure the quality of a church by the quality of childcare.

Nona D. of Milwaukee is a forty-six-year-old divorced woman. She has no children, but she does have an opinion about their needs. "Before I became a Christian, I visited several churches," she told us. "Either through the comments of others or my own observations, I usually could tell how well children were treated at the churches. And you know, the churches that had top-notch preaching, worship services, and friendly people were the churches that had the best nursery facilities. If they didn't care about the kids, they usually were lousy in other areas."

As you would expect, however, parents of young children were the most outspoken. A pastor from Illinois recently visited my hometown of Louisville, Kentucky. He and his wife have a two-year-old daughter. They decided to visit a church with the perspective of the unchurched.

> It seems that many unchurched people measure the quality of a church by the quality of childcare.

Scott told us the story: "We were ten minutes late to the worship service. It was raining, so we were anxious to find a parking place near the nursery. The problem was that there was no signage that gave us a clue where the nursery facilities were."

Scott's horror story continued: "We went into the foyer of the sanctuary looking for directions to the nursery, but no one was there. We went into a side hallway with no lights on. We followed the hallway into the darkness for some time until we saw a light coming from beneath a door. When we opened the door, we saw six boys in a dirty room. The boys were wild, jumping off chairs and screaming as an elderly woman watched passively."

Scott and his wife quickly decided that they would never leave their daughter in the dirty room with the wild animals. "If we had not been Christians, even mature Christians, we would have gone home. But we decided to go to worship with our two-year-old."

Fortunately (or so they thought), someone showed them the "quick way" back to the sanctuary. The member opened a door for them to enter and quickly closed it behind them. Much to their horror they were facing the entire congregation. The preacher had already begun his sermon and was just six feet from them.

"There were probably one hundred people there, and I could feel all two hundred eyes staring at us. We hung our heads and made our way to the back of the sanctuary straight out the door to our car," Scott said with disgust. "What if my wife and I had not been Christians?"

The formerly unchurched told us repeatedly how difficult it was for them to visit a church. And those who had young children were especially sensitive to their kids' needs. Though I knew prior to this study the importance of adequate childcare in churches, I did not realize how deeply emotional this issue was for the unchurched. After hearing the responses of the unchurched, I am no longer surprised that nearly one-third of the respondents commented without prompting about childcare. They raised the following issues.

Figure 4.4

**First Impression Issues Mentioned in Interviews:
Quality Children's Facilities**

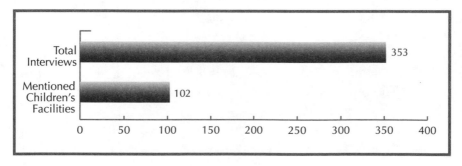

- Safety is the number one concern. Parents want to know that no dangerous toys or other items are in the children's rooms. They want to be certain that only the parents can get to the child. They insist on some type of identification system to pick up children. They want to be certain that sufficient adult workers are present so that no harm comes to their children.

- Easy accessibility to their children is their second concern. The formerly unchurched told us that they would not leave their children if they were separated from them by a great distance, particularly several buildings.

- The third most frequently expressed concern was the ability to be notified if needed. Their first choice was a pager; their second preference was a number notification monitor.

- The apparent concern and attitude of adult workers were mentioned next. Phyllis M. of Texas told us that she walked away from one church when an indifferent adult worker met her.

- Cleanliness was also mentioned frequently. "You could tell quickly if the church cared about a sanitary environment for the kids," Phyllis said.

Also cited by several of the formerly unchurched was how up-to-date the children's area was. Old furniture, broken toys, worn carpet, and 1980s baby beds are a sure sign of neglect.

First Impression Issue #4: Organization or Chaos

Charlie R. of central Louisiana told us there were two nondenominational churches in the mid-size Louisiana city. Azalea Community Church was his first visit; the Church of Greensprings was his second. "Azalea was a mad house," Charlie offered without apology. "The service started late, the music was messed up, the person running the sound system was incompetent, and most of the people participating in the leadership of the worship service seemed clueless," he observed.

"I visited the Church of Greensprings the next week. What a difference!" Charlie exclaimed. "You could tell that everything had been given careful attention. They had both wonderful organization and the opportunity for spontaneity. Yeah, everything was planned, but they were so sincere. You didn't get the impression that they were just performing," Charlie concluded.

Charlie started attending the Church at Greensprings and eventually accepted Christ. And he was one of several formerly unchurched who told us that one of his first impressions was the organization of the church, particularly the organization and flow of the worship service.

Over one hundred of the formerly unchurched noticed the attention churches gave to having a well-planned worship service, as noted in figure 4.5. These former seekers told us that such attention to detail was an indication that the church was serious about its mission. Charlie noted, "I have been in the corporate world for over twenty years. I can tell in any company or church if the organization has a sense of purpose. One of the big factors for a church is its worship services, where the most people gather at any one time. If that isn't planned well, you can be sure that the church members do most everything else poorly."

Figure 4.5

First Impression Issues Mentioned in Interviews: Organization in Worship Services

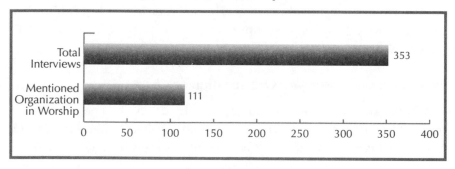

First Impression #5: Greeters and Welcome Centers

"Nothing makes me more uncomfortable," Jean T. said, "than walking into a place where I'm a total stranger." The Houston resident found a Methodist church that eased her fears. "When I got out of my car, some people in red vests greeted me and gave directions to the worship center. And when I entered the building, I was greeted by more of the red-vest gang." Jean continued, "The church is not huge, about 400 in attendance, but they have a better way of greeting people than a lot of big churches I attended. They also built a small welcome center that has information about the church and usually has someone to greet you there as well."

Sam Walton knew his customers' needs and desires. He built Wal-Mart to become one of the world's largest retailers by always seeking to be sensitive to the needs of the consumer. The friendly greeters at the Wal-Mart entrance are but one small part of the legacy of customer orientation he left the company.

Churches do not have to compromise any biblical values to be sensitive to the needs of the unchurched. Greeter ministries in particular can be implemented with relative ease. In nearly one-third of our interviews, the formerly unchurched shared with us positive first impressions of when the church had a good greeter ministry and a welcome center. They gave us the following insights.

- Ushers who hand out bulletins are not always greeters.
- A good greeter ministry requires good training.
- Many churches tend to ask older members to be greeters when a balance of ages is best.
- A good welcome center keeps current information about the church, a map of the church, and gives away items.
- Many of these churches had greeters placed in numerous strategic places, including the parking lot.
- Effective churches seek the friendliest members to be greeters.
- Many churches ask new members and new Christians to be greeters. Their enthusiasm is often contagious.

Figure 4.6

First Impression Issues Mentioned in Interviews: Greeters and Welcome Centers

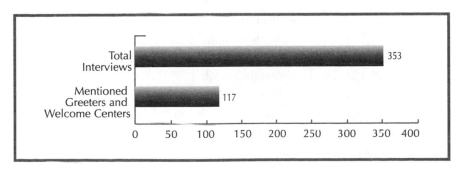

One-third of the formerly unchurched told us that they were impressed with a church's greeter ministry or welcome center. A helpful hand, a friendly smile, and good directions make an eternal difference.

The Issue is Excellence, Not Compromise

My first pastorate had seven people in attendance. Hopewell Baptist Church lies between Madison and Hanover, Indiana, a sparsely populated rural area. I have little doubt that God used the preaching of his Word and the sharing of the gospel as his primary vehicles to grow our church, but he also used an unusual incident as a catalyst to growth.

The church records indicated that no one had accepted Christ in years. The facilities were beautiful for a country church; the stones that were used to build the church had come from a clear stream flowing near the church property. But the facility was in terrible shape. The grounds showed no care, and the little parsonage clearly revealed signs of years of neglect.

We started trying to do ministry with excellence. We began a weekly newsletter. We took turns cleaning the church and mowing the lawn. We started bringing in high-quality guest musicians. We began an outreach ministry for the first time in a generation. Attendance increased to forty.

Then we decided that in order to get some major projects completed, we would have an all-day work day two weeks from Saturday. Word spread throughout the rural community that Hopewell was back on its feet, that the building was clean, and that the people were reaching out to others. A number of people who were not members showed up for the Saturday work day. One of those people was Steve.

Steve was married to Nancy, who had returned to the church after several years of absence. Steve was a hard worker. At the end of the day, I expressed my deep appreciation to Steve for all that he had done. As the crowd began to disburse, I noticed that Steve was reluctant to leave. I approached him and asked him if I could help him in any way. A simple "uh-huh" from Steve prompted us to walk into the church.

"What can I do for you?" I asked Steve. Reluctantly he responded. "I never thought much about church people until I heard what y'all were doing at Hopewell. Nancy comes home excited every time she goes to church. I came up here today 'cause I was curious."

Steve paused, and then I asked him to continue. "I reckon I was surprised to be around a bunch of church folks who had so much fun and seemed so happy. I wish I was that happy."

Now I understood. How I could have been so blind is a mystery to this day. "Steve," I asked, "would you like me to show you how to become a Christian?" His response was a simple but eternally profound, "Yep."

Steve's baptism started a new round of growth in the church. At the end of one year our attendance was seventy, ten times higher than when I started. Steve was attracted to people who cared, people who sought to make the church a better place, people who were willing to clean a dirty building for the Savior.

Steve was attracted to excellence. I think I forgot that lesson for a while, but now I am reminded again. The formerly unchurched are right: the church that seeks to be a church of excellence in all things will see God's blessings. And the difference in the lives of many will be eternal.

CHAPTER 5

Why They Returned and Stayed

I'm a new Christian, a little over a year. But I just can't seem to find a church where I can connect and feel comfortable enough to stay.

—"KingsGirl" in the WWJDX7
Internet Chat Room

John Ott is the senior pastor of Parkway Wesleyan Church in Roanoke, Virginia. The story of Parkway is a story of miraculous growth and changed lives. I had the opportunity to provide church consultation services for the church in 2000.

Typically when I am called in to do a consultation, it is because a church has either a major problem or a major opportunity. For Pastor Ott the issue at hand was a tremendous opportunity. Parkway Wesleyan Church, through nothing less than a series of miracles, was able to purchase an eighty-five-acre site on a beautiful and elevated area in one of the most visible points in Roanoke. The question in Pastor Ott's mind centered on timing and preparation for the move. The church would be relocating and building on a site seven times larger than its present site. The pastor needed to know if the church was ready.

Frankly, I know of few leaders as visionary and dynamic as John Ott. From a human perspective, I could understand clearly why the church grew as rapidly as it did under his leadership. But the pastor wanted to address the church's readiness. One of the primary issues we discussed was retention of members, particularly new Christians.

"In the last church I pastored several years ago," John reflected, "we led hundreds of people to Christ. But it was a frustrating experience because so few of them would stay in the church. I almost gave up on personal evangelism programs because of it."

John Ott's story is not unusual. If the surveys of religious interest have any validity, America is a very religious nation. Over seven out of ten (71 percent) Americans consider themselves to be "spiritual" people. When asked if they considered themselves "Christians," 85 percent responded affirmatively. And a like number (83 percent) said that religious faith is very important in their lives.[1]

Despite the strong affirmations of religious identity, particularly Christian identity, we have seen almost no change in church attendance for a decade in America. In 1991 almost half (49 percent) of adults in America attended church services in a typical week. By 1996 the number had declined significantly to 37 percent. In 1999 the number of Americans attending church in a given week was up slightly to 41 percent (see figure 5.1).[2]

> Despite the strong affirmations of religious identity, particularly Christian identity, we have seen almost no change in church attendance for a decade in America.

The plight of the American church is an increasing sense of religious values among the people of the nation, with little concern if this religious expression takes place in the context of the institutional church. Yet the biblical mandate calls for Christians to gather together (Hebrews 10:25). Why in our nation do we have religious people who are not "churched" people?

The assimilation issue is complex. No single answer explains the church's failure to "close the back door." The formerly unchurched, however, gave us keen insights into the reasons people stay in or leave churches. We also completed in 1999 a major research project on assimilation from the church's perspective.[3] The combination of information and data from the formerly unchurched and from churches with high retention complemented each other. Together they painted a clearer picture of how churches reach and *retain* people.

The formerly unchurched in this study were extremely discerning. Sometimes when I speak to church leaders, I get the impression that they view unchurched people as totally ignorant about the church and how it

Figure 5.1

Church Attendance Among American Adults, 1991–1999

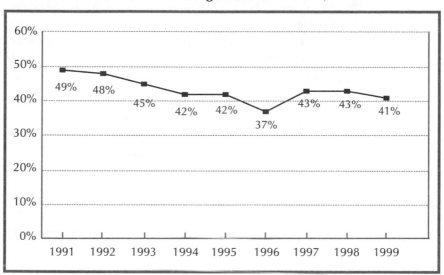

operates. To the contrary, the unchurched seem to have insights to which longtime church members are oblivious. We found this perspective particularly true on the issue of assimilation.

For the remainder of this chapter we will focus on six key issues for retaining members and for increasing return visits among guests. Some of the issues have obvious overlaps, and none can stand alone effectively. Nevertheless, the formerly unchurched told us that if a church gives attention to all six factors, retention will increase. To the first of those factors we now turn.

Why They Returned

Issue #1: Doctrine Clarified

Paddy is a second-generation immigrant. Her spiritual pilgrimage is unlike any of the formerly unchurched we interviewed. She adopted the Buddhist beliefs of her parents until she left home for a job and to be on her own. While at home one Saturday two Mormon missionaries visited her. Paddy was attracted to the friendliness and strong moral values of the Mormons. At age twenty-one she was baptized in the Mormon church even though she "didn't really understand what they believed." She left the church three years later.

She subsequently started attending a Church of Christ with a friend. She joined this church because of the built-in relationships she had. Once again, she was "clueless about their beliefs." Paddy was baptized but left the church two years later.

For nine years Paddy attended no church, but "people and partying" could not fill the emptiness in her life. She tried another church, Landwood Community Church, near Denver. For the first time in her life she heard clearly the gospel of Jesus Christ. She became a Christian and was baptized a third time. "But this time I knew why I was being baptized—not because of friendly people or friends in the church," Paddy told us, "but because I knew what I believed and who I believed in."

From Buddhist to Mormon to Church of Christ to an evangelical non-denominational church, Paddy's path has been anything but typical. At the time of our interview, she had been at Landwood Community Church slightly less than two years. It is therefore too early to conclude that she will stay active in the church. We do know, however, that Paddy returned to Landwood, joined Landwood, and continues active at Landwood for one key reason: she understands clearly what the church believes, and she affirms the church's beliefs.

In previous "churches" (including her Buddhist and Mormon ventures) she became a part of the fellowships because of nondoctrinal reasons. She was a Buddhist because her family is Buddhist. She became a Mormon because she hungered for their family-like caring. And she joined the Church of Christ because she had a friend who belonged there. But at Landwood Community Church Paddy had no previously established relationships. And though the people were friendly, Paddy, by her own admission, was "searching for truth." She found truth in Christ at Landwood.

Perhaps surprisingly to some readers, doctrine was the major factor in attraction and retention of the formerly unchurched. In a culture that prides itself on its religious pluralism, we found that perhaps millions of Americans are on a quest for objective truth. Because this issue was the most often mentioned factor in both the reaching and retention of unchurched people, we will devote the entirety of the next chapter to the reality that doctrine really matters. For now the reader simply needs to hear that churches that are unambiguous in their beliefs and clear on their teachings of them are the churches that see more of their visitors return and more of their attenders join.

Issue #2: High Expectations

Sam T. is a member of a Southern Baptist church in Columbia, South Carolina. He visited numerous churches from the time he graduated from college to his thirty-second birthday. The death of his father led him on his "umpteenth spiritual journey in a decade." Sam explained: "It seems like anytime something happened in my life, I was off to another church. But I just couldn't connect with any of the churches."

Sam's story changed when he visited White's Fork Baptist Church. "What a difference there was at White's Fork," Sam emphasized. "The first time I visited there it was very clear that they took church seriously," he said. "The folks at White's Fork believe that they can make a difference through the church, and they don't expect anybody to be on the sidelines."

Sometimes the conventional wisdom to reach the unchurched has been to lower expectations, to tell guests that we really do not expect anything of them. Such seeker friendliness may be effective for a short while, but it seems to be a sure formula for a wide open back door. Churches like White's Fork Baptist Church take a different approach. They make clear to even first-time visitors that they are a high-expectation church.[4] And contrary to some conventional wisdom, the unchurched are more likely to return if they understand the church expects much of their members. Notes Sam, "I may not have realized it at the time, but I was looking for a church that expected something of me. And you know, it's a shame that many of God's churches don't realize that there are many people like me."

After our research team had studied two thousand churches for over four years, the "high-expectation" factor became clear. Now, with 20–20 hindsight, I wonder why we did not recognize this factor as a common-sense issue. People have no desire to be a part of something that makes no difference, that expects little. And, frankly, many churches have dumbed down church membership to the point that it has no meaning at all.

Our research of the formerly unchurched complemented our study of two thousand churches. When high expectations are communicated to members, the unchurched are attracted to these churches that have meaningful membership. One such church among the churches we have received information on is Carron Baptist Church, an African-American church in Washington, D.C. They actually require their members to agree to a church covenant that mandates the following:

- To read the Bible daily.
- To pray with and for members of your family daily.
- To attend all worship services unless hindered by health or circumstances beyond your control.
- To abstain from gossip, backbiting, murmuring, or negative talk.
- To respond to conflict and disagreement according to biblical precepts.
- To share your faith regularly; to invite people to church.
- To participate in Bible study/Sunday school.
- To be in agreement with the church's doctrine.
- To be involved in at least one ministry in the church.
- To tithe.
- To abstain from alcohol and illegal drugs.
- To be sexually pure.

The unchurched that visit Carron Baptist Church quickly discern that it is a high-expectation church. Yet they keep returning, keep joining, and the church continues to grow.

High assimilation churches communicated that their Christian community expects much of everyone. Members are expected to live and minister in a way that is consistent with New Testament teachings. They are expected to attend worship and Sunday school or small groups regularly, adhere to doctrine, be involved in ministry, attend new member classes, and if they are new Christians, participate in some type of mentoring or discipleship relationship.

> Churches with high expectations not only reach the unchurched but retain them as well.

Our research indicates a clear trend. Indeed, with the information we have gleaned from two thousand effective churches and the unchurched, the evidence is staggering. Churches with high expectations not only reach the unchurched but retain them as well.

Issue #3: An "Entry Point" Class

Veronica B. is a Northern California native, though she had never lived in Sacramento until two years prior to our interview with her. Veronica is an accountant for a Fortune 500 company that has offices around the world. She was transferred to the Sacramento office, much to her delight.

"I'm now only two hours from my home. I get to see my parents at least once a month," she told us.

Veronica's description of her religious upbringing was "nominal Methodist." She knew that she was not a Christian before she ever visited the Presbyterian church in Sacramento. "I understood the gospel long before I became a Christian, but I put off any decision," she said.

Veronica visited the church at an invitation of a coworker. Veronica had no intention of returning for a second visit until she heard the pastor say that the church would be offering a class for anyone interested in membership or finding out more about the church. He described the entry-point class as "a no-obligation seminar."

Why not? she thought. Veronica had an interest in learning more about churches, so this opportunity seemed good. The pastor led the Sunday afternoon class. She would learn that day that the class was required for membership but open to anyone like her who was merely interested in finding out more about the church. She was impressed with the organization of the class and with the informative notebook that was given to each participant. And she was surprised by how much was covered in the three-hour class.

Nearly half of the two thousand churches we looked at offered or required a new members' class. When we asked them the topics they covered, the responses in order of frequency of topic covered were:

1. Doctrine of the church (67.0%).
2. Polity of the church (66.0%).
3. Examination of the church constitution (64.6%).
4. Explanation of Lord's Supper/Communion/baptism (63.5%).
5. Explanation of the church covenant (63.2%).
6. Policies for church discipline (62.5%).
7. Expectation of members after joining (58.7%).
8. History of the church (56.5%).
9. Tour of the church building (56.4%).
10. Denominational information (if applicable) (51.6%).
11. How to become a Christian (49.1%).
12. Tithing/financial support of the church (47.4%).
13. Method/meaning of baptism (41.1%).
14. Requirements for membership (38.9%).
15. Ministry opportunities in the church (37.2%).

16. Introduction to spiritual disciplines (35.2%).
17. Introduction to the church staff/leadership (33.7%).
18. Explanation of the church's mission and or vision (32.6%).
19. Inventory of spiritual gifts (29.5%).
20. Structure/support of missions (21.4%).
21. Brief evangelism/witnessing training (18.6%).

Veronica's fascination with the new members' class led her to come back to the church. She accepted Christ two months later and continues as an active member today. "I made the decision about the church with my eyes wide open," she told us. "I knew that they expected much from members because of what I heard in the class. And I really like being a part of a church that expects something of me. I'd be disappointed if they didn't."

How important is the new member class in the retention of the formerly unchurched and other new members? Figure 5.2 is revealing.

Figure 5.2

The Relationship between a New Members' Class and Retention

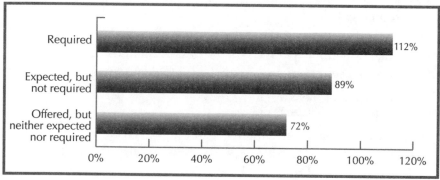

Though our study cannot draw dogmatic conclusions, the relationship between assimilation effectiveness and new members' classes is amazing.

Our research team examined the retention level of new members over a two-year period. As figure 5.2 shows, churches that require persons to enter membership through a new members' class have a much higher retention rate than those that do not.

To understand our concept of retention rate, an example might clarify the issue. A church in Oklahoma had average attendance of 300 in 1999. During 2000 the church added 45 new members, but the average attendance increased to 360 by the end of the year. In other words, attendance increased by a number greater than the number of new members. We would interpret the data to indicate that this church had a retention rate above 100 percent. (To see our precise calculation of this ratio, see note 4.)[5]

> The relationship between assimilation effectiveness and new members' classes is amazing.

Now note the retention rate of churches that require a new members' class. They are actually experiencing numerical growth greater than the number of new members added each year. The churches that encourage or expect, but do not require, a person to attend a membership class have a retention rate of 89 percent. This rate is lower than the 112-percent rate of the churches requiring membership classes, but healthy nevertheless. If a church merely offers a new members' class but neither requires nor expects people to attend, the retention rate drops to 72 percent over two years. And while 72 percent is lower than 89 percent and much lower than 112 percent, it is still a very good retention rate. Most church leaders would be delighted to have nearly three-fourths of their new members still active in the church two years after joining.

How does a new members' class impact the assimilation rate of churches? The question is best answered by reminding the reader of the second issue noted in why the formerly unchurched returned: high expectations.

The new members' class communicates expectations prior to a person joining the church. Presenting expectations early on was deemed to be much more effective than communicating them later in a member's tenure. And the new members' class, perhaps more than any other venue, was the vehicle by which expectations were most effectively communicated.

Issue #4: Small Groups and Sunday School

Undoubtedly you have heard or read that relationships are the most effective means of reaching and retaining the unchurched. With this point we have little disagreement. What many of the pundits fail to tell us, however, is the *how* of getting the unchurched or formerly unchurched established in relationships in the church. The process can be frustrating.

When I was the senior pastor of a church in Birmingham, Alabama, I tried to connect new members and particularly those with little church background with longer-term members of the church. We tried a "deacon family" ministry plan in which each deacon had the responsibility of developing relationships with and ministering to families, including new members. The plan had modest success at best.

We next attempted an "adopt a new member" ministry. Members volunteered to develop relationships with new members—to spend time with them and to help get them get assimilated in the church. This plan simply disappeared in less than a year.

What we discovered the hard way is that you cannot program relationships. They must develop naturally. But the church must provide avenues and opportunities for new members to get to know others in the church. Our research team discovered two primary vehicles for the formerly unchurched to connect with others: small groups and ministry involvement. We will discuss ministry involvement in the next section. Small groups are the focus of this part of the chapter.

Figure 5.3 shows that the formerly unchurched to whom we spoke typically found a Sunday school or some other small group where they developed relationships. The numbers are not mutually exclusive, but the evidence is strong that some type of small-group involvement was deemed very important to the formerly unchurched. Carol, for example, came from a second-generation unchurched family. She started visiting Advent Presbyterian in a small Tennessee town after her mother died. "For the first time in my life, I found myself interested in religious things," Carol told us. "Mom's death was the issue that pushed me to look for a church, but I was thinking about it for several months." What made her choose Advent Presbyterian? "Simple," she responded. "There are not a lot of churches in this town. I visited the four largest churches, and Advent was my favorite."

When we asked Carol what made her choose Advent over the other churches, she gave us several factors. But there was one factor that led her to speak with enthusiasm several times in our conversation. "I love my Sunday school class," Carol gushed. "Every woman in the class is in the same boat I'm in. We're all married, but our husbands don't attend church. We're really a tightly knit group," she mused.

As we invited Carol to explain further her enthusiasm for her Sunday school class, several factors emerged. The big issue, of course, was the friendships she had made in her class. The relationships she had developed were among the major factors assimilating her into the church. But

Figure 5.3

Number of Formerly Unchurched Involved in Sunday School or Other Small Groups

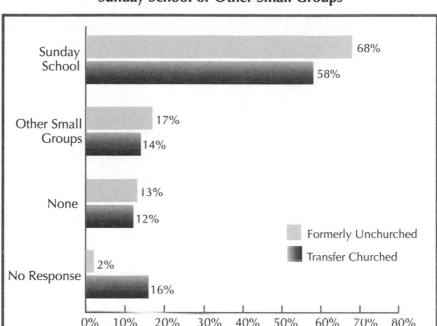

Carol also told us that she appreciated the Sunday school format that allowed her eleven-year-old daughter and nine-year-old son to be in a Bible study class concurrent with hers. "It might be a problem if I had to ask Rob [her husband] to keep the kids every week while I go to Sunday school. I'm glad they go with me," she said.

Another positive factor about Carol's Sunday school class is its connection with the worship service. "Rob is being pretty patient with what he calls my 'God thing.' I have to be careful not to overdo it. I can go to Sunday school and worship and be back at the house just as he starts moving around. It wouldn't work if I had to be out more than once each week," she told us.

We found an overwhelmingly convincing relationship between effective assimilation and involvement in small groups. Most of our data was on Sunday school; we do not have sufficient information at this point to draw conclusions about small groups or cell groups outside the Sunday school.

Two key research projects, one by George Barna[6] and a recent project by our team, combine to draw a fascinating conclusion. Involvement in small groups, such as Sunday school, is key to assimilation, yet churches have been largely unsuccessful in getting most of their members involved in these small groups. We found, for example, that new Christians who immediately became active in Sunday school were five times more likely to remain in the church five years later than those who were active in worship services alone. (We did not include those who moved to another community or those who died in the "dropout" category.) Figure 5.4 shows this sharp contrast in assimilation effectiveness for new Christians.

> We found an overwhelmingly convincing relationship between effective assimilation and involvement in small groups.

Figure 5.4

Percentage of New Christians Who Remain Active in the Church Five Years After Joining

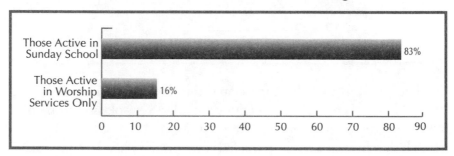

With this type of data, one might expect churches to give high priority to getting new members involved in a small group immediately. We certainly found the formerly unchurched to have an enthusiastic view of small groups, particularly Sunday school. Yet, as George Barna's research indicates, churches are doing a poor job of getting members into small groups. According to his data, adult Sunday school attendance has been flat for a decade.[7]

Attendance at worship services has also remained flat. Four out of ten adults (41 percent) attended worship services in 1999.[8] In rough terms, the combination of our data and Barna's data indicates that churches are involving only about one-half of their worship attenders in a Sunday school

118

Figure 5.5

**Percentage of Adults in America
Attending Sunday School, 1991–1999**

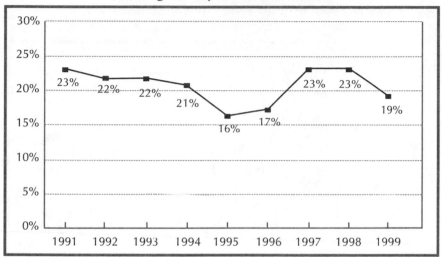

Figure 5.6

**Percentage of Adults in America
Involved in Small Groups, 1993–1999**

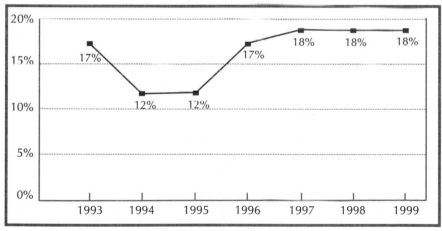

class. The data portrays a slightly worse picture for small groups other than Sunday school. For three consecutive years, the number of adults involved in *any* type of small group or cell group other than Sunday school has remained flat at 18 percent.

Our data on the formerly unchurched indicate over eight out of ten (84 percent) of those involved in small groups are also involved in a Sunday school class. Many of the formerly unchurched involved in small groups are doing double duty by also attending Sunday school.

Over eight of ten of the formerly unchurched in non-Sunday school small groups are also in a Sunday school class.

The picture is clear: the formerly unchurched "stick to" a church when they get involved in a small group. Let us pray that more churches will learn this lesson.

Issue #5: Clarity of Purpose

I have been dean at the Southern Baptist Theological Seminary since 1992. Each morning I wake up with excitement and anticipation about my place of work and ministry. I can honestly say that this position is the most rewarding, fulfilling, and even fun place I have ever been.

Undoubtedly, I could point to many factors that make this ministry so exciting. The professors at Southern are second to none. A collegiality exists among us that is unlike any place I have ever known. The students are great as well. Another thing that makes my ministry so enjoyable is what I call the trust factor. President Albert Mohler and Vice President Daniel Akin have given me much responsibility. They do not micromanage me; instead, they give me significant leeway to lead my school and to cast a vision for the work of the Billy Graham School of Missions, Evangelism, and Church Growth.

But if I had to point to any one factor that keeps me excited about my ministry at Southern Seminary, it is the vision and clarity of purpose for the mission of the school. Under Albert Mohler's leadership, three issues have become perfectly clear. First, we will be uncompromising on our doctrinal and biblical positions. Second, we will pursue excellence in all that we do, in particular in the teaching and training of God's ministers. Third, we will be a Great Commission–focused seminary. Our priorities in training men and women will include missions and evangelism. A certain excitement springs from having a vision, from knowing where we are going. And because I have such purpose, I have a desire and anticipation to come to work each day.

New church members, particularly the formerly unchurched, express similar sentiments. Notes Eric F., a new Christian at a Wesleyan church in Michigan: "I get pumped coming to church. You can feel the excitement. We're on a mission for God, and we know where we're going."

Though we did not specifically ask the formerly unchurched if they sensed a clear vision or clarity of purpose, seven out of ten of those interviewed provided comments that indicated they understood the direction and purpose of the church. Sample comments include:

- "We are a church that focuses on reaching the unchurched."
- "We have a bunch of ministries that are designed to minister to people's needs and to share Christ with them."
- "Our pastor never stops telling us how important our prayer ministries are to reach people."
- "Our church believes that reaching young families is really important. We spent over a million dollars on a state-of-the-art preschool building to reach these families."
- "Everybody in the church is asked to repeat our vision statement during the worship services at least a dozen times a year."

We recently asked hundreds of laypersons in effective evangelistic churches across America (see the introductory chapter for our definition of effective evangelistic churches) to name the purposes of a church. We did not put a limit on the number of responses they could give. We then asked the same question of a like number of laypersons from churches that did not meet our evangelistic criteria. We were looking for any responses that could be identified as the five purposes of the church: evangelism, discipleship, fellowship, ministry, and worship (we have subsequently added prayer as a sixth purpose of the church). A precise response was not necessary. For example, a response of "teaching the Bible" would be satisfactory for the discipleship purpose.

The results were revealing. Over 90 percent of the laypersons in the evangelistic churches were able to name at least four of the five purposes of the church. But only 17.7 percent of the laypersons in the nonevangelistic churches were able to identify at least four of the five purposes.

Figure 5.7a and 5.7b

Named the Purposes for Which a Church Exists

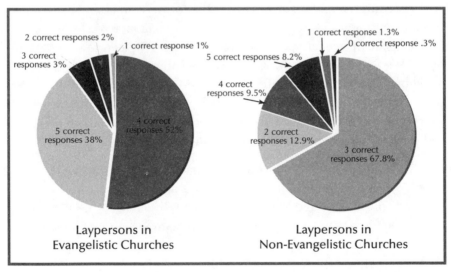

Laypersons in
Evangelistic Churches

Laypersons in
Non-Evangelistic Churches

Churches that are effective at reaching and retaining people typically are clear about their purposes. Ann, a formerly unchurched woman from Boston, told us: "I was attracted to the church because you know where they stand and where they're going. I'm staying at the church for the same reason."

Issue #6: Ministry Involvement

When we asked the formerly unchurched the straightforward question, "What keeps you active in the church?" their responses were enthusiastic. Sixty-two percent of those interviewed gave us a response that indicated their ministry involvement to be the glue that held them to the church.

The comments from the formerly unchurched were not only numerous, they were enthusiastic as well. Below are but a few sample responses to the question "What keeps you active in the church?"

- "Serving in the children's ministry."
- "Being active in the singles' ministry."
- "My ministry in the crisis pregnancy center."
- "I volunteer for Logos on Wednesday night."
- "Teaching children's church."
- "Being involved in the youth program."
- "Involvement in FAITH."
- "I am a care group leader in Sunday school. I can't believe I have grown from not being a Christian to ministering to other Christians in less than two years.

From the perspective of the formerly unchurched, being involved in ministry has been the key factor in their assimilation in the church. When

Figure 5.8

What Keeps You Active in the Church?

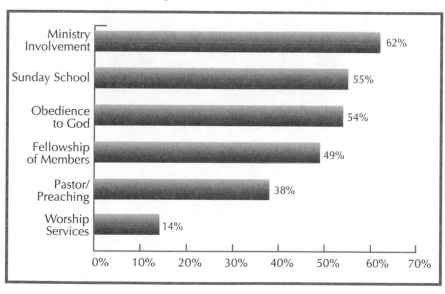

123

we tallied all 353 responses to our interviews, the impact of ministry involvement became obvious. More than any other factor, the formerly unchurched told us that their service and ministry in the church keeps them coming back each week.

Figure 5.8 (on the previous page) shows the different responses to the question "What keeps you active in the church?" Because of the nature of the interviews, most of the formerly unchurched gave us multiple responses.

While no single issue can explain why the formerly unchurched stay at a particular church, these new Christians make one point perfectly clear. Get them involved in ministry and they are much more likely to stay.

"Don't Keep Me on the Sidelines"

If a theme is obvious in this chapter, it is well reflected in the words of forty-five-year-old Tom B. of Oklahoma, a formerly unchurched person in a Nazarene church: "Don't keep me on the sidelines. Let me get involved." The formerly unchurched deeply desire to be a part of a church that makes a difference. They want to be involved in small groups, Sunday school, and ministry. They want to participate in a church that has clear direction and vision. And they do not mind, indeed they desire, churches that expect them to do ministry for God in the church where they met Christ.

CHAPTER 6

Doctrine Really Matters

*I like this chat room. I finally found some Christians
who are willing to stand for what they believe.*

—"FiFOAC" in the WWJDX7
Internet Chat Room

Billy Graham. The mere mention of his name evokes an immediate response, usually a positive response. And one of the "what if?" questions about the famed evangelist relates to his struggle with the issue of biblical authority in the summer of 1949. Billy Graham had been engaged in numerous conversations with his friend Chuck Templeton, a minister who was doubting the veracity of Scripture.[1]

Notes Graham: "I had similar questions arising from my own broadened reading habits. I wanted to keep abreast of theological thinking at mid-century, but brilliant writers such as Karl Barth and Reinhold Niebuhr really made me struggle with concepts that had been ingrained in me since childhood. They were pioneers in what came to be called neo-orthodoxy."[2]

Billy Graham's primary struggle was over neo-orthodoxy's "redefinition of inspiration to allow for a Bible prone to mistakes and to subjective interpretation."[3] At a conference coordinated by Henrietta Mears, Graham had yet another encounter with Chuck Templeton, who spoke boldly to the young evangelist: "Billy you're fifty years out of date. People no longer accept the Bible as being inspired the way you do. You're going to have to learn the new jargon if you're going to be successful."[4]

Confused and hurting, Billy Graham took a late-night walk in the woods near the San Bernardino Mountains. Though he does not recall the specific words of his 1949 prayer, Graham says the essence of his conversation with God was something like this: "O God! There are many things in this book I do not understand. There are many problems for which I have no solutions. There are many seeming contradictions. I can't answer some of the philosophical and psychological questions Chuck and others are raising."[5]

> Surprisingly, the formerly unchurched indicated a greater interest in doctrine than longer-term Christians.

But in an act of faith and trust, Billy Graham decided to trust the totality of God's Word. He said: "Father, I am going to accept this as Thy Word— by *faith!* I'm going to allow faith to go beyond my intellectual questions and doubts, and I will believe this to be your inspired word."[6]

The evangelist "sensed the presence and power of the Holy Spirit." He knew that he was now ready to do God's work. "In my heart and mind," he said, "I knew a spiritual battle in my soul had been fought and won."[7]

Billy Graham believes that his ministry never would have been blessed by God had he not, in faith, trusted all of the Bible's teachings. What one believes about the teaching of the Bible is called doctrine, and this issue was also far more important in the minds of the formerly unchurched than many have believed.

The Importance of Doctrine
to the Formerly Unchurched

As our research has indicated throughout this book, doctrine is important to the formerly unchurched; it was also important to them when they were lost and unchurched. "Even before I became a Christian," Cheryl S. told us, "I was really interested in what churches believed. I had enough common sense to know that they weren't all exactly alike. I wanted to find a church that would stick to their guns on their beliefs."

Surprisingly, the formerly unchurched indicated a greater interest in doctrine than longer-term Christians. As figure 6.1 shows, 91 percent of the formerly unchurched thought that doctrine was important; 89 percent of the transfer churched expressed the same sentiments.

Figure 6.1a and 6.1b
Was Doctrine Important in Your Decision to Join the Church?

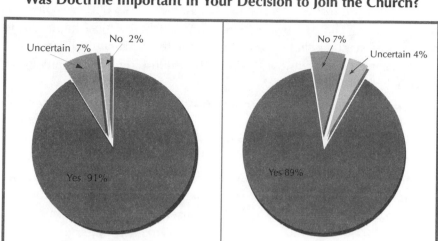

Formerly Unchurched   Transfer Churched

Not Just Any Doctrine

The formerly unchurched, however, were not just interested in the facts of the doctrine; they were insistent that the churches should be uncompromising in their stand. These facts fly in the face of an increasingly pluralistic and theologically tolerant culture. It seems as if, when one takes the step from being firmly unchurched to at least being an inquirer, attitudes change. The seeker desires to discover truth and the conviction among Christians about the reality of God, Jesus, and the entire supernatural realm. Jorge C. spoke rather bluntly about the issue: "I visited a few churches before I became a Christian. Man, some of them made me want to vomit! They didn't show any more conviction about their beliefs than I did. And I was lost and going to hell!"

The formerly unchurched were clear. They not only were interested in learning about doctrine, they were attracted to conservative, evangelical churches that were uncompromising in their beliefs.

Dean Kelley Was Right

In 1972 Dean Kelley wrote a landmark and hotly debated book called *Why Conservative Churches Are Growing.* The very fact that Kelley, an executive with the more liberal National Council of Churches, even acknowledged the growth of more conservative churches was significant. But Kelley went further, describing the characteristics of these conservative churches. The first characteristic, obviously the most important to Kelley, was "a total belief system." In simple terms, Dean Kelley was saying that conservative churches believe the Bible and make no apology for their beliefs.

Kelly further described four other distinguishing features of conservative churches. First, they have a distinctive code of conduct. This code of conduct emanates from the conviction of the beliefs in the churches. Second, they practice "strict discipline." Again, the churches are doing nothing more than practicing what they believe. Third, conservative churches commit significant resources to their causes. Of course, the very existence of a cause is the result of belief in Scripture, which shapes the cause. Finally, they have missionary zeal. What church could not have missionary zeal if the people believe in eternal salvation through Christ alone and eternal damnation without Christ as taught in Scripture?

> "I can find plenty of compromise in the world, but I expect the church to stand for something."

The formerly unchurched we interviewed probably never read *Why Conservative Churches Are Growing*. But they echoed in sentiment what Kelley articulated in facts. Churches that are lukewarm in their doctrinal conviction do not attract the unchurched. "I can find plenty of compromise in the world," Rob M. of West Virginia told us, "but I expect the church to stand for something."

The Barna Study

George Barna and the Barna Research Group have made tremendous contributions toward the study of the church and its mission field. Recently he noted that the unchurched are, for the most part, still unchurched. Churches are doing little, he says, to make a dent in the unchurched population. This is the reason we believe our study on the formerly unchurched to be so critical. Instead of asking unchurched people, most of whom will not move to the ranks of the churched, how we can reach them, we are asking those who have already been reached what happened in their lives.

In the same research publication in which Barna laments the failure of the church to reach the unchurched, he reports on a study entitled "What People Say They Want from a Church."[8] Admittedly, the data from the two studies cannot be combined. One study looks at the unchurched, the other asks Christians who attend church what draws them to their church. Though the comparison may be "apples and oranges" to some extent, the combined studies offer interesting insights.

On the one hand, Barna continues to proclaim that the unchurched are still unchurched. On the other hand, he notes that those in churches say the most important issue for them is theological beliefs or doctrine. We have adapted Barna's data to show the six factors most important to people in the church.

Figure 6.2

Importance of Factors in Selecting a Church

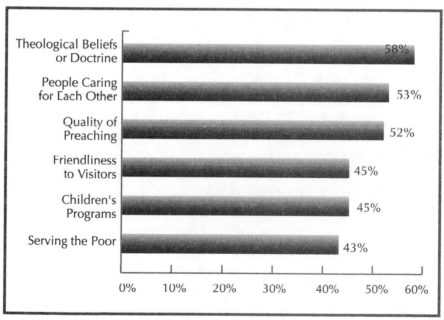

The formerly unchurched agree with Barna's research. Doctrine is important. Both our research and Barna's research indicate it is the single most critical issue in reaching people. When will churches in America grasp this reality?

Looking for Absolutes

Because almost nine out of ten formerly unchurched told us that doctrine was the major factor in their choosing a church, we delved further into this issue. "Why," we asked, "is doctrine so important to you?" The most frequent response was their desire to know truth or absolutes.

Janet D. is a stay-at-home mom living in the Cincinnati area. She was raised in a home with no church background, and her parents are "friendly agnostics." Janet's parents never communicated any particular sense of truth to her. "I'm just not sure on what authority they base their values."

Janet and Lyle were married seven years ago, and they now have two sons. Janet expressed to Lyle her desire to find for their children some type of environment that had a clearly defined value system. Lyle had grown up occasionally attending a Southern Baptist church across the Ohio River in Kentucky. An affable fellow, according to Janet, Lyle was glad to help her on this quest.

"I began my search for truth under the guise that my kids needed clear boundaries," Janet said. "But the search was really for me." Of course, neither Janet nor Lyle were Christians at this point.

Janet described the frustration of her upbringing: "My parents didn't have a clue. The schools I attended, from kindergarten to college, almost seemed to have a disdain for absolutes. And all the friends I hung around with were as clueless as I was. Here I was twenty-nine years old, and I felt like a kid lost in a big store."

Naturally religion and churches were on Janet's mind as paths to pursue. But she did not know where to turn. She was fortunate. The first church she and Lyle visited gave her the answers she had been seeking. "God must have been looking after me. I could have gone a thousand different ways. But I just remembered seeing this church from the interstate and thinking that it looked nice," she reflected.

The church of choice was a warm, evangelical, nondenominational community church. Attendance was about six hundred, and the church put a lot of resources into its children's ministry. Both Matt and Brett, their sons, instantly connected with the church. And Janet knew she had found the perfect place right away.

"It was unbelievable. The church made clear their positions on doctrinal issues in their publications. Pastor Eric spoke clearly about the church's position in his sermon. I had to decide that either all of the people at the church were deluded or that I had found the answers I was seeking. I chose the latter."

Janet and Lyle accepted Christ a few weeks later. Doctrine had brought them to the church, and it keeps them there today.

Frankly, most of the stories we heard from the formerly unchurched are not like Janet's story. Most of those we interviewed did not understand explicitly that they were searching for absolutes as they visited churches. Selena T., for example, was one of those rare cases where her husband became a Christian before she did, six months earlier to be exact. She started attending the worship services to be with her husband, and she was immediately impacted by the pastor's sermons.

> Doctrine is the content of belief; certitude is the conviction of belief. In nearly one-half of our interviews, the formerly unchurched gave us some indication that certitude was an important reason they chose a church.

"Jeff is an incredible preacher," Selena spoke enthusiastically. "His style of preaching and delivery is good, but the content of his sermons is great. I began listening carefully to his words and realized that I had never really considered what I believed about God or eternal matters." She continued, "More than anything else, I became a Christian because I was drawn to a church that taught clearly the Word of God. That's why I answered in the first interview that I identified with the beliefs of the church."

Sensing Certitude

Closely related to the matter of doctrine is the issue of certitude. Doctrine is the content of belief; certitude is the conviction of belief. In nearly one-half of our interviews, the formerly unchurched gave us some indication that certitude was an important reason they chose a church.

One question we routinely asked in our interviews was, "What brought you back to the church?" We received answers such as the following relating to the issue of certitude.

- "The church is uncompromising on the Word."
- "The pastor spoke the Word of God as truth. Didn't 'fluff-up' sermon. Called 'sin' sin in a loving way."

131

- "You could tell that the people really believed what was taught and preached."
- "All the material they give visitors in the worship service tells you clearly that the church has convictions about what it believes."
- "I have never been to a Sunday school class where the teacher was so well prepared and taught with so much authority and conviction."

In some of the church consultations in which I have been involved, interviewing the pastor briefly or listening to one sermon tells me immediately what one problem may be—no sense of certitude. The words may be similar to another pastor's sermons, but conviction is lacking. The pastor may not have had a "Billy Graham crisis."

The formerly unchurched told us with clarity that they recognized certitude or lack of certitude even before they became Christians. Sean R. is a civil engineer in a mid-sized town in South Carolina. Sean was one of many formerly unchurched men who told us that their wives were the single greatest influence in getting them to visit churches.

"Marilyn was lovingly persistent, I always say," Sean said. "She didn't nag me, but I had no doubt that she wanted me to visit church with her. Every now and then, I would be the good husband and follow her to a church."

Sean continued, "I tell you, Thom, I honestly can't remember anything about the other churches I visited. Maybe I was so spiritually dead that I don't remember anything about them. Or maybe the churches were so dead that they made no impact on me."

Everything changed when Sean and Marilyn visited the Southern Baptist church on the edge of town. "I was mesmerized by the sermon. And it wasn't just Hal's delivery. The first time I heard him, I thought, *this guy really believes this stuff.* I guess I really surprised Marilyn when I told her I wanted to go back for another visit."

Sean returned to church several times. The conviction with which Hal spoke convinced Sean to explore Christianity. Six months after their first visit, Sean accepted Christ. When we spoke to him, his enthusiasm for his faith was obvious. "I get excited thinking about where I am now. But I also know that there are a lot of churches out there where no conviction exists. I've been to some of them. You're never going to convince a lost person to become a Christian unless the church is totally sold out on its beliefs. Man! There sure are a lot of wishy-washy churches out there."

Anecdotally, the formerly unchurched seemed to be more cognizant of the certitude of belief present in churches than did the transfer churched. In our interviews with the transfer churched, we did not have nearly as many comments about the importance of doctrine nor the level of conviction about doctrine.

Stories like Sean's were not uncommon. Not only was doctrine important to the formerly unchurched, but the certitude about the doctrine was noticed as well. And in many cases, the formerly unchurched told us that the evidence of clarity and conviction of doctrine was most obvious in the pastor. To that issue we turn.

The Pastor, Doctrine, and Certitude

We heard hundreds of comments about doctrine from the 353 formerly unchurched we interviewed. Some reflected on written documents in which the church made clear its doctrinal position. Others told of how a small group or Sunday school class communicated clearly a conviction or stand on doctrinal positions. A few spoke of conversations they had with church members in which doctrinal conviction was evident. Yet the overwhelming number of comments regarding doctrinal certitude was tied to the pastor. In part 2 we will hear from pastors and learn of their doctrinal convictions. For now we will look at what the formerly unchurched sensed about the pastor when they visited a church.

First, these new Christians told us, the pastors mentioned doctrinal issues with frequency. "One thing that impressed me about Mark [the pastor] the first time I came to Southwick Church was his willingness to tackle tough issues in his sermon," Bill P. of Maryland told us. He continued, "I remember the first sermon really well. It was about Christ being the only way of salvation. He hit that issue straight on. And honestly that was something I had been struggling with."

Bill told us that, over the course of his visits the next several weeks, he heard Mark take on many doctrinal issues. "It seemed like every opportunity Mark had, he mentioned something about biblical beliefs," Bill said. We heard many similar stories from the formerly unchurched. Pastors considered the understanding of major doctrines critical to the health of the church. Thus, the formerly unchurched heard doctrinal issues with frequency.

Bill continued, "One of the things that attracted me to Southwick was that you had no doubt where the church stood. Just listen to Mark a few weeks and you'll know."

A second issue related to pastors and doctrine is one that has already risen in this chapter, the issue of certitude. As we have noted at several points, the formerly unchurched have a keen awareness of the level of conviction present in church members and staff. But they most readily noticed the level of conviction when the pastor spoke.

Bill, like many of our interviewees, did not hesitate to speak his mind. In the course of our interview about Southwick, the church he joined, Bill decided to tell us about a church he did not join.

"I didn't have a church background," Bill said, "but I sure could tell a lot about churches after a visit or two. There was this one church where the preacher went through all sort of gyrations to say nothing. It was like he was afraid he would offend somebody. Personally, I was offended that he was such a dud. I could've turned on the TV and watched *The Simpsons* and learned as much about the Bible!"

Bill became more animated in his conversation. "Why do these guys even get into the ministry if they don't believe anything? It seems like it would be a matter of integrity for them to believe in what they do. What a shame!"

One other issue arose frequently as the formerly unchurched spoke about the pastor and doctrine. It is the factor we have dubbed "speaking the truth in love." Numerous times we heard how these pastors were strong in their convictions but gentle in spirit. As Bill spoke of his pastor, Mark, he said: "You know where he stands, but you also know he cares about you. He isn't some ranting and raving legalist." We will continue this theme at the end of the chapter, where we will see that speaking the truth in love is a factor that includes more than the pastor alone.

Doctrine and Assimilation

It is too early to make any certain conclusions about how well the formerly unchurched will assimilate into the churches they joined. Most of those whom we interviewed were at the church only a short time. The early evidence, however, is impressive. We can say with a high degree of certainty that clearly articulated doctrine attracts the unchurched. And we can also say, based on the results thus far, that doctrinal conviction assimilates the formerly unchurched as well. How then does doctrine affect the closing of the back door?

First, we were told, no one desires to be a part of an organization or cause based on uncertainty or ambiguity. Leslie C. of Missouri notes, "Why should I waste my time being a part of something that doesn't really make a difference?" To the contrary, doctrinal certainty and clarity engender commitment. A cause or a purpose is evident, and many desire to be a part of the cause.

Second, one of the reasons the formerly unchurched were attracted to the churches they joined was the churches' unambiguous declaration of absolutes. In a world of relativity, many seekers desire to know that a black and white reality does exist. That same clarity of absolutes that attracted the unchurched keeps them in the church.

Third, churches with doctrinal certitude tend to be activists in their beliefs. When these churches know with certainty that salvation comes only through Christ and believe that those without a personal relationship with him are hell-bound, they are more likely to be evangelistic. Their evangelistic passion reflects their conviction about what they believe. And their continuing role of activism tends to keep those who desire to be a part of a greater cause.

Speaking the Truth in Love

In all of our 353 interviews with the formerly unchurched, we never heard the effective churches described as harsh, legalistic, or the like. These churches were firm in their convictions, said the formerly unchurched, but were also gentle in spirit. As indicated above, this characteristic was evident in the pastors of the churches, but it extended well beyond any one person.

Southeast Christian Church of Louisville, Kentucky, mentioned earlier, is one of the largest congregations in North America. Though Senior Minister Bob Russell refuses to take any personal credit for the phenomenal growth of Southeast, one cannot help but see his influence. God has used him in many ways, but "speaking the truth in love" is certainly an example set by Bob Russell for more than thirty years.

Bob's influence has spread to the congregation. For the past three decades, Southeast has been a moral and Christian lighthouse in the

Louisville metropolitan area. The church has been the recipient of intense criticisms from liberal media and liberal religious groups for its positions on abortion, homosexuality, the exclusivity of salvation through Christ, and other "hot-button issues." Despite the criticisms, the large congregation has maintained a spirit of love and grace. Many of the harshest critics express surprise at the gentle and loving spirit of the church when they visit.

Southeast Christian's ministries have made a profound impact on the Louisville community. Their ministries are far too numerous to list in this book. Suffice it to say, the influence of these ministries has been pervasive for many years. The congregation knows that holding to truth with conviction is not mutually exclusive with being a people demonstrating Christlike love.

In 160 of the 353 interviews, slightly under half, the formerly unchurched described the churches they eventually joined as churches that were uncompromising in their convictions but Christlike in their demeanor. "I had this image of Southern Baptists as mean-spirited and legalistic," the outspoken Frank N. of Georgia told us, "but the church I connected with is anything but that. The church does have a clear doctrinal stand, but they are also one of the most loving groups of people I have ever been around," he concluded.

Yes, Doctrine Really Matters

Perhaps some people will be surprised to hear of the importance of doctrine in reaching the unchurched. The formerly unchurched, however, left little doubt of the importance of doctrine in their accepting Christ and choosing a church. They spoke with clarity of the issues that were important to them.

- More formerly unchurched spoke of the importance of doctrine in their decision-making process than any other factor.
- The doctrine that attracted the formerly unchurched was not just any belief system, but a theology that could best be described as conservative, evangelical, and uncompromising.
- Many indicated that their interest in doctrine was a consequence of their desire to discover absolutes in a culture where few absolutes are perceived to exist.

- Those who spoke of the importance of doctrine could discern easily where churches were strong or weak in their affirmation of beliefs. The formerly unchurched were attracted to churches that had doctrinal certitude.
- The pastor was the key person to whom the formerly unchurched looked for certitude of beliefs. They did not look to the pastor alone, however, but to the entire congregation.
- It appears that doctrinal conviction not only attracts the unchurched, but it may have a major role in their assimilation after they become Christians.
- Without exception, when the formerly unchurched told us of their attraction to churches with doctrinal conviction, they never described the spirit of the churches with such negative words as *harsh, judgmental,* or *legalistic.* When they described the spirit or ethics of the people of the church, they typically used words that could best be summarized as "speaking the truth in love."

The evidence is clear, if not overwhelming: doctrine really matters. Church leaders will ignore this reality to their church's peril. The insights of the formerly unchurched have been intriguing and helpful. An entire set of strategies could be developed from the information we gleaned from them. But unless church leaders are willing, even eager, to do that which is necessary to reach the unchurched, the information is of little value. In other words, leadership is critical. In part 2 we will hear from the leaders of churches that reach the unchurched. Insights from these leaders, combined with the insights of the formerly unchurched, paint a clear picture of what it takes to reach the unchurched population for Christ.

PART TWO

Leaders of Churches That Reach the Unchurched

In part 2 we look at the leaders, particularly pastors, of churches that are reaching the unchurched. In chapter 2 we saw the critical role pastors play in churches that reach the unchurched, but we looked at pastors from the perspective of the formerly unchurched. In these next five chapters we hear from the pastors themselves.

As I indicated in chapter 2, I was hesitant to place yet another burden on already busy pastors. But because the formerly unchurched told us that pastors had a key role in their coming to know Christ personally and in their choosing a particular church, we added a dimension to this research project not originally anticipated. We interviewed not only the formerly unchurched, but also the leaders of the churches that reached them. Their insights are indeed worth hearing.

CHAPTER 7

A Profile of the Unchurched–Reaching Leaders

*Most of you Christians don't know how to think,
especially the ministers.*

—"Zarathum O" in the U4Christ
Internet Chat Room

Michael W. is a seminary-trained pastor who considered joining the denomination of the seminary he attended. But when the opportunity arose to lead a nondenominational church in a mid-size town in Illinois, he accepted the call to the church instead of taking the denominational path.

The pastor considers his seminary training valuable. "I wouldn't trade my time at the seminary for anything," Michael said. "I was not very pro-seminary when I got there, but I really saw the benefit of intensive training in Bible, theology, church history, and other basic courses." But Michael does affirm the often-heard criticisms of seminaries: "It just didn't prepare me for the real world, especially leadership issues and mean church members," he mused. "Also, I didn't have a clue how to reach lost people and unchurched people. Maybe I expected too much of seminary training," he reflected.

Michael has been at his church twelve years, a significant tenure in light of the fact that the average church tenure of a pastor in the United States is 3.8 years.[1] "The first year was great," Michael recalled, "a true honeymoon. But then all hell broke loose!" He quickly told me that he was not using the word *hell* profanely. He literally meant that the best description of his next two to three years was "hell-battling spiritual warfare."

"The criticisms were intense, and the opposition was ugly." I could tell by the tone of his voice that old wounds were opening even a decade later. "I know that many of the mistakes were my own doing," Michael confessed.

> The average church tenure of a pastor in the United States is 3.8 years.

"I moved too fast at times, and I copied some churches' methods instead of transferring principles. But I paid the price. No Christian should be saying things like some of my members said to me," he said softly.

"What happened next?" I asked. I was hesitant to push further on the issue, but I knew that many pastors and church leaders could benefit from his story.

"There was a major move to get rid of me. It failed, but it left the church pretty torn apart," he said.

"So what did you do?"

"I probably 'quit' the church twenty times. But when it came time to resign officially, I couldn't do it. God just wouldn't let me go," Michael recalled.

With some of the most vociferous dissenters gone, Michael provided "a new type of leadership." This new leadership was no less committed to reaching the lost and leading a church to make a difference in the world, but it was more patient and incremental in its approach. "I really changed the most in the area of communication," Michael said. "Everything was on the table. No more surprises for the church. We talked things out until everybody was sick of hearing about it," he laughed.

My research team at the Billy Graham School at the Southern Baptist Theological Seminary has looked at more than four thousand churches across America. Unfortunately, we rarely see leaders with Michael's tenacity. His story is truly the exception.

"We didn't grow at all for over four years," he told us. The church had about 150 in attendance when I got there. Nearly five years later our attendance was 140. But it was a different congregation. Some of the troublemakers left, and some fired-up new people joined. And some of the members who were there before I got there really got on board with the new direction of the church," Michael said with more enthusiasm.

The "new direction" of which Michael spoke was a passionate vision to reach the lost and unchurched. Changes were made in the activities of the church. "So much of what we were doing was playing church," he said. The worship style was modified from a traditional format to a more blended style. "We did that gradually," Michael said. "It was more of a transition in quality than style." The expectations of church members to be involved in ministry gradually rose as well. "We're finally able to tell people that membership means ministry. We've got no room for members on the sidelines," Michael told us.

A growth pattern that can best be described as steady rather than explosive began in Michael's fifth year of ministry. Now in his twelfth year of ministry, Michael pastors a church with more than six hundred in attendance.

"We're not a megachurch," Michael said. "But for the past few years I've felt like we are a church. If we become a megachurch, fine, but that's not my ultimate purpose. I've learned that joy does not come from being the biggest. I just want our church to be a church that honors God," Michael said with conviction.

Listening to Unchurched-Reaching Pastors

The formerly unchurched told us with clarity to listen to the pastors whose churches are reaching the unchurched. So we did. In fact, we listened to exactly 101 of these leaders in extensive written and telephone interviews. The pastors represented the churches we studied, roughly in proportion to denominational affiliation of those churches.

Figure 7.1

Denominational Affiliation of Pastors Interviewed

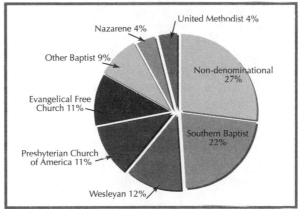

The churches these leaders served ranged in age from almost brand new to over one hundred years. We thus attempted to hear from a cross section of newer churches, newer established churches, and older established churches.

Further descriptions of these pastors demonstrate the variety of leaders to whom we spoke.

- 72% were Anglos; 14% were African-Americans; 9% were Hispanic; 4% were Asian; 1% were "other."
- The churches represented by these pastors came from a variety of demographic settings: large city suburban; large city urban; medium city suburban; medium city urban; small city; town; and open country.
- The pastors ranged in age from twenty-eight to sixty-four, with over 80 percent in ages ranging from thirty-eight to fifty-five.

We realize that 101 pastors do not represent precise demographic slices of America. Like our study of 353 churches, this portion of our study is more depth than breadth. Nevertheless, we feel that these leaders do well represent pastors of churches that are reaching the unchurched.

Again, the effective churches represented by these pastors had to meet two criteria. First, the church had to have a minimum of twenty-six conversions in the year we studied. These conversions represented people who not only moved from the status of lost to saved, but also unchurched to churched. Second, the church had to have a conversion ratio of less than 20:1, calculated by dividing membership or attendance, whichever is higher, by the number of conversions in a year. This ratio attempts to answer the question, "How many of the church's members does it take to reach one person for Christ in a year?"

In these next five chapters, we will look at specific issues related to these leaders. In this particular

Figure 7.2

Age of Churches Served by Pastors Interviewed

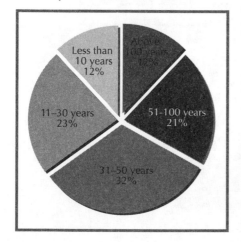

chapter, we will provide a brief checklist of items to paint a picture of pastors whose churches reach the unchurched.

Are the Interview Results of the Leaders Consistent with the Results of the Formerly Unchurched?

The first "big-picture" issue that we sought to address in our study was the consistency of our findings in interviewing two different groups. Were the insights of the 101 pastors different from those of the 353 formerly unchurched, or were the two groups consistent in their responses? The responses were not only consistent, but *highly* consistent. Indeed, we found no major contradictions in comments from the two groups.

> Were the insights of the 101 pastors different from those of the 353 formerly unchurched, or were the two groups consistent in their responses? The responses were not only consistent, but *highly* consistent.

Two caveats, however, must be noted. First, we did not ask the same questions of both groups. Although some issues were similar, we were primarily focusing on leadership issues with the pastors. Second, though we found amazing consistency in the responses of the two groups, the perspectives were sometimes different. The clearest example of different perspectives is in the issue of the importance of the pastor in churches that reach the unchurched. Both groups affirmed the important role the pastor played, but the formerly unchurched often viewed the pastor's role in reaching them to be more critical than the pastors themselves stated.

Lauren R. of Virginia, a formerly unchurched mother of four, offered a typical expression of this issue: "I cannot stress how important the influence of Pastor Rick was in my accepting Christ. His preaching and enthusiasm made me return again and again."

Rick affirmed in our interview that his leadership is important in reaching the unchurched. He cited John Maxwell—one of America's prominent authorities on leadership—as an influence, saying, "Everything rises and falls on leadership." But Rick saw a bigger picture than Lauren described. He mentioned the importance of an unleashed laity in reaching the unchurched, of a quality worship service, and of a church that had

> The average tenure of an unchurched-reaching pastor is 11.8 years, over three times longer than the typical American pastor.

a theology of true lostness for those who do not have a personal relationship with Jesus Christ.

Ultimately, however, we found no real contradictions between the two groups. Perspectives were sometimes different and levels of importance assigned to different factors may have varied, yet the two groups agreed on how the unchurched were reached.

The Tenure Issue

I mentioned briefly at the beginning of this chapter the pastoral tenure issue. Our surveys of pastors across America indicate the average tenure of a pastor to be 3.8 years. But the average tenure of an unchurched-reaching pastor is 11.8 years, over three times longer than the typical American pastor.

Figure 7.3

Tenure of American Pastors

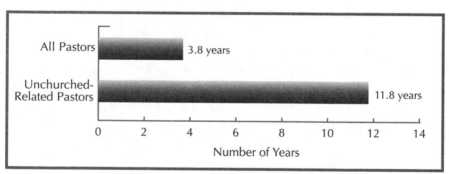

Approximately one-half of the pastors we interviewed had been at their churches for six to ten years, but 42 percent had a tenure of over ten years, for an average tenure of nearly twelve years. The average tenure of the pastors of unchurched-reaching churches was very close to the tenure of pastors in a previous study we conducted on effective churches.[2]

While our data cannot prove a causative relationship between pastoral tenure and evangelistic effectiveness of churches, a positive correlation is evident. Obviously effective leadership has a longer-term approach. All battles do not have to be won in a day. All opportunities do not have to be seized in a week.

The Education Issues

Most of the pastors (87 percent) who led these effective churches were seminary trained. As I indicated earlier, the pastors typically affirmed the benefit of seminary education in the classical disciplines. They tended to be critical of seminaries for not equipping them in leadership, conflict management, time management, evangelism and church growth, and other practical issues. "I almost got killed in my first church out of seminary," a Southern Baptist pastor told us. "Why didn't the seminary prepare me for those not-so-well-intentioned dragons?"

Figure 7.4

Tenure of Pastors of Unchurched-Reaching Churches

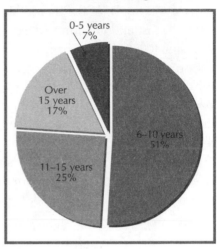

Nevertheless, our research team was surprised that nearly nine out of ten of those pastors have at least a master's degree from a seminary. Four out of ten have a seminary doctoral degree. Because our research team is seminary-based, we have been careful not to express a bias in favor of seminary education. Our most objective assessment therefore is that seminary education was important to those leaders but that the education was woefully lacking in leadership and practical issues.

Figure 7.5

Highest Education Level of Pastors of Unchurched-Reaching Churches

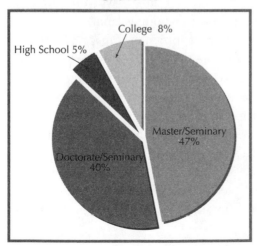

The "Passion Factor"

One issue that defied objective measurement is what we describe as "passion." Though we cannot quantify the pastors' sentiments, all of our interviewers spoke of the incredible intensity obvious in these pastors to reach the lost and unchurched world.

Listen to a Southern Baptist pastor from the Orlando area: "My heart just breaks when I think of the number of lost people within five miles of our church. Your statistics may indicate that we're doing a good job of reaching the unchurched, but I know how many we're not reaching. Some days I am driven to the point of tears when I realize how many hell-bound people I pass every day."

These leaders are passionate about reaching lost and unchurched people. We will more fully explore this issue in the next chapter when we look at "What makes these people tick?"

A Week in the Life of a Leader Who Reaches the Unchurched

Though we will also develop this issue more fully later, the likes and dislikes of these leaders are fascinating. For example, we were told by one Wesleyan pastor to speak to Ron D., a layman who, according to this pastor, "keeps me honest about keeping my priorities by just watching his own lifestyle."

We asked the leaders of these churches to tell us how they spent each of 168 hours in a week's time. While most of our interviews were with pastors, Ron was one of several laypersons with whom we spoke.

"Churches waste so much time in stupid meetings," he offered rather forcefully. "We spend a lot of time talking about what we should be doing rather than just doing it." He said that he and fifteen others in the church are accountable to each other for developing relationships with the unchurched and for sharing Christ with them eventually. "We do meet for an hour or so each week," he said, "but the sole purpose of our meeting is to talk about what we've done to reach people rather that what we should do." The passion to reach the lost and unchurched is obvious in how these leaders spend their time. In the next chapter we will delve more fully into the time priorities of these leaders.

"Have You Read Lately ...?"

Most of the leaders we interviewed were avid readers. Though books were not the most influential factor in their lives, they have had a formative role in their leadership development.

There is little doubt from our surveys and interviews that the book of greatest impact in recent years has been *The Purpose-Driven Church* by Rick Warren. Why was this book so influential? Jim R., a nondenominational church pastor from the Nashville area, notes: "Rick's book was a wake-up call to me. For years I have tried to maintain different programs in my church. I realized after reading *The Purpose-Driven Church* that my leadership was program driven instead of purpose driven. I guess more than anything the book got me back to biblical basics."

Though the formerly unchurched we interviewed did not indicate that they had read *The Purpose-Driven Church*, their comments indicated that the churches they joined were purpose driven. "You go to some churches to find they're just going through the motions. But when I came to this church, I could tell that they had their act in order," said Tommy H. of Mississippi. "They really understood what a church is supposed to be doing." And, yes, when we ask the pastor of Tommy's church to name the influential book or books in his ministry, he named *The Purpose-Driven Church*.

While Rick Warren's book was the runaway most influential publication in the lives of these leaders, seven others were also mentioned frequently. These books are shown in figure 7.6.

Figure 7.6

Most Influential Books in Ministry Rated by Leaders of Unchurched-Reaching Churches

1. *The Purpose-Driven Church* by Rick Warren
2. *My Utmost for His Highest* by Oswald Chambers
3. *Knowing God* by J. I. Packer
4. *Fresh Wind, Fresh Fire* by Jim Cymbala
5. *The Master Plan of Evangelism* by Robert Coleman
6. *Pilgrim's Progress* by John Bunyan
7. *In His Steps* by Charles Sheldon
8. *Mere Christianity* by C. S. Lewis

Preaching ... Again!

The formerly unchurched said so, the data said so, and the pastors themselves said so: preaching is a major factor in reaching the unchurched. In fact, preaching is so important that we devote the entirety of chapter 11 to the topic. For now we will preview the issues from the perspective of the pastors.

- Preaching, by far, is the most exciting task of the pastors. They told us without hesitation that they looked forward to preaching more than any task.
- Sermon preparation was one of the greatest consumers of their ministry time.
- As we have found in previous studies, the dominant preaching style was expository among pastors whose churches were effectively reaching the unchurched. By no means, however, was expository preaching the only preaching style (more on this issue in chapter 11).
- Communication skills were seen as critically important to these pastors. Not all of the pastors saw themselves as naturally good communicators. Most of them, however, saw the need to work constantly at improving their communication skills.

Theologically Conservative

The leaders of churches that reach the unchurched are theologically conservative. Indeed, it is their understanding of sin separating humanity from a holy God that drives them to reach out to the unchurched with the gospel message of Jesus Christ. These leaders unhesitatingly affirm the exclusivity of salvation through Christ; only one held to a more inclusive position, that is, salvation possible in ways other than explicit faith in Jesus Christ.

> It is their understanding of sin separating humanity from a holy God that drives them to reach out to the unchurched with the gospel message of Jesus Christ.

These leaders tended to hold a conservative view about the inspiration of Scripture. About eight out of ten leaders held to full inerrancy. They believed the Bible was true in all areas, not only in religious areas, but in science and history as well. Almost one out of five held a

Figure 7.7

**Leaders of Unchurched-
Reaching Churches:
Beliefs in Salvation**

Figure 7.8

**Leaders of Unchurched-
Reaching Churches:
Beliefs of Scripture**

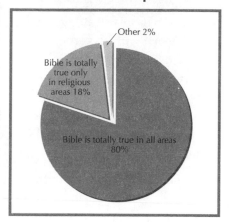

more limited inerrancy view, that the Bible was true in the religious sphere but contained possible errors in other areas.

Leaders Who Desire to Be Better Leaders

The American church of the 1950s readily accepted pastors who had few leadership abilities. The primary concern was that church leaders have sufficient pastoral skills to visit the sick, perform weddings and funerals, and preach, and have sufficient listening skills to help people carry their burdens in times of need. The pastor probably had responsibility for no more than 150 people.

The church of the twenty-first century, however, demands strong pastoral leadership skills. The society is no longer predominantly Christian; it is largely pluralistic. The moral values of the community usually contradict the values of the church. Conflict is now the norm in the church. And the number of people who come from a totally unchurched background has accelerated since 1955, from nearly no one to four out of ten since 1955. The world has changed, and the demands placed on pastors have increased and changed, yet some elements of pastoral ministry remain constant. Preaching remains primary, and evangelism is still needed whether the date is 1955 or 2005.

Jerry W., at age sixty-six, was the oldest pastor in our study. He has the perspective of four decades of ministry. "I would struggle if I were just entering the ministry today," he said. "So much has changed. When I first entered the ministry, I could preach and minister to the people and they would be happy. Today I have to preach, minister to the people, develop a strategy, reach the unchurched, keep the budget balanced, work with dysfunctional families, understand facilities needs, keep deacons happy, attend a zillion meetings, be active in the community, be active in the denomination, and be a good family man when I have time."

A distinguishing feature of the leaders whose churches reach the unchurched versus those who do not was the desire of the effective church leaders to improve their leadership skills.

- They are more likely to read books to improve their leadership skills.
- They are more likely to seek continuing education.
- They usually have someone to whom they confide and consult, a mentor relationship of some sort.
- It is not unusual for them to seek to improve themselves in areas in which they have no formal training, such as finance or administration, for example.

As we will discuss more fully in chapter 9, these leaders face the same difficulties articulated by other leaders. The most often cited issue was conflict and criticism. A Nazarene pastor told us: "I wish I could say that criticism doesn't bother me, but it does. Just this past week one of the leaders in our church went over a list of complaints with me. I've been depressed since then. I guess I'm just too thin skinned." He is not alone. Over 70 percent of the pastors surveyed indicated that criticism and conflict bother them significantly.

> Over 70 percent of the pastors surveyed indicated that criticism and conflict bother them significantly.

The Intentionality Issue

The leaders of these churches that reached the unchurched demonstrated a leadership style that can best be described as intentional. We have a data base of interviews with two thousand pastors of churches that did not meet our evangelistic criteria cited earlier. These pastors did not generally have specific plans for evangelistic ministries, for prayer ministries, or for reaching the unchurched, to name a few.

In contrast, the leaders of churches that reached the unchurched were focused and intentional in their efforts to reach and minister to the people. Though they articulated their belief that only God's power is sufficient, they never used that as an excuse for inactivity or failure to plan. Noted Caleb M. of Florida: "We take the five purposes that [Rick] Warren uses, and we review monthly how we are doing in each one. If we're weak in evangelism, we increase our efforts in evangelism. We don't believe that ministry just happens. It has to be intentional."

Figure 7.9

Importance of Selected Characteristics in Leading the Local Church

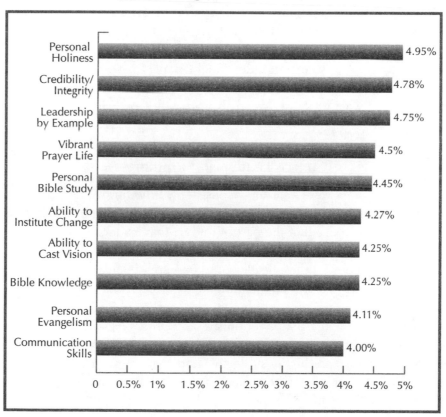

What Really Matters

We asked the leaders of the effective churches to rate personal characteristics as they relate to leadership in the local church. We listed twenty-two different characteristics and asked the pastors to rate the factors on a scale of 1 to 5. The scale of importance looked like this:

1. Not very important
2. Somewhat important
3. Important
4. Very important
5. Absolutely necessary

Figure 7.9 (on the previous page) shows the top ten characteristics as rated by the pastors of unchurched-reaching churches.

Though these leaders did not diminish the importance of typical leadership issues such as conflict management, administrative acumen, and strategic planning, the most important characteristics they listed were spiritual disciplines. Three of the first five characteristics were related to their own personal spiritual growth: personal holiness, vibrant prayer life, and personal Bible study. An independent Baptist pastor in Florida told us: "We can have all of the right tools for ministry, but it all counts for nothing if we do not have a close daily walk with God."

The Unchurched-Reaching
Church Leader: In Summary

The interviews were amazingly consistent. Whether we talked to the formerly unchurched, pastors, or lay leaders, we received information that rarely contradicted. All of the parties told us that leadership was critical in reaching the unchurched.

As we interviewed these leaders, our research team spoke of similar issues that simply cannot be quantified and placed on a chart or graph. Some of our interviewers described the leaders in subjective terms such as "dynamic," "energetic," or "enthusiastic." Others used more spiritual descriptions like "godly," "Spirit-filled," or "anointed." We realize that these expressions are highly subjective and that we must be careful in expressing them in a research project. Nevertheless, we must report that there is something different about these leaders that we cannot quantify;

God's presence can be sensed in their lives. And because they are providing leadership in churches that reach the unchurched, we desire to know as much about them as possible.

What motivates these leaders? What makes them tick? What is different about their lives when compared to leaders of other churches? These questions were on our minds when we interviewed them. In the next chapter we will hear their responses.

CHAPTER 8

What Makes These Leaders Tick?

Isn't a good pastor an oxymoron?

—"Wobam" in the U4Christ
Internet Chat Room

I am the father of three great sons. The years 1980, 1982, and 1985 were joyous years as Sam, Art, and Jess came into this world. Each of my boys has his own strengths and gifts. But this story is about my middle son, Art.

Of these three boys, Art is the quiet one. His relatively few comments are typically limited to funny one-liners—unless he is focused on sharing Christ with someone.

Art developed a relationship over the course of two years with a young man I will call Alan. When Alan arrived as a new student, Art took it upon himself to befriend this teenager who had no friends at the school. I cannot recall how many times Art would ask me questions about the Bible or the gospel, particularly if the questions arose in the context of his concern for Alan. My son was intensely concerned about Alan's eternal destiny, for the young man readily admitted he was not a Christian.

Art was not alone in his concern for Alan's salvation. Some of Art's Christian friends joined in the attempts to witness to Alan. But, at least from a proud parent's perspective, it was Art to whom Alan was most drawn. And it was Art who provided the constant witness in lifestyle and words.

One early evening Art called me to come to his room, not a typical request for the then high school senior. My son pointed to a brand new, leather-bound study Bible on his bed. Alan had purchased the gift and left it in Art's car. Holding back tears, Art looked first at me, then at the Bible, then said quietly, "He's so close, Dad; he's so close." In a moment when I have rarely felt closer to my son, I prayed with him for Alan's salvation.

Art has a passion for lost persons. He has a heart to reach the unchurched. He believes that anyone who does not have a personal relationship with Jesus Christ is headed for an eternity in hell. His theology drives his life, and his heart has a love for people that desires that none should perish.

The Pastor/Leader Factor

In the churches that are reaching the unchurched, you will find a leader who has a passion for reaching the lost. You will find someone whose heart breaks at the thought of anyone going to hell. In most of the churches we studied, that leader was the pastor. But that person may have been a key lay leader.

> In the churches that are reaching the unchurched, you will find a leader who has a passion for reaching the lost. You will find someone whose heart breaks at the thought of anyone going to hell.

Our interviews, however, focused particularly on the role of pastors in reaching the unchurched. The interviews with the formerly unchurched left us with the clear message that pastors played a critical role in their accepting Christ and joining the church. In this chapter we hear more from the perspective of the pastors. Our focus is on the pastors' motivational drives. What makes these leaders tick?

After we have examined the four key motivational forces of the pastors for reaching the unchurched, we will have a fascinating look at the top fifteen lessons these pastors have learned in reaching the unchurched. For now, let us turn to the major driving force behind these pastors as they lead their churches to reach the lost and unchurched.

The Theology Factor

The church consultation was about to end in frustration. Not only was I, the consultant, frustrated, but so was the pastor whose church had retained me. I had been asked to come to the Texas church because of the church's twelve-year decline in attendance.

The demographics of the community were good. In the past ten years the population within a five-mile radius of the church had increased over 80 percent, the buildings were in good shape, and the visibility of the church on a major thoroughfare was the envy of the other church leaders in town. But the church I was studying had declined from 1,300 in worship attendance to 700 in the past twelve years.

The consultation process includes a church health inventory (see appendix 5) devised by our consultation firm, The Rainer Group. We distribute the 130-question survey to at least 15 percent of the adult attendance. Several of the questions are theological in nature: Is Christ the only way of salvation? Can adherents of other religions go to heaven? Is hell a literal place?

When I received the results from this particular church, I knew I was in a precarious situation. My clearly defined invitation was to discover the sociological or methodological problems with the church and offer a sure-fire prescription to remedy the dilemma. But this church had no major sociological barriers. And no quick-fix methodology would help their situation. The surveys we had distributed were clear: the vast majority of the members did not believe that Christ was the only way of salvation, and almost 80 percent of the members did not believe in hell.

"Hal," I said to the pastor, "the key issues I see in your church's decline will not be corrected with new methods, buildings, or programs. The main problems are theological." I then told the pastor of our survey results.

The frustration, even anger, that he expressed caught me off guard. Hal first talked about the "intolerant view" that held to one narrow way of salvation. He ridiculed the idea that a loving God would ever send someone to hell. "It's a mythological place!" he exclaimed.

I tried to reason with Hal. "Look," I said, "let's put aside for the moment our theological differences. Can you really expect your members to evangelize if they believe in ways of salvation outside of Christ? Do you expect them to respond with passion and urgency if they believe in no eternal punishment?" My words were spoken in vain. Our discussion ended with Hal muttering something about not paying my consultation fee. That, I thought, was the least of my concerns.

Motivation #1: A Theology of Lostness

We showed a glimpse of the theological beliefs of unchurched-reaching pastors in the previous chapter. With only one exception out of the 101 we interviewed, these leaders believed that John 14:6 is literally true: Jesus Christ is the only way of salvation, and explicit faith in him is imperative.

These leaders believed not only in the "salvation" emphasis; they also believed in the "lostness" factor. For most of these leaders, it is not enough to say that Jesus saves; they also believe that those who do not put their faith in Christ are eternally lost. Hell is a clear reality in this theology of lostness. The number one articulated motivational drive of these leaders was a theology that held that only Jesus saves, and anyone outside of Christ's salvation is eternally damned.

This next story requires no fictitious names. With his reluctant permission, I tell the story of Pastor Al Jackson of the Lakeview Baptist Church in Auburn, Alabama. Since Auburn University is the chief rival of my alma mater, the University of Alabama (mortal enemy may be a more accurate description of our true feelings), I am somewhat grieved to admit that anything good can come out of Auburn. But the heart of this pastor needs to be heard.

A few years ago I was having lunch with Pastor Jackson in an Auburn restaurant. Our conversation began with idle chatter until Al started talking about a man his church was trying to reach. The pastor's deep concern for this non-Christian was evident. Then the reality of the man's lostness seemed to hit Al, and tears welled in his eyes. Al spoke quietly with a broken voice, "I can't stand the thought of him dying without accepting Christ."

The clear and compelling motivational drive articulated by leaders like Al was a theology of lostness. No programs, methods, or approaches to ministry can substitute for a broken heart.

Motivator #2: Passion and Enthusiasm

The first motivation leads to the second. A broken heart for lost people engenders passion and enthusiasm for outreach. I do about 150 speaking engagements a year. Inevitably those who hear me speak learn something about my wife and three sons, because I am passionate and enthusiastic about my family. I have been told that my enthusiasm impacts others positively.

Effective leaders are genuinely enthusiastic about reaching people for Christ. A Nazarene pastor in California shared with us: "I don't want to ever say that our evangelistic efforts depend on me. That would take the focus off the author of salvation." He paused for a moment, collecting his thoughts, then continued. "I have to say, though, when the congregation senses my enthusiasm to reach the unchurched, they tend to respond. And when I get distracted from focusing on the main things, the church tends to lose its focus as well."

We asked all of the pastors to articulate the senior pastor's role and responsibility in personal evangelism. Listen to the numerous comments related to modeling passion and enthusiasm:

- "The senior pastor must model personal evangelism by being enthusiastic about developing relationships with the unchurched."
- "The senior pastor must always be passionate about reaching lost people. If he isn't, who will be?"
- "I am supposed to urge the people to be faithful and consistent to be bearers of the Good News. If I'm not excited about it, my congregation won't be."
- "My key responsibility is to create an environment for evangelism by my enthusiasm for the task."
- "The senior pastor is first the inspirer, the exhorter, and the encourager for evangelism by his own enthusiasm."
- "The senior pastor must have a passion for the lost, be active in personal evangelism, and lead the staff and congregation by example."
- "If I'm not excited about [reaching the unreached] then most of the congregation will not give a rip about it."

Motivator #3: Accountability in Personal Evangelism

As my fellow deans and the president of our seminary gather for our weekly executive cabinet meeting on Wednesdays, Dr. Ted Cabal and I have a brief conversation before the meeting begins. "How did you do this week?" Ted asks me. I respond by telling him about my conversation with the waitress. "How about you, Ted?" I inquire next. He shares with me how he distributed tracts in an area of town and made himself available to anyone who had questions.

This weekly exercise, no more than five minutes in length, is a brief accountability session in which Ted and I share with each other our endeavors in personal evangelism and reaching out to the unchurched. I must admit that there have been a few times when I have told Ted that

> If there was a single characteristic that separated the pastors of effective churches from other pastors, it was the issue of accountability in personal evangelism.

I have not been faithful in sharing Christ. Just my articulation of such words is sufficient rebuke to motivate me to get my priorities right for the upcoming week.

If there was a single characteristic that separated the pastors of effective churches from other pastors, it was the issue of accountability in personal evangelism.

Only two out of every one hundred pastors in the comparison group (churches that did not meet our criteria to be an effective evangelistic church) had established some type of accountability for their own personal evangelism. But 43 percent of the pastors of the effective churches had established such relationships.

If there was a single characteristic that separated the pastors of effective churches from other pastors, it was the issue of accountability in personal evangelism.

Leslie M., pastor of a fast-growing nondenominational church in Pennsylvania, emphasized the importance of accountability relationships: "We have staff meetings every Monday morning. Before we even have prayer,

Figure 8.1a and 8.1b

Do You Have an Accountability Relationship Established for Your Own Efforts in Personal Evangelism?

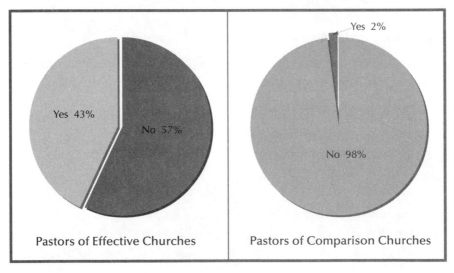

Pastors of Effective Churches   Pastors of Comparison Churches

all ministers share about their witnessing for the previous week. We do this before praying, because if a minister has not shared his or her faith during the week, he or she then has the opportunity to repent in prayer in front of the rest of us."

Motivator #4: Excellence in All Things

The leaders of these churches that are reaching the unchurched will do whatever it takes, within the boundaries of Scripture, to reach the lost. And they realize that the unchurched have expectations of excellence if they make the bold step to visit a church.

Said an Assembly of God pastor: "We don't want them to find mediocrity if they visit us. Besides, aren't we supposed to be excellent in all things we attempt for God?"

Other leaders told us that an attitude of excellence engenders an atmosphere of excitement, which in turn encourages church members to invite their friends. A Southern Baptist deacon in Georgia told us, "For over twenty years we would never see more than two or three visitors a week, even though we held an average attendance over three hundred during these years." But those years, he said, preceded the arrival of Denzil T., the church's current pastor. The deacon continued: "When Denzil came, he started emphasizing excellence in all things. In music, in our buildings, in our programs, in our grounds—you name it. He said that if we couldn't do something excellent for God, then we shouldn't do it at all."

For the next several months, the attitude of excellence began to take hold in the church. The facilities started looking nicer. Someone volunteered to landscape the grounds. The musicians in the church became enthused about improving their ministries. This new attitude in turn excited the once struggling congregation. The deacon explained: "You know what I did for the first time in years? I invited my neighbor to church. I guess I was never really too excited about the church before now."

Though no single factor can explain the phenomenal growth of Southeast Christian Church in Louisville, Kentucky, Senior Minister Bob Russell's commitment to excellence is certainly a contributing factor to the church becoming one of the largest congregations in North America. A recent study of the church found that members invited guests almost every week.[1] The members at Southeast Christian are excited about their church, and one reason for their excitement is the excellence evident in all the church does.

Fifteen Lessons from the Leaders
Whose Churches Reach the Unchurched[2]

What makes these leaders tick? A theology of lostness. Passion and enthusiasm. Accountability in personal evangelism. Excellence in all things. What do these leaders do with their motivation? In the remainder of this chapter, we will look at fifteen lessons shared with us by the leaders of churches that reach the unchurched. If some of the lessons sound familiar, it is because the formerly unchurched shared similar sentiments.

Lesson 1: Authenticity

Over nine out of ten of the pastors interviewed told us that their own personal integrity was a major factor in reaching the unchurched. "The unchurched look at leaders just like anybody else does," said Sam P., a Methodist pastor from Texas. "If they don't see authenticity in our own lives, how can they expect the church to be real?"

> *Lesson 1:*
> **Authenticity of the Pastor**
> ***92%***
> responded

Just as we heard from the formerly unchurched, the leaders of these churches realize that they must demonstrate honesty and vulnerability from the pulpit and in conversations with the unchurched. Sam elaborated further: "On occasion I let the people know of my own struggles and weaknesses. I don't believe I should be confessional frequently, but it lets the unchurched know we're humans just like they are."

One related issue to authenticity that arose frequently was the appropriate use of humor by the pastors. "I tell you," an opinionated pastor told us, "you find a church that's reaching people, and you'll find a church that laughs together. A preacher doesn't have to be a clown, but he sure needs a sense of humor."

> *Lesson 2:*
> **The Imperative of Personal Evangelism**
> ***88%***
> responded

Lesson 2: The Imperative of Personal Evangelism

As we learned earlier, 75 percent of the formerly unchurched told us that someone from the church they joined shared Christ with them. The leaders of the church confirmed this reality from their perspective. A Southern Baptist pastor from Louisiana stated bluntly: "So you're now doing a study on the unchurched? You probably won't quote me on this, then, but I think most church leaders are basically stupid about reaching the unchurched. You know what they need to do? Tell lost people about Jesus. Witness to them. I mean, what kind of idiot expects to reach lost people without telling them about Jesus?"

> Church members are hesitant to invite people to church, to develop relationships with the unchurched, if they are not excited about their own church and their own walk with God.

Almost nine out of ten church leaders affirmed what 75 percent of the formerly unchurched told us. Without an intentional, organized effort to share the gospel with non-Christians, most lasting efforts to reach the unchurched are in vain. The comments of Earl B., a formerly unchurched man from Tampa, Florida, are instructive: "I thank God that my church sent people out to share Jesus with me. I thank God they were trained how to share the gospel with me. I thank God they loved me enough to be obedient to the Lord."

Lesson 3: Relationships Again

Much of what the leaders said confirms our earlier material from the unchurched. More than eight out of ten of the pastors we interviewed indicated their keen awareness of the impact of reaching the unchurched through relationships. The struggle articulated by many of these leaders, however, was the "how" of encouraging such relationships. Though no one simple response was given, there seems to be agreement that church members are hesitant to invite people to

> *Lesson 3:*
> **Yes, Relationships Are Important**
> *84%*
> responded

church, to develop relationships with the unchurched, if they are not excited about their own church and their own walk with God. The development of relationships with the unchurched, it seems, cannot be programmed. Such relationships are the result of the "overflow" of God's presence in a Christian's life.

Lesson 4: An Atmosphere of Love and Acceptance

The leaders to whom we spoke were highly motivated to lead their churches to become havens of love and acceptance for the unchurched. A Nevada pastor told us: "The stories of hurting people who come to our church are incredible. We have no advertising budget, but people just keep coming. We do not compromise our beliefs whatsoever. But we do tell people over and over again that Jesus accepted them where they were, that he forgives sinners." A Wesleyan pastor shared the compelling story of a woman who simply showed up at their church with the unusual greeting, "Billy Graham sent me." Upon further inquiry, the members heard an amazing story.

> *Lesson 4:*
> **An Atmosphere of Love and Acceptance**
> *79%*
> responded

Gloria S. was ready to take her life. She had untold numbers of prescription drugs that she had saved for this moment. Her life was a heart-wrenching story of drug abuse, failed relationships, and multiple rejections. Gloria turned on the television lest any apartment neighbors hear her make any noises as the drugs did their deadly work.

In the sovereignty of God, the television turned on to a Billy Graham crusade. A telephone number was on the bottom of the screen for anyone needing help. Gloria called the number before she took the pills.

The wise counselor for the Graham organization recognized that Gloria was suicidal. She told Gloria to find a church immediately, that someone would help her. The Wesleyan church was on the list of churches the Graham organization had that were near Gloria.

Gloria decided to put off her suicide and try the church the next day; after all, the next day was Sunday. Again, in God's perfect timing, Gloria ran into the pastor just before the worship service began. "Billy Graham sent me," she told him.

"Billy Graham saved me from killing myself," Gloria told us, "but my church showed me how to be saved from my sins." What was it about the church that made Gloria want to listen to them? "The love of the people was incredible. I never knew someone as dirty as me could ever receive love again. The people accepted me just as I was." She paused for a moment, then continued. "I have seen Jesus. He is in the faces of all these people who love me."

Lesson 5:

The Pastor Must Model Personal Evangelism

72%

responded

Lesson 5: The Pastor Must Model Personal Evangelism

Some pastors learned the hard way, they told us. They tried the latest church-growth model, attended conferences, and bought books on the church, but they still had anemic results in reaching the unchurched.

Over seven out of ten pastors we interviewed shared with us the critical importance of their modeling personal evangelism. Said Wesley, a nondenominational pastor from Michigan: "I used to beat up the people pretty badly from the pulpit. Then God convicted me that we would never reach the unchurched unless I myself was obedient to the Great Commission. It seems like we reach people for Christ when I'm obedient; and it seems like the church is dead when I'm disobedient."

Lesson 6: Enthusiasm and Joy Are Present in Churches that Reach the Unchurched

Lesson 6:

Enthusiasm and Joy Are Present

68%

responded

"You'll never go into a church that's reaching people," the Evangelical Free Church pastor told us, "unless there's a lot of joy and enthusiasm present. It feeds on itself. A joyous church motivates people to invite the unchurched. And when the unchurched are reached, the joy grows. It's a great cycle!"

The obvious question, of course, is how the cycle ever begins. Different leaders offered different insights.

- "It begins when the pastor becomes personally evangelistic."
- "In our church the right atmosphere was created after we got serious about prayer."
- "When I [the pastor] spend enough time in sermon preparation, God seems to honor the worship services with his presence."
- "If you provide ways for people to grow as Christians, they will be more joyous."

Lesson 7: Do Not Compromise the Essentials

"Yeah, I went through a phase in ministry that I called 'Bible-lite' years. I dumbed down my preaching and didn't ask much of the people for fear that I'd offend them. Big mistake! Our back door opened wide," a pastor from Oklahoma exclaimed. We heard similar stories from over 60 percent of the pastors we interviewed. Not only does an unchallenging message fail to attract the unchurched, but we learned from the formerly unchurched that such an approach actually deters them from returning. As we saw earlier, the formerly unchurched are attracted to churches with a strong belief system.

> *Lesson 7:*
> **Do Not Compromise the Essentials**
> *63%*
> responded

"It seems like there are two groups out there arguing how to reach lost people," an Indiana pastor told us. "On the one hand, you've got the seeker-movement people who devise a bunch of methods to reach the unchurched. Then you've got the strong doctrinal group that says preach the Word faithfully and God will reach these people." But this pastor had come to his own conclusion: "I'll tell you what I do. I won't compromise a lick of doctrine to reach the unchurched, but I'll also do everything we can with methods, programs, and ideas to reach them. As I see the Bible, it doesn't teach either/or; it teaches both/and."

Lesson 8: Have Small-Group Opportunities Available

While some church leaders debate the best type of small group, most of them agree that some type of small-group organization must be in place both to reach and to assimilate the unchurched. A number of church leaders viewed their small-group organization as indispensable in reaching the unchurched. And while more leaders in our study favored Sunday schools as their primary expression of small groups, most of them saw the outreach potential of numerous groups.

> *Lesson 8:*
> **Small-Group Opportunities**
> *60%*
> responded

Greg M., a pastor from Kentucky, probably the most loquacious interviewee we encountered, insisted that all small-group leaders in his church report to a team captain every other week. "Accountability is the key," Greg spoke before we asked the question. "When we tell our small-group leaders that their groups are responsible for reaching out, they nod and say okay. But when we tell them they will have a report session every two weeks, they really get moving!"

Lesson 9: Reaching People in Crisis

A significant number of the formerly unchurched told us that their first reason for visiting a church was a crisis in their lives. This book opened with the story of Donna C. and the tragedies of her divorce and subsequent financial struggles. If you recall, it was Donna's mother who influenced her daughter to visit a certain church, but it was Donna's crisis that gave her a desire to seek to fill a void in her life.

Lesson 9:
Reaching People in Crisis
57%
responded

One factor is certain about the leaders of these churches that reach the unchurched: they are highly creative in their attempts to reach the unchurched. A Baptist church in West Virginia has a hospital ministry to new mothers, an attempt to reach these young families in their "positive crisis." A West Coast Evangelical Free Church has reached more unchurched through its crisis pregnancy ministry than any another approach. And a Wesleyan church in the Midwest offers its beautiful sanctuary to prospective newlyweds at a very modest fee—but only if they agree to four sessions of premarital counseling.

> One factor is certain about the leaders of these churches that reach the unchurched: they are highly creative in their attempts to reach the unchurched.

The lesson is clear: the unchurched are more likely to seek a church at a point of crisis. Innovative churches have discovered ways to have a presence in these crisis moments.

Lesson 10: Reaching the Unchurched through Quality Childcare

In my role as a church consultant, I tell church leaders that quality preschool and children's facilities are imperative. Bright and safe modern rooms with new furniture, equipment, and toys, along with unquestionable security features, are demanded by discerning parents today, especially unchurched parents.

Lesson 10:
Reaching People through Quality Childcare
57%
responded

Well over half of the leaders we interviewed indicated their *strategy* to reach the unchurched through quality childcare. "Parents today want the best for

169

their children," indicated an independent Baptist pastor from Louisiana. "It is amazing how much they care for the spiritual well-being of their children but neglect themselves in this area," he said. "We decided to allocate heavy dollar resources into updating our preschool and children's wing. Boy, has it paid off! We're now reaching many of these young families who have no church background," he exclaimed.

We received mixed opinions from the church leaders about the effectiveness of a "mom's day out," a day care, or a five-day preschool as an evangelistic tool. Some leaders indicated that these ministries typically lose their evangelistic focus and cater to Christians only. Others said the ministries tend to become a tail wagging the dog. But still some said that, with highly intentional efforts, these weekday ministries can be evangelistically effective.

Lesson 11: Focus Evangelistic Efforts on Children and Youth

Our research team's studies indicate that 81 percent of those who accept Christ do so before the age of twenty.[3] Whether this number is an indicator of receptivity to the gospel at a young age or the ineffectiveness of the church to reach adults, the case for focusing evangelistic resources on young people is compelling.

> **Lesson 11:**
> **Focus Evangelistic Efforts on Children and Youth**
> **52%**
> responded

Noted a nondenominational church pastor from Minnesota, "We don't neglect the adults, but we have seven specific ministries a year designed to reach teens and children." Over one-half of the pastors indicated that their churches had specific strategies to reach children and youth, the largest unchurched group in America.

> **Lesson 12:**
> **Utilize a Discovery Class to Reach the Unchurched**
> **48%**
> responded

Lesson 12: Utilize a Discovery Class to Reach the Unchurched

In a previous study, our research team found that new members' classes were highly effective tools in closing the back door.[4] Many leaders of the effective churches told us that they use these classes for dual purposes: entry into membership and an inquiry class for prospective members including the unchurched.

Such an approach makes sense in light of the strong desire of the formerly unchurched to learn doctrine, to know more about the church, and to learn biblical issues. While some leaders of churches created two separate classes, almost all of those we interviewed indicated the ease by which one class can be used for two purposes.

Lesson 13: Find an Evangelistic Leader

"I have been the senior pastor of four churches in thirty-two years," the Southern Baptist pastor from Texas told us. "In every church, I've looked for and prayed for someone who is passionate about evangelism. God has answered my prayers. And when you turn that person loose, the gates of hell begin to fall." Four out of ten pastors we interviewed indicated that through an intentional process or by an unsought blessing, an evangelistic leader has emerged. "You wouldn't believe the difference it makes in the church," the pastor told us, "when you have both the pastor and a key layperson being evangelistic champions." Yes, we would.

> *Lesson 13:*
> **Find an Evangelistic Leader**
> *41%*
> responded

Lesson 14: Marketing Tools Alone Are Ineffective

I frequently come in contact with people whose primary vocation is to sell marketing tools to churches. Their products are quality products: direct-mail pieces, visitor cards, and response letters, to name a few. And every marketing person whom I have met tells prospective purchasers that such tools are to be used *in conjunction with* a comprehensive evangelistic strategy. Still some church leaders think neat, well-packaged marketing tools are all they need to reach the unchurched. Even some of the leaders of the effective churches confessed their own mistakes of depending on marketing tools alone. "I went four years in ministry trying to find a quick fix," a North Carolina pastor told us. "I've learned my lesson. There is no substitute for concerted prayer, godly obedience, and a lot of hard work!"

> *Lesson 14:*
> **Marketing Tools Alone Are Ineffective**
> *37%*
> responded

Lesson 15: Patience Is Required

We rarely met or interviewed church leaders who said their churches' growth was easy. Many expressed to us their seasons of dryness, growth plateau or decline, and frustration. We heard stories of how a number of these leaders felt like they could not continue in their place of ministry. Yet those who remained faithful and persistent in their places of ministry told us about breakthroughs on some occasions and slow but steady growth at other times.

Lesson 15:
Patience Is
Required
33%
responded

Reaching the unchurched world, they said, is hard work. It requires a life of prayer and an evangelistic spirit. It also requires leadership skills, and many of the church leaders shared with us that they found themselves ill-equipped to lead their churches. Leadership is vital, they said, but many were not prepared. So what did they do? The answer is the subject of our next chapter.

CHAPTER 9

Raising Leadership Issues

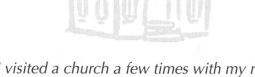

*I visited a church a few times with my neighbors
when I was ten or eleven years old. The pastor
was a mean jerk. I said I would never go back.*

—"Born2Bwild" in the Born Again 3
Internet Chat Room

The church-planting strategy team called me to consult with them about concerns over their new churches. God had blessed the denominational group with abundant financial resources. But, as many know who are familiar with new church work, money can be a curse as well as a blessing. Financial dependency can be the factor that hinders a new church from becoming an indigenous, reproducing church of its own.

As I met with the strategy team, we poured over the statistics, funding levels, and growth of each new work. We looked at the most successful churches, the failed churches, and the churches headed down a precarious path.

What, asked the strategy team, are the reasons for success or lack of success of each church? All of the churches were planted in areas with solid demographic growth and with potential for future growth. Why would one church grow and another church never get off the ground? I had my suspicions, so I asked the strategists to go through an exercise with me.

Without looking at demographic issues, we discussed many of the church planters. How did they do in their assessments, the process by which each prospective church starter is evaluated for new church work? On a subjective level, how would you describe their personalities? If we compared a "successful" church planter with one who did not experience success, how would you describe the differences between the two church starters?

As we went through this exercise, one issue emerged with clarity. The success or failure of these church planters depended significantly on their leadership abilities. And two leadership issues were more prominent than others: Does the church planter demonstrate evidence of visionary leadership capability? And does the church starter show in his background an exceedingly strong work ethic? If the strategy team answered yes to both of these questions, without exception we saw a successful church plant.

In our studies of over four thousand churches, my research team and I repeatedly have seen the incredible impact leadership has on the effectiveness of a church. Almost all of the pastors of the effective churches we studied had two traits in common: they were theologically conservative and had strong leadership skills. In most cases, the presence of only one of these characteristics was not sufficient to produce an effective church.

In this chapter we will look specifically at leadership issues: How did these leaders develop their leadership styles? Who or what influenced them? How do the effective leaders manage their time? What tasks do they enjoy? What tasks do they abhor? Do they mentor others? Are they motivated by others?

Another Study ... Similar Conclusions

Though our study was unique in its approach to interviewing the formerly unchurched, other researchers continue to make valuable contributions toward our understanding of the church. I return to the many good studies by the Barna Research Group. One research project in particular yielded conclusions similar to our study of the unchurched.[1] When respondents were asked to identify the reasons they chose to attend a church service, the top ten responses, listed in order, were:

1. The theological beliefs and doctrine of the church.
2. How much the people seem to care about each other.
3. The quality of the sermons that are preached.
4. How friendly the people in the church are to visitors.
5. How involved the church is in helping poor and disadvantaged people.
6. The quality of the programs and classes for children.

7. How much you like the pastor.
8. The denomination the church is affiliated with.
9. The quality of the adult Sunday school classes.
10. The convenience of the times of their weekend services.[2]

Two of the top ten issues were related to the pastor. The other factors were direct results of the pastor's leadership. Regardless of the party asked—the formerly unchurched, pastors, other leaders, or laypersons—the responses are similar. Leadership is important, if not critical, in reaching people, particularly the unchurched.

Leadership Defined

Before we delve further into leadership issues, let us hear from the leaders themselves on definitions of leadership. Note the consistency in many of the definitions.

Leadership is . . .

> "the art and science of influencing people."
> "the God-given ability/gift to motivate people to accomplish God's goals."
> "active involvement in influencing people."
> "influence that helps people get to where they need to go."
> "the ability to influence others."
> "the ability to cast vision and influence people to join you in a preferred future."
> "having people follow you over a period of time."
> "the ability to motivate followers to a specific end."
> "the gift of generating followership."

Several parts of the definition of leadership were common in many of the responses. More than any other component, having "followers" seemed to be the key to being a leader. Obviously, he or she who has no followers is not a leader.

A second common element in the definition was "influence." Many of the leaders of these churches seem to have been influenced by John Maxwell's definition: "Leadership is influence."[3] But these leaders accepted this definition with more than mental assent. A Colorado pastor said it succinctly: "If I'm not influencing people, I'm not a leader."

175

The third most common element of the leadership definitions was "vision." The influence of George Barna was evident here, as numerous pastors defined vision to be a "preferred future."[4] We have found a significant level of confusion among church leaders related to the concept of vision. Noted a pastor from New York whose church did not qualify as an effective church in our study: "Vision is the in thing. You have to have an exact idea where the church needs to go to lead it. But honestly, I don't know how to get the vision. I pray. I work. I read books. I attend conferences. But I just don't get it."

Though most definitions have some level of specificity in them, the leaders of the effective churches did not seem concerned if they did not know the specific direction the church was going. A pastor from Illinois said, "The vision I communicate to the church is one of reaching more people and ministry to more people. I really don't know all the details on how we'll get there."

For this pastor, the "preferred future" is simple. The church will reach and minister to more people. He has no grandiose schemes or elaborate programs to specify how the church will meet its general goal. Repeatedly we heard that the most effective vision casting was delivered in broad, general terms, even though most definitions of vision call for specificity.

Who Influenced Whom?

If leadership is influence, it is interesting to note the key influences on the leaders themselves. In our survey of the leaders of these churches, we asked the respondents to rate the most influential factors of influence. We show on the next few pages the top four influences. Then we comment on one factor that was not influential.

More than any single factor, successful church experiences were rated the most significant influence by these leaders on their own leadership development. In particular, many leaders told us how successful experiences in reaching the unchurched shaped their ministries. "Yeah, I tried a bunch of the latest fads," said the slow-speaking Mississippi pastor, "but what really affected me was getting our church involved in a regular personal evangelism program. I led the way, and the church followed. Now we're finally reaching people."

Another church leader told us about a ministry his church was using to help members become more sensitive to reaching the unchurched.

"We developed an accountability system to reach unchurched people," he told us. "The whole process of trying it, promoting it, and working out the bugs was a true learning experience. And now that it's working, we have become somewhat of a model for other churches."

Shawn Corzine (his real name) is the associate pastor of a large Southern Baptist church in the San Antonio area. He completed a doctor of ministry degree under my supervision at Southern Seminary. One of the assignments our students are required to complete is a lengthy personal leadership assessment. They must address the greatest influences, positive or negative, on their ministry and leadership style.

Figure 9.1

Rate the Influence of Experiences of Success in Church Work As a Factor in Your Development As an Effective Leader

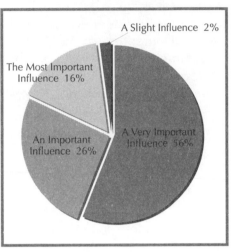

Shawn says a pastor named Bailey Stone had the most positive leadership influence on his life. "Growing up in Midland, Texas, I sensed a call from God to go into ministry. Bailey Stone was a pastor who immediately took me under his wing. When I would return home from college and seminary, he would call me, and we would spend several hours together," Shawn reflected.

"I would like to follow his example in my own ministry," Shawn told me. "I now know how incredibly busy he was, yet he saw shaping my life and ministry as a priority for his own ministry.

Almost seven out of ten of the leaders we interviewed said that a mentor was the most important or a very important influence on their lives and ministry. If the category "an important influence" is included, 83 percent of the leaders considered the relationship of a mentor to be a key factor in their own leadership development.

As the formerly unchurched clearly communicated to us, a critically important factor in reaching the unchurched is the attitude and passion of a leader. In numerous interviews we heard that the enthusiasm these leaders exude was caught from a mentor. As we will see at the end of this chapter, many of the leaders learned this lesson well. They are spreading the enthusiasm of reaching the lost to a new generation.

"I was thirty years old, fresh out of seminary, and full of myself," Chip reflected. Chip is a forty-two-year-old pastor of a nondenominational church in Ohio. "When I attended [a megachurch] conference, I said to myself, 'This is it! This is how we're supposed to do church.' I went back to my church convinced that we would change the world in a year."

> Almost seven out of ten of the leaders we interviewed said that a mentor was the most important or a very important influence on their lives and ministry.

Chip introduced the new ideas to a skeptical leadership and began eliminating some existing programs, changing worship styles, and reconfiguring official leadership patterns. Within a few weeks Chip and the church were in crisis.

"The conference leader made everything sound so easy." Chip reflected. "When everything came crashing down I was totally caught off guard." The traditionalists opposed the more contemporary worship style. The leaders of the programs revolted when their areas were eliminated. And the old guard leadership in the church almost succeeded in firing Chip.

"I survived the experience, but I am scarred from it. More than anything, I've learned from the experience," Chip mused. "I've learned that you can never communicate too much information. I've learned that what works in one context may not work in another. And I've learned to consult with others and to seek input and wisdom."

A majority of the leaders indicated that a negative experience

Figure 9.2

Rate the Influence of a Mentor As a Factor in Your Development As an Effective Leader

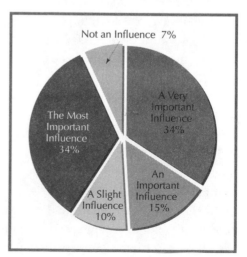

Not an Influence 7%

A Very Important Influence 34%

The Most Important Influence 34%

An Important Influence 15%

A Slight Influence 10%

or a failure had shaped their ministry and leadership significantly. One church leader put this issue into perspective. "When you're dealing with reaching lost people, you will get opposition and you will have failures. Sometimes the opposition will be nothing less than spiritual warfare. Satan obviously opposes any efforts to reach people for Christ. But sometimes the opposition will be fellow Christians. Perhaps they resist change. Or perhaps we leaders don't do a very good job at leading them to change."

The church leader paused for a few moments and then said, "The key for me, and the key for many other church leaders has been learning from our mistakes and failures. Anyone who is trying to reach lost and unchurched people will make mistakes. The only people who don't make mistakes are those who don't try anything. The real issue is whether or not we learn from our mistakes. Two steps backwards is okay," he concluded, "as long as you take three steps forward."

Figure 9.3

Rate the Influence of Experiences of Failure in Church Work As a Factor in Your Development As An Effective Leader

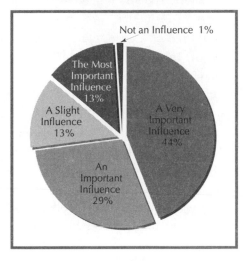

> A majority of the leaders indicated that a negative experience or a failure had shaped their ministry and leadership significantly.

We were surprised when the leaders of the effective churches told us that participation in a conference or seminar was a highly influential factor in their leadership development. Slightly more than half indicated that the conference was a "very important influence. Only 3 percent said it was not an influence at all.

While conferences and seminars often are criticized for various reasons, the leaders of the churches that are reaching the unchurched have benefited from them. We were impressed with how well the leaders could glean principles from the conferences yet know how to apply and contextualize the lessons learned in their own churches.

Before we leave the subject of influence on the leaders of effective churches, let us note two other positive factors that came close to being ranked as "the most important influence" or "a very important influence": leadership expert (49 percent) and books on leadership (41 percent).

Though I am not pleased with the

> Only three out of ten of those we interviewed indicated that college or seminary training positively impacted their leadership development. And four out of ten told us the influence was slight or not a factor at all.

responses regarding another factor in leadership development, integrity demands that I report it. Only three out of ten of those we interviewed indicated that college or seminary training positively impacted their leadership development. And four out of ten told us the influence was slight or not a factor at all.

We who teach in or lead colleges or seminaries have much work to do. While the leaders praised the seminaries in particular for their training in classical disciplines, they consistently told us they were ill-equipped for the real world of power groups, multiple expectations, and angry church members. Fred W., a Southern Baptist pastor, noted: "I definitely needed training in Bible and theology, and I'm grateful to my seminary for its help in that area. But I had lousy people skills when I graduated, and many of my professors knew it. I got fired from my first year in ministry and went a year and a half without a ministry job. My training wasn't much use when I didn't have a job."

Figure 9.4

Rate the Influence of Participation in a Conference or Seminar As a Factor in Your Development As an Effective Leader

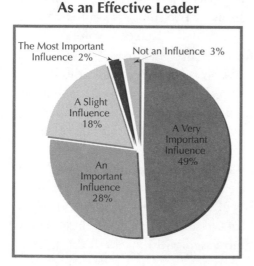

The Most Important Influence 2%
Not an Influence 3%
A Slight Influence 18%
A Very Important Influence 49%
An Important Influence 28%

Figure 9.5

Rate the Influence of Training in College or Seminary As a Factor in Your Development As an Effective Leader

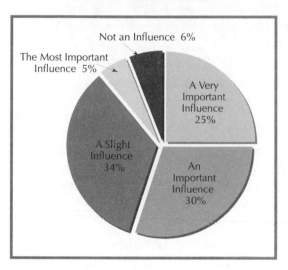

Those Leaders Have Style!

A critical issue for us to discern is *how* these leaders of churches that are reaching the unchurched lead. The level of consistency in our survey responses told us that certain leadership styles are more effective in reaching the unchurched than others. We listed and defined ten different leadership styles for the leaders of the churches to use in assessing themselves. The ten styles are:

Delegator oriented—leads by assigning tasks in nearly every situation.

Dream oriented—spends a lot of time dreaming big dreams with little concern for completion.

Goal oriented—has high interest in setting goals and pushing for completion.

Knowledge oriented—leads by superior knowledge and understanding rather than by example.

Loner oriented—would rather work alone and risk accomplishing little.

Organization oriented—is organized above all else, every detail
checked.

Relationship oriented—has high interest in people, feelings, and
fellowship.

Suggestion oriented—leads by making suggestions to others.

Task oriented—has high interest in production and getting things
done.

Team player oriented—must work in a group or be a part of a
team effort; leads primarily by example.

We combined the categories of "completely characteristic" and "very
characteristic" in the responses of leaders whose churches are reaching
the unchurched. Note the ten factors in order of responses.

A clear leadership pattern emerges in the leadership styles of those we
surveyed. Those leaders are driven to accomplish goals. They set the tone

Figure 9.6

Which of the Following Describes Your Leadership Style?

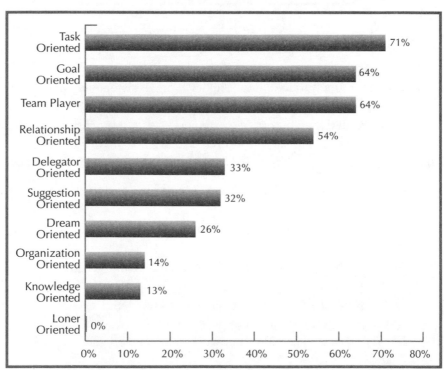

for lofty visions, establish goals to attain those visions, and then work with grist and determination to accomplish their goals.

But the leaders do not seek to accomplish tasks in a void. They realize the importance of relationships and team effort in accomplishing tasks. True, these leaders are driven. But they are not driven to the point of running over those to whom they minister and with whom they work.

Note the dramatic drop in responses in figure 9.6 after the first four leadership styles. The two big issues for these leaders were the accomplishment of goals and making certain work was done in the context of a team.

A comparison of the leadership styles between the effective church leaders and the churches that did not meet our criteria for effective evangelistic churches is interesting. The big difference between the two groups is that the effective church leaders are more task driven and goal oriented. Many of these leaders indicated that such a style was learned from others rather than a part of their natural abilities.

Figure 9.7

Top Four Leadership Styles

"Effective" Church Leaders	"Comparison" Church Leaders
1. Task Oriented	1. Relationship Oriented
2. Goal Oriented	2. Suggestion Oriented
3. Team Player	3. Team Player
4. Relationship Oriented	4. Organization Oriented

Time on Their Side

Leadership gurus will tell you that a primary skill of effective leaders is the ability to manage time. With that in mind, we asked the 101 leaders to provide us an hour-by-hour calendar of a typical 168-hour workweek. A pastor of a nondenominational church in Utah commented, after completing this assignment, "This was an eye-opening exercise for me. I've always prided myself on being a good time manager, but I saw significant room for improvement."

Our researchers were impressed with the time management skills of effective leaders. Perhaps the best way to show their skills is to compare their use of time with that of leaders of the churches in the control group.

Figure 9.8a and 9.8b

Composition of a 168-Hour Week

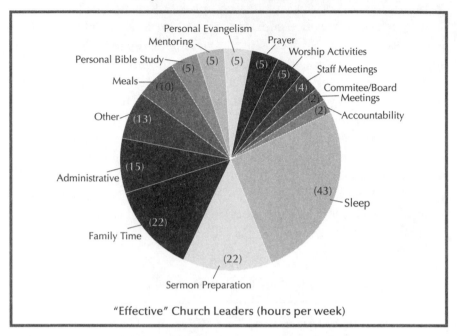

"Effective" Church Leaders (hours per week)

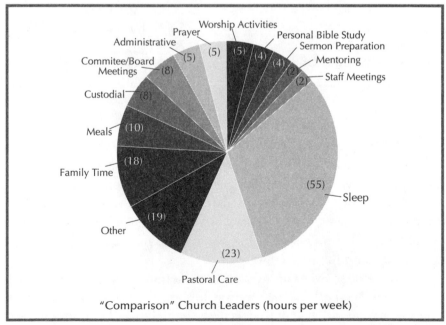

"Comparison" Church Leaders (hours per week)

Note the significant differences between the two groups:

- Leaders of effective churches sleep slightly over six hours per day; other church leaders sleep almost eight hours per day.
- Effective leaders spend twenty-two hours in sermon preparation time compared to four hours for the other group.
- The effective church leaders spent ten hours each week in pastoral care compared to thirty-three hours for the comparison group leaders. Pastoral care included counseling, hospital visits, weddings, and funerals.
- Effective leaders average five hours each week in personal evangelism. Most of the comparison group leaders entered "0" for their weekly time in personal evangelism.
- Comparison group leaders spend eight hours a week—more than an hour each day—performing custodial duties at the church. The typical custodial duties included opening and closing the facilities, turning off lights, and general cleaning of the building.
- Leaders of the effective churches find the necessary time to focus on priority items. They spend more than twenty hours each week in sermon preparation, but they give equal time to family activities. They make certain they devote almost an hour each day to personal evangelism. They allow others in the church to be involved in pastoral care and custodial responsibilities.

The time allocation of effective leaders seems to complement the way they described their own leadership styles. These leaders are goal oriented and task driven. In order to accomplish their goals, they cannot do many of the responsibilities often expected of pastors. They cannot make every hospital visit. They cannot counsel everyone. And they cannot perform all the custodial duties many may expect of them. But as leaders they can see that those things get done. And that leaves them more time for the Great Commission work of reaching the unchurched.

Do Leaders Believe They Are Leaders?

One other question we asked the church leaders concerned their view of themselves: "How would you rate your overall effectiveness as a leader?" Their responses are shown in figure 9.9.

None of the leaders we surveyed indicated that their leadership was "only slightly effective" or "not effective at all." The lowest rating they gave themselves was "effective." Our interview team's subjective assessment of the leaders was "confident but not cocky." These leaders do have a certain presence that is noticed immediately, but they are rarely arrogant. They seem to understand that their strengths come from a source other than themselves.

Figure 9.9

How Would You Rate Your Overall Effectiveness As a Leader?

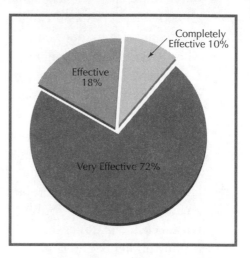

What are their strengths? Do they have significant weaknesses? If they could relive certain situations, what would they do differently? The answers to these questions cannot be given in just a few sentences. For that reason we make it the subject of our next chapter.

CHAPTER 10

An Honest Look at Their Personal Strengths and Weaknesses

I have always believed in God, but not in an individual Jesus. Now I am looking into Jesus with this really cool pastor that has his act together.

—"Lutman07" in the Christian Home Internet Chat Room

Mary Beth L. attends a growing Georgia church near the South Carolina border. Though the church has no denominational affiliation, "it seems like the Southern Baptist church I attended as a child," said Mary Beth. The thirty-two-year-old mother of two was fairly active in church until her parents divorced. She was eight years old at the time of the divorce and shared that, "I never returned to church again until the past two years."

Mary Beth became a Christian only five months prior to our interview. We asked her the questions you have heard throughout this book. Of course the key question was, "What was the single greatest factor that led you to choose this church?" Her response was quick and straightforward, "That's easy. The pastor."

Of course we wanted more details. What specific issues related to the pastor attracted her to the church? His preaching? His personality? His vision-casting ability? "All of these things were important," she told us, "but more than anything else was Bruce's transparency, his willingness to admit mistakes; he is just a real person."

The "real person" description was stated numerous ways in our interviews with the formerly unchurched. Many of these new Christians expressed surprise at leaders' openness and transparency about mistakes.

Noted Mary Beth, "I expected a 'holier-than-thou' pastor, and I saw just the opposite. I remember the second time I heard him. He told the church about a mistake he made. I was floored that a pastor would admit he had any weaknesses."

Though our research team did not necessarily have the same level of surprise as Mary Beth, we were keenly aware of the "real person" issue as the leaders responded to our questions. These leaders of effective churches readily shared not only their perceived strengths, but their weaknesses as well.

The information you are about to read profoundly impressed me. The next few pages are a mini-manual of leadership principles that are not theoretical but come from the real-life experiences of leaders of effective churches. We will hear self-appraisals of their leadership skills, both strengths and weaknesses.

The Strengths of Leaders Whose Churches Reach the Unchurched

Our questions to the leaders of the effective churches were open-ended. Two simple questions led to many insightful responses:

> What do you feel your greatest strengths are in the area
> of leadership?
> What do you feel your greatest weaknesses are in the area
> of leadership?

Of all the possible responses, twelve strengths were cited by at least 50 percent of the leaders, and twelve weaknesses were cited by at least half of the pastors. Our research thus presents twenty-four insightful leadership factors to help us better understand how to reach the unchurched.

Strength #1: The Ability to Cast Vision

"When I came to the church nine years ago," the Ohio pastor told us, "the church did not have a clue where it was going. The leaders told me that they were willing to follow me anywhere if I could just tell them where we needed to go."

As I indicated in an earlier chapter, the ability to cast vision does not always mean that the leader knows precisely where the church should go. He may communicate that obedience to the Great Commission is imperative, that reaching the unchurched is not an option, and that ministering to those in need is the cultural mandate for the church. But the leader of the church may not have a clear idea where this obedience to God may lead. I once asked Bob Russell, pastor of the huge Southeast Christian Church in Louisville, Kentucky, how he developed a vision to become one of the largest churches in North America. His response? "I didn't." He explained to me that he never once planned to be pastor of such a large church. "We just tried to be obedient to what God called us to do and to do everything with excellence."[1]

Strength #1:
The Ability to Cast Vision
72%
responded

Two elements of vision casting were mentioned frequently. First, the leader is confident. Such confidence comes from experience and from a sense of God's presence in the vision. Second, the vision is communicated with passion and inspiration. "When Pastor Paul talks about the vision for our church," Helen D. observed, "the whole church gets fired up. We believe in God's vision for our church because the pastor is so enthusiastic about it."

Yet rarely did we hear of a leader who had developed a precise plan to lead a church to growth. One point, however, is clear: regardless of the lack of detail, the communicated vision in almost all of our surveys included a clear and compelling picture of reaching lost people. The formerly unchurched were reached in no small part due to the vision of a leader who passionately communicated the urgency to reach the lost.

We asked the leaders of these churches to categorize their leadership style as sustaining, reactionary, or visionary. *Sustaining* refers to a style that seeks to preserve the status quo. *Reactionary* is a style that responds when needs become apparent. And the *visionary*

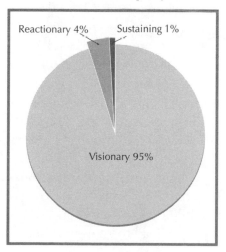

Figure 10.1

Which Label Best Describes Your Leadership Style?

Reactionary 4%   Sustaining 1%

Visionary 95%

style anticipates needs before they are apparent. Figure 10.1 (on the previous page) shows how the leaders responded.

No matter how we asked the question, the leaders said that they were visionaries, a response that agreed with what the formerly unchurched had told us.

Strength #2: A Sense of Humor

The formerly unchurched indicated that they were attracted to a particular church because of the personality and transparency of the pastor. And often they mentioned that the personality included in part a sense of humor. The surprise from our perspective, however, was the number of leaders who mentioned humor as a strength. Nearly seven out of ten leaders noted this strength, the second most frequently mentioned characteristic of leadership. "Many of the unchurched expect a real straight-laced pastor when they finally visit a church," a Nazarene pastor told us. "They are really surprised to find we are human just like they are. A sense of humor tends to disarm those who may be uptight about being in church."

Strength #2:
A Sense of Humor
68%
responded

Strength #3: Work Ethic

Hardly a day goes by that I do not receive a call, e-mail, or letter from a church seeking a pastor or some other staff member. Inevitably most of the inquirers ask me if I could recommend someone who has a strong work ethic. Recently I received this e-mail: "Dr. Rainer, I commend the trend where ministers insist on spending more time with their families. I think it is a great need. But if our last three staff members are any indicators of a minister's work ethic, we are going to have trouble finding someone who will put in a forty-hour work week."

Strength #3:
Work Ethic
67%
responded

Though only two-thirds of the church leaders we interviewed mentioned a strong work ethic as one of their leadership strengths, I believe that all of those leaders are hard workers. Whether I interviewed them myself or read the notes and surveys from other interviewers, one factor came through clearly: these leaders work long and hard for the churches they serve.

Figure 10.2 provides credible evidence for the work ethic of effective church leaders. After analyzing the 168-hour week of leaders of both the effective churches and the "comparison" churches, the contrast in work weeks is notable.

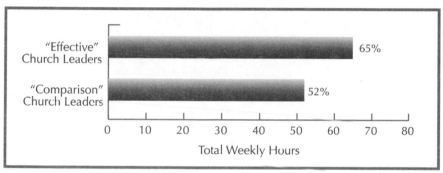

Figure 10.2

Average Weekly Hours Worked at Church

The thirteen-hour difference between the two groups of leaders could mean as many as 650 hours in a fifty-week year. And on a more subjective level, the time-management analysis of the previous chapter indicates that the effective church leaders are making better use of the time they give to their churches. For example, eight of the fifty-two hours given to the church by the comparison group are for custodial duties, particularly opening and closing the church several times a week.

Strength #4: Persistence

The pastor of a nondenominational church in Maryland told us his leadership strengths could be summed up in one word: *persistence.* "I have been at this church for fourteen years. I've made some stupid mistakes, and I've done a few good things. As I look back over fourteen years, I can see that God has blessed me despite me. Too many of my fellow pastors run to another church at the first sign of trouble. I'm glad I stuck it out."

Strength #4:
Persistence
65%
responded

As noted earlier, the tenure of the pastors of the effective churches is significantly longer than that of the pastors of the control churches. As the Maryland pastor indicated, the longer tenure allows leaders to overcome mistakes. But the persistence issue was more than just hanging on for several years. These leaders were tenacious in their attempts to get God's work done well at the churches they served. Dan, a New York pastor, told us: "The old cliché is to make lemonade out of lemons. I believe that God will bless our projects if we are faithful to him. So even when something doesn't go the way I like, I see it as an opportunity to leave a closed door and find a new open door."

Strength #5:
Leadership by Example
59%
responded

Strength #5: Leadership by Example

"Never ask the people of the church to do something you wouldn't do yourself!" a Tennessee pastor exclaimed.

A Virginia Presbyterian pastor told us, "One of my greatest leadership strengths is my willingness to lead by example. I have a lot of weaknesses," he added with modesty, "but that is my greatest strength." More than any other factor, a majority of the pastors said that they had to model personal evangelism. Listen to some of their comments.

- "The senior pastor must model personal evangelism to the staff and congregation."
- "The pastor should set the example by seeking to lead one person to the Lord each week."
- "I must set the pace in personal evangelism. I can't expect the people to do what the pastor is not doing."
- "The pastor must be a soul winner. Personal evangelism is both taught and caught."
- "I must establish relationships with non-Christians so that the people in the church will see my lifestyle modeled."
- "The pastor is a player/coach. He shows evangelism by example then encourages and exhorts others to do evangelism."

The issue of leadership by example was most conspicuous in the comments on personal evangelism, but it was not limited to that one issue. We received a plethora of responses related to prayer, personal Bible study, ethical issues, and family issues, to name a few. We heard clearly that the pastor must be a biblical example, practicing what he preaches.

Strength #6: Integrity

One pastor told us a story of tragic consequences. He began counseling a young lady alone. After three sessions with her, the pastor realized her problems were well beyond his counseling competencies. When he told the young lady that he would need to refer her to a professional counselor, she became distraught. Within a few days she was claiming that the pastor had made sexual advances toward her. Though the charges proved unfounded, his reputation was ruined. Under pressure he resigned.

> More than any other factor, a majority of the pastors said that they had to model personal evangelism.

We interviewed this pastor five years after the tragic event. Though he now leads a growing evangelistic church, the pain is still very evident in his voice. "If a pastor's integrity is ever questioned by many, it is next to impossible to be a leader. I learned the hard way that I must not only avoid evil, but I also must avoid any appearance of evil."

Strength #6:
Integrity
57%
responded

A number of the formerly unchurched we interviewed spoke of their initial skepticism of ministers because of what one coined "the televangelist syndrome." The leaders of those churches seemed well aware of their need to model the biblical mandate of being one who is above reproach. Such is the reason many responded to our inquiry about their leadership strengths with phrases like "integrity," "high moral character," and "reputation." And though over four out of ten did not specifically respond to our questions with words like "integrity," most of them did indicate the importance of high character in being a leader in ministry.

Strength #7: Change Agent

Every leader we interviewed had a story about change. And over half of them indicated that one of their leadership strengths was the ability to lead change.

Strength #7:
Change Agent
57%
responded

One pastor told us: "I used to work in the corporate world before God called me into the ministry. Change is difficult in the business world; it's almost impossible in the church."

Why is change so difficult for churches? For some churches, we were told, the issue is one of a desire for stability in a world of rapid change. "You can see it in their eyes and hear it in their voices," a Minnesota pastor told us. "The church is their place of constancy and refuge. When we start changing things in the church, we are messing with their only source of stability. Rather than accuse these people of being stuck-in-the-mud traditionalists, we need to be more sensitive to the pain they are experiencing."

A northern California pastor, however, had another perspective. "The main issue is that the people who are screaming about change are just lazy and disobedient. It's a lot easier to be comfortable than to be obedient. Following Christ is costly. Many people just don't want to pay the cost."

Figure 10.3 shows how both the effective churches and the comparison churches respond to change.

Do the pastors of the effective churches lead churches that were willing to change even before they became pastor? Or do the effective leaders provide leadership that makes the churches more receptive to change? Although our research team could not make a definite conclusion, we thought that leadership was a stronger factor than a church's being more open to change.

Our assessment of this issue is based largely on interviews and surveys in which the leaders shared with us their approaches to leading. We asked them to describe briefly the steps they take for leading their churches through change. Though we received no identical responses, we found many similarities. A typical step-by-step process to lead change went something like this:

1. Pray.
2. Present ideas to key leaders and seek input.
3. Present ideas to entire congregation and seek input.
4. Communicate plan redundantly over a lengthy period if possible.
5. Implement plan.
6. Evaluate.

The leaders of the effective churches realize that the success or lack of success in implementing change is critical in reaching the unchurched.

Figure 10.3a and 10.3b

How does your church typically respond to a challenge to change?

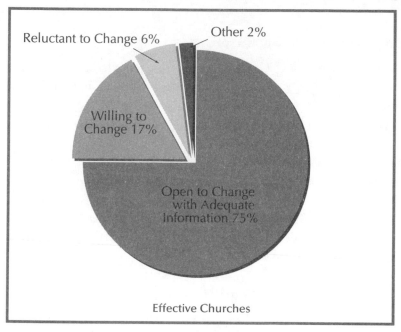

Effective Churches

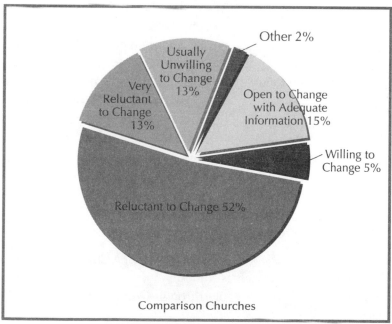

Comparison Churches

"Your 1950s church won't get it," an Alabama pastor said. "Churches that refuse to change will not reach the unchurched. They will be completely irrelevant."

Strength #8: Love of God's Word

At first glance, to love God's Word may not seem to be an obvious leadership trait. We were surprised to learn that over one-half of the leaders we interviewed believed that their love of God's Word would fit in the category of a leadership characteristic, but the leaders explained their points well.

> *Strength #8:*
> **Love of God's Word**
> *54%*
> responded

An Assembly of God pastor could be a spokesperson for most of the leaders we interviewed: "Obedience to God's Word is one of my leadership strengths. I can't be a leader unless I have an authority to lead from. I lead from the authority of the Word of God."

Strength #9: Communication Skills

The formerly unchurched told us they were attracted to the churches they joined in part because of the communication skills of the pastors. Those same church leaders agreed. "In today's high-tech, super-communication world, communication skills are needed more than ever," John C., a Baptist pastor told us." "You can't expect to hold the attention of the unchurched if you're a poor communicator."

> *Strength #9:*
> **Communication Skills**
> *53%*
> responded

More than one-half of the pastors indicated that communication skills were key to the success of their leadership. And they told us that these skills were particularly needed to reach the unchurched.

Strength #10: Faith/Optimism

"What impressed me about the pastor of Valley Community Church," Natalie commented, "was his confidence in God. He made me almost believe that anything was possible through God ... and I wasn't even a believer at the time!"

Slightly over one-half of the pastors indicated their faith in God was a leadership strength. "I have taken what many people would call stupid risks. We recently entered into a building program that is a huge step of faith," the Texas pas-

> *Strength #10:*
> **Faith/Optimism**
> *52%*
> responded

tor enthused. "We will have to grow in our budget by 25 percent within two years to be able to carry out this project. But I am convinced that God will provide. And the people of the church have followed my leadership. They are convinced too."

Some of the leaders were careful as to how they articulated this particular strength. Noted a New Jersey pastor, "I know that my faith and optimism are strengths God has given me. But I don't want you to tell people who read your book that my theology is the power of positive thinking or name-it-and-claim-it."

Faith and optimism are contagious. More than one leader told us they challenge their churches to do something so great that it is doomed to failure unless God is in it. And "BHAGs" were mentioned by one-fourth of the leaders. BHAG comes from the classic book on leadership *Built to Last* and means "big, hairy audacious goals."[2] Most churches modify the phrase to "big, holy, audacious goals." Noted the New Jersey pastor, "I challenge the people to one BHAG a year. We have never failed to meet our goal."

Strength #11: Relational Skills/Love of People

In the year 2000 I made a decision as dean of the Southern Baptist Theological Seminary that our faculty would add a required course in leadership that would cover such topics as conflict management, financial management, and interpersonal skills. The latter topic in particular was one that I knew to be of urgent import. I have seen, both as a dean and as a church consultant, some of the brightest people blow opportuni-

> *Strength #11:*
> **Relational Skills/ Love of People**
> *52%*
> responded

ties for effective leadership because they have poor interpersonal skills.

A majority of the leaders to whom we spoke cited interpersonal skills as one of their strengths. An executive pastor from Ohio told us: "I've got five good friends who graduated with me from seminary. Two have lost their jobs and are not in ministry. Another is in a difficult situation in a church. I believe the common factor in all of my friends' problems is their failure in relating to people. Their problems are a lesson for me. I'm trying to improve my relational skills even though I think I'm pretty good at it."

Strength #12:
Team Building/Mentoring

"If I had not made a major change four years ago," a Southern Baptist pastor told us, "I would have concluded my ministry without doing a major duty of a pastor: mentoring one or more men." We interviewed and surveyed some of the busiest leaders in Christian ministry. Many of them struggle to find the time to mentor others in much the same way that Paul mentored Timothy. Yet because many of these leaders were themselves mentored by others, they see the vital need to train and counsel people in the ministry of the gospel.

> *Strength #12:*
> **Team Building/ Mentoring**
> *50%*
> responded

> Our research has shown a trend of increased interest in mentoring over the past six years.

Our research has shown a trend of increased interest in mentoring over the past six years. Some Christian leaders mentor those who are specifically called by God to vocational ministry. Others focus their mentoring efforts on laypersons, to better equip them for their work in the local church. We would not be surprised to discover a few years from now that even more leaders view mentoring as one of their leadership strengths.

The Weaknesses of Leaders Whose Churches Reach the Unchurched

We did not know what type of response we would get to the question: "What do you feel your greatest weaknesses are in the area of leadership?" Would the leaders of these effective churches recognize weaknesses? Would they admit them? Would they be reticent to share their weaknesses if they did admit them?

Somewhat to our surprise, not only did these leaders recognize and admit their mistakes, but they were happy to share their weaknesses with us. If anything, our sense of their comments was that they were too hard on themselves. Sometimes we could not get them to stop talking about their deficiencies.

A majority of the leaders of the churches that reach the unchurched listed twelve weaknesses just as they listed twelve strengths. The most frequently mentioned weakness may surprise some people, but the fact that it was at the top of the list did not surprise the leaders we interviewed.

Weakness #1: Pastoral Ministry

Almost three out of four leaders told us their number one leadership weakness was providing personal pastoral ministry. Our definition of pastoral ministry included counseling, doing hospital visitation, and performing weddings and funerals, to name a few of the responsibilities. "If I get a consistent criticism," a Nevada pastor told us, "it is my failure to live up to the expectations to minister to each person individually. But if I live up to all of their expectations, I wouldn't have time for sermon preparation, personal evangelism, and just plain ol' dreaming. I constantly live with this tension but refuse to give up time from the other responsibilities."

You will remember from chapter 9 that when we looked at how leaders spent their 168-hour week, we discovered that leaders of effective churches spent 10 hours per week in pastoral care while leaders of the comparison churches spent 23 hours doing the same type of ministries.

> **Weakness #1:**
> **Pastoral Ministry**
> **73%**
> responded

"It finally hit me one day," said Tom J., a senior pastor from Oklahoma. "I was doing all of the hospital visits, counseling, home visits, and nitpicky ministry for two reasons. First, I received affirmation for doing it. Second, I avoided criticism for not doing it. Neither is a legitimate reason for doing things the way I was doing them."

He paused for a moment, and his tone indicated a serious reflection. "But you know what really got to me? I realized that I was being disobedient to Scripture. When I try to do all the ministry, I am depriving the people in the church of their God-given call to do ministry."

So why did the leaders of the effective churches say pastoral ministry was their number one leadership weakness? The issue, it seems, is one of balance. "I am constantly dealing with the tension," Jack M. of eastern Tennessee told us. "I know my primary calling, according to Acts 6, is to be in prayer and the ministry of the Word. But when the critics tell me I am not caring enough, I wonder if I am too insensitive to their needs. I wish I was a strong enough leader to know just exactly what to do."

Weakness #2: Lack of Patience

The fifth weakness noted by effective church leaders was that they are task driven. We will look at that issue shortly. Because they are task driven, over seven out of ten of the leaders indicated they were also impatient to see objectives accomplished.

Contributing to this dilemma is the fact that most American churches are notoriously resistant to change. Frank M., a Southern Baptist pastor from Kentucky, exclaimed, "Sometimes things in my church seem like they are moving in slow motion. I am dealing with a situation now where we made some changes in the order of worship and a woman in the church shouted at me with anger after the service. Being a pastor in this church has really tested my patience."

> **Weakness #2:**
> **Lack of Patience**
> **71%**
> responded

The mix of an intransigent church with a task-driven leader can be lethal. "Several years ago, Dr. Rainer, I read your book *Eating the Elephant*,"[3] Frank shared with me over the telephone. "If I learned anything from the book, it was the need to have a long-term view in the church you serve so that you can be patient in the slow process. I'm trying to be patient, but it's about to kill me!"

Weakness #3: Dealing with Staff

Most of the effective church pastors we interviewed had at least one other part-time minister on the church staff. Thus, most of the pastors in our study had to deal with staff. And seven out of ten leaders considered their staff leadership skills to be weak.

> **Weakness #3:**
> **Dealing with Staff**
> **70%**
> responded

One of the open-ended questions we asked in our leadership survey was worded as follows: "Name some specific leadership decisions you have made in your church that had a negative impact and result." The number of responses related to bad decisions with staff were numerous:

- "I made some terrible staff choices."
- "I did not get involved in staff hiring. It was a big mistake."
- "No area of ministry frustrates me more than dealing with staff. I feel so inept."
- "My worst mistakes in ministry have mostly been related to issues with the ministry team."
- "The two greatest conflicts I have had in ministry had to do with firing a staff member and not dealing with a weak staff member."

The leaders of the effective churches clearly voiced their lack of training and preparation in dealing with staff members. "I was never taught how to be a supervisor mentor or leader to staff," an Idaho pastor told us. "And that's the area where I've made the most mistakes."

Weakness #4: Dealing with Criticism

Today is Tuesday as I write this chapter. Though I no longer serve as a pastor of a church, I have served several churches as an interim pastor. This past Sunday I was sharply rebuked and criticized in the present church where I served as interim pastor. I made some minor changes in the worship service, and a church member, in an emotional outburst, said I had betrayed the church.

Weakness #4:
Dealing with Criticism
67%
responded

The criticism came in a highly public setting. I think I did a pretty good job of maintaining my composure, and, to the best of my knowledge, I was Christlike in my responses to her. So what is my point? It is now forty-eight hours later, and the criticism is still bothering me. In my role as a senior pastor of four churches, as an interim pastor of six churches, and presently as dean of a seminary, I have had my share of critics. I guess I have learned to deal with criticism, but I sure have a leadership weakness in that I let it continue to bother me for days, even weeks after the event.

The results of our leadership survey indicate that I am not the only leader who struggles with criticism. Nearly seven out of ten of the leaders we interviewed noted this issue as one of their own leadership weaknesses.

But, as an Evangelical Free Church pastor told us, the great danger is letting criticisms paralyze our ministry.

"I went nearly an entire year," he told us, "making decisions based on conflict avoidance. I got so burned initially with criticisms that I was determined not to rock the boat. Our church had its worst year that year."

When we asked him how he deals with criticism today, he gave us his formula:

1. Pray for a Christlike spirit even as the criticisms are being directed at you.
2. Pray after the criticism for wisdom to deal with it and to have love for the critic.
3. Seek God's wisdom to discern if the criticism is valid or petty. If it is valid, seek to change and respond to the criticism positively.
4. If the criticism is not valid, move on with your items and plans. Do not be hindered or paralyzed with fear.
5. Allow our God in his own way and time to deal with critics.

"Reaching the unchurched is spiritual warfare. Attacks and criticisms are to be expected," the pastor said wisely, "but we cannot give up on the Great Commission just because our feelings have been hurt."

Weakness #5: Always Task Driven

In chapter 9 we saw the self-description of pastors' leadership styles. A clear pattern emerged. The dominant leadership style noted was "task oriented." We defined task oriented as "high interest in production and getting things done." According to the definition, one might not expect this leadership issue to be a weakness. But the leaders we interviewed spoke of a leadership style that was always task driven, sometimes to the exclusion of relational issues.

Weakness #5:
Always Task Driven
64%
responded

"I get so focused on a project," Jeremy T. of North Carolina told us, "that I often fail to take people's feelings into consideration. It's good to be task driven, but it's not good to be so driven that you forget about people."

The issue, it seems, is one of balance, much like the issue of pastoral care ministry. A task-driven leader is typically a successful leader. But

Figure 10.4

Which of the following describes your leadership style?

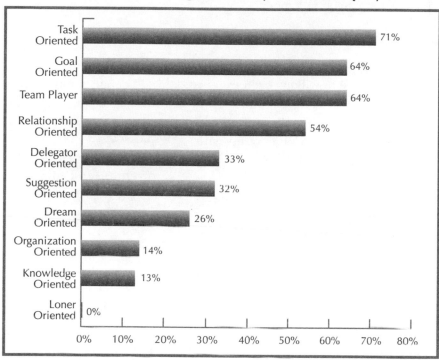

pastoral care and ministry cannot be totally neglected as the goal is sought and the task is accomplished.

Weakness #6: Too Little Time for Prayer

The leaders of the effective churches and of the comparison churches spent on the average five hours per week in prayer. The effective church leaders, however, were highly self-critical of their time in prayer. Nearly two-thirds of those we interviewed readily identified their lack of time in prayer as a weakness.

Weakness #6:
Too Little Time in Prayer
63%
responded

The pastors noted the relationship between being too task driven and spending little time in prayer. "I know in my mind and heart that I should pray more," said a Texas pastor, "but I get so involved in visions and goals for the church that I let prayer get neglected."

Still, on the average, these leaders spend nearly forty-five minutes a day in prayer. I suspect that quantity exceeds the time in prayer of the typical American churchgoer.

Weakness #7: Paying Too Little Attention to Details

"I'm a big-picture person," a nondenominational pastor from Minnesota told us. "I'm willing, even eager to delegate details to others. On the one hand, that's good, because I can provide the big vision for the whole church. But sometimes I get in trouble because I don't follow up with those who are supposed to be taking care of all the details."

Weakness #7:
Paying Too Little Attention to Details
61%
responded

Again, some of the greatest strengths of leaders can turn into weaknesses if they are carried to an extreme. A leader who is too task driven can neglect pastoral ministry and prayer and become too impatient. And a "big-picture" leader can become ineffective if he never pays any attention to detail.

Weakness #8: Moving Too Fast

This weakness comes as no surprise after hearing the first seven weaknesses. A leader who has tendencies to be impatient and task driven is more likely to move too rapidly for many churches. Nearly six out of ten leaders noted this issue as a leadership weakness.

We heard numerous tales of horror from the leaders about their leadership moving too far ahead of the rest of the people in the church. "I was so excited about reaching the unchurched in our community," a Georgia pastor told us, "that I came up with about ten major changes in the church in one year. I lasted in that church for two and a half years before the deacons asked me to leave. I was devastated and finally destitute."

Weakness #8:
Moving Too Fast
59%
responded

The Southern Baptist pastor, however, learned his lesson. He neither withdrew from leadership in his next church, nor did he move too fast. "I'm learning to stay just ahead of the people, but not to move so fast that it scares them to death." The maxim is well stated: A good leader stays far enough in front

204

> A good leader stays far enough in front of the people to lead but not so far in front that he is mistaken for the enemy and shot in the rear.

of the people to lead but not so far in front that he is mistaken for the enemy and shot in the rear.

Weakness #9: Poor Relational Skills

Only one strength was also stated as a weakness. Many of the leaders of these churches have both strong and poor relational skills. How could one leader be both good and poor in interpersonal skills?

"I tend to be pretty friendly to visitors, particularly unchurched people. And I'm also outgoing to church members on most occasions. The times that have gotten me in trouble is when I've lost my cool with church members who tried to hijack some things we were trying to do." These words came from a Colorado pastor who expressed concern over his occasional outbursts of anger.

Weakness #9:
Poor Relational Skills
57%
responded

Though these leaders did list poor relational skills as their ninth weakness, our evaluation of how they relate to others was quite positive. The leaders seemed pretty hard on themselves for infrequent temper flare-ups.

Weakness #10: Time Management

Our research team was surprised that the leaders of effective churches would note time management as a leadership weakness. But, as we have seen of numerous points in their self-assessments, these leaders tend to be highly self-critical.

Where do they struggle in time management? They worry about their lack of family time. They express concern that

Weakness #10:
Time Management
54%
responded

they spend too little time in Bible study and prayer. But, more than any issue, they say they need to spend more time in personal evangelism. Even though the leaders on the average spend five hours a week in personal evangelism, they typically feel that they do not do enough.

"I know you surveyed me and interviewed me because our church is reaching some unchurched people, and I'm grateful for that. But I know that we can do a lot more. I'm just not happy with my time commitment in this area," said one pastor.

Perhaps the struggle, more than a sign of weakness, is an indication of leadership strength. Can anyone truly say that he or she has mastered his or her use of time? The fact that these leaders struggle in many areas could be indicative of their desires to improve in many areas.

Weakness #11: Failure to Develop a Strategic Plan

Slightly more than one-half of the leaders told us that they did not plan for the long term well. Some of them articulated specifically their failure to develop a strategic plan for their churches' future. "Sometimes, I think

> **Weakness #11:**
> **Failure to Develop a Strategic Plan**
> **53%**
> responded

I'm making up the rules as I go," an Illinois pastor told us. "Every attempt I make to develop a three- or five-year plan seems to fall flat. It seems like I deal with the crisis of the moment."

One of the reasons the leaders expressed concern over this perceived weakness was related to their passionate desire to reach the unchurched. "I need something to keep me on focus to reach people for Christ," the Illinois pastor continued. "If I could just get a plan in place, I think I would have a more intense and intentional focus to reach the unchurched."

Weakness #12: Failure to Communicate Well

"You would think I would learn, but sometimes I just don't get it," a nondenominational church pastor confessed. "Three of my biggest problems in ministry occurred when I pushed an issue without communicating to key people in the church, or even the whole church. The problem is that I did this not once or twice, but three times."

> **Weakness #12:**
> **Failure to Communicate Well**
> **51%**
> responded

The task-driven personality of these leaders sometimes fails to take communication issues into consideration. The very ambition and desire to reach people that sets these leaders apart from others can also work against them.

"When I move so fast that the people don't know what's going on, I run into obstacles, criticisms, and apathy. I'm trying to learn," one pastor told us, "that you just can't communicate too much."

Listening to Leaders

These leaders are in churches that reach the unchurched. The formerly unchurched left no doubt of their importance in reaching lost and unchurched people. They have shared with us openly and candidly their strengths and weaknesses. Their insights are invaluable to reach the world of the unchurched.

The formerly unchurched spoke strongly of the critical role preaching played in reaching them. For that reason we have devoted an entire chapter to the leaders' perspectives on the task of preaching. Their insights are fascinating. Let us turn to the next chapter and listen to them carefully.

Leadership Self-Evaluation Chart

How would you rate your leadership skills in these areas of strength?

1. The ablity to cast vision   1 2 3 4 5 6 7 8 9 10
2. A sense of humor   1 2 3 4 5 6 7 8 9 10
3. Strong work ethic   1 2 3 4 5 6 7 8 9 10
4. Persistence   1 2 3 4 5 6 7 8 9 10
5. Leadership by example   1 2 3 4 5 6 7 8 9 10
6. Integrity   1 2 3 4 5 6 7 8 9 10
7. Ability to lead change   1 2 3 4 5 6 7 8 9 10
8. Love of God's Word and obedience to it   1 2 3 4 5 6 7 8 9 10
9. Communication skills   1 2 3 4 5 6 7 8 9 10
10. Faith in God/optimism   1 2 3 4 5 6 7 8 9 10
11. Relational skills/love of people   1 2 3 4 5 6 7 8 9 10
12. Team building/mentoring   1 2 3 4 5 6 7 8 9 10

(1=lowest; 10=highest. Unchurched-reaching pastors typically rate themselves as 8 or higher.)

How would your rate yourself in these areas of potential weakness?

1. Providing personal pastoral ministry   1 2 3 4 5 6 7 8 9 10
2. Lack of patience   1 2 3 4 5 6 7 8 9 10
3. Dealing with staff   1 2 3 4 5 6 7 8 9 10
4. Dealing with criticism   1 2 3 4 5 6 7 8 9 10
5. Task driven to detriment of relationships   1 2 3 4 5 6 7 8 9 10
6. Too little time in prayer   1 2 3 4 5 6 7 8 9 10
7. Paying too little attention to details   1 2 3 4 5 6 7 8 9 10
8. Moving too fast beyond the congregation   1 2 3 4 5 6 7 8 9 10
9. Poor relational skills   1 2 3 4 5 6 7 8 9 10
10. Struggles with time management   1 2 3 4 5 6 7 8 9 10
11. Failure to develop a strategic plan   1 2 3 4 5 6 7 8 9 10
12. Failure to communicate well   1 2 3 4 5 6 7 8 9 10

(1=not a weakness; 10=a significant weakness. Scores above 4 indicate a need for improvement.)

CHAPTER 11

Preaching That Connects with the Unchurched

I don't particularly like going to church, but I got to admit that I don't mind listening to the dude preach.

—"Galino4" in The Way
Internet Chat Room

Bob's story proved to be one of the most fascinating stories of the interviews I personally conducted with the formerly unchurched. He had caught the wave of the technology boom at a good time, and his start-up company would soon be traded publicly. Analysts predicted that his net worth would soar to the hundreds of millions of dollars.

But wealth was not new to Bob. A successful inventor, he already had a taste of being a millionaire. The pleasure was fleeting; joy was still elusive. Bob's failure to find joy in the material world was a crushing blow. "I worked the first forty years of my life with a singular aim: to become a millionaire before I turned forty. I succeeded, but I found no joy. I began wondering if I would ever be happy."

When Bob met Alicia, he again thought that he had found happiness. Indeed, he was so infatuated with her that he thought his life's journey for happiness was over. He was wrong.

"Alicia and I were very much in love," Bob confirmed. "Yet the more we talked, the more we realized that we were still missing something in our lives. That's when we decided to visit a church." The church they chose to visit was a large nondenominational church not far from their homes on the east side of town.

"We didn't choose the church because it was big or because it had a bunch of programs. We were just looking for answers. We picked this church because our neighbors recommended it."

How did they react to the church? "It was unbelievable," said Bob. "It was like the pastor was preaching right at us. I would look at Alicia and she would look at me. We were both thinking, 'How can this guy know what's going on in our lives?'"

The connection with the preacher did not end with that one service. "We figured that we would give the church another try. So, for the next several weeks, we sat in amazement as each sermon spoke directly to us. It was like the few thousand other people weren't there, and the preacher was connecting directly to us."

Preaching That Connects

Bob's story is similar to many interviews with the formerly unchurched. But our purpose in this chapter is to hear from the preachers themselves. The formerly unchurched were unequivocal in their beliefs that preaching was key in bringing them to Christ and to the church. But how do the preachers view the role of preaching?

Before we hear from the preachers, we must remember that not all the unchurched hear preachers, especially on a regular basis. The way the formerly unchurched described their pilgrimage could be illustrated as follows.

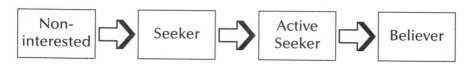

On the rare occasions when a "noninterested" unbeliever heard a sermon, the formerly unchurched told us, the preaching typically had no impact. But when the believer began to seek religious truth, the sermons had some meaning. By the time the nonbeliever was an active seeker, attending church on a regular basis, the nonbeliever tended to hang on every word of the sermon, that is, "if the sermon was worth a flip," an Idaho formerly unchurched person told us. What criteria determine if the sermon is indeed "worth a flip"? We have heard from the perspective of the formerly unchurched. Let us now hear from the preachers. How do they view the role of preaching?

Preaching Must Be a Passion

The leaders whose churches are reaching the unchurched are passionate about preaching. Most of them, when asked about the call of God in their lives, refer to it as a "call to preach." For them, preaching is their primary activity and calling.

In our surveys of pastors of effective churches and pastors of comparison churches, we asked: "Which of the following tasks do you find most exciting and challenging? Least exciting and challenging? Please mark three tasks in each column." The choices included:

Administration	Pastoral care
Budgeting	Personal evangelism
Building campaigns	Preaching
Committee meetings	Staff leadership
Discipleship/training of members	Visitation
Future planning	Other (fill in the blank)
Goal setting	

The pastors of the effective churches overwhelmingly voiced that preaching was their most exciting and challenging task. Note the differences between these pastors and the pastors of the comparison churches.

The contrast between the pastors of the effective churches and the pastors of the comparison churches is stark. Ninety-three percent of the pastors of the effective churches named preaching as one of their most exciting tasks compared to 70 percent of the pastors of the comparison churches.

> Personal evangelism was not named in the top ten most exciting tasks by the pastors of the comparison churches.

The effective pastors' passion for preaching is obvious. Their second most exciting task drops from 93 percent to 58 percent, represented by personal evangelism. Interestingly, personal evangelism was not named in the top ten most exciting tasks by the pastors of the comparison churches.

Not many of the pastors of the effective churches or the pastors of comparison churches rated preaching as a "least exciting task," but the contrast is still evident. Only 2 percent of the pastors viewed preaching negatively in the effective churches; 17 percent did so in the comparison

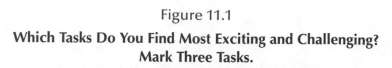

Figure 11.1

Which Tasks Do You Find Most Exciting and Challenging? Mark Three Tasks.

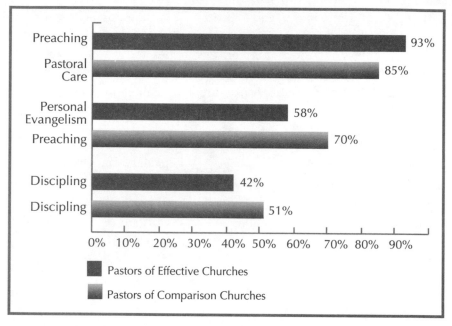

churches. Still none of the leaders of the churches rated preaching in their top three "least exciting tasks."

Pastoral care, which included counseling, hospital visits, weddings, and funerals, was the third least exciting task of the effective church pastors but the most exciting task of the comparison church pastors. Personal evangelism, however, rated second in the most exciting tasks of the effective church pastors; but the same was the third least exciting of the comparison church pastors. The two groups obviously have different priorities.

There can be little doubt that the pastors of churches that reach the unchurched are excited and passionate about preaching. A Nevada pastor told us, "Nothing in ministry gets me more fired up than preaching. Quite frankly, I have trouble getting motivated for a lot of the pastoral ministry stuff. I determined several years ago that I had to be an 'Acts 6 pastor.'"

Several of the leaders of these churches made reference to Acts 6:1–7. In that passage the Jerusalem church is confronted with the problem of inadequate ministry; the widows of Greek origin are not receiving food

Figure 11.2

Percent of Pastors Rating Preaching As a "Least-Exciting Task"

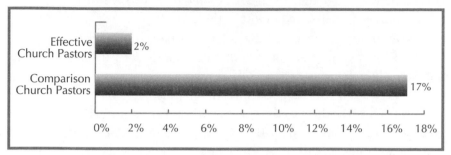

Figure 11.3

**Which Tasks Do You Find the Least Exciting and Challenging?
Mark Three Tasks.**

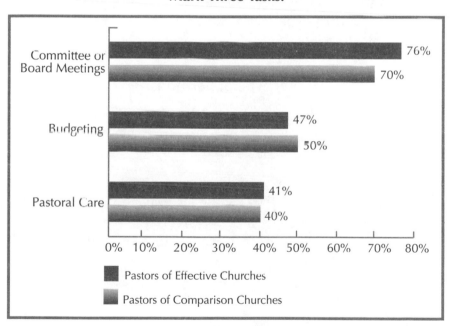

from the church, but the native Hebrew widows are. The apostles, instead of increasing time in ministry to unbearable hours, decide to spread the ministry to the laity, "whom we may put in charge of this task" (6:3 NASB).

What then will be the primary ministry of the Twelve? "But we will devote ourselves to prayer, and to the ministry of the word" (6:4 NASB).

Andy, a nondenominational church pastor from upstate New York explains: "My first calling is to be in the Word and to preach. And if I'm going to have enough time to do what I need to do in the Word, the people in the church will have to do most of the ministry."

The argument to be an Acts 6 leader does have biblical merit. Acts 6:7 indicates three vital results of the unleashing of the laity to do the work of ministry while the leaders devote themselves to the ministry of the Word. First, "the word of God kept on spreading" (NASB). Second, more people accepted Christ: "the number of the disciples continued to increase greatly in Jerusalem" (NASB). But perhaps the most fascinating result is that the Jerusalem church began reaching "hardcore" unchurched people. The text indicates that "a great many of the priests were becoming obedient to the faith" (NASB). The Jewish priests were likely among those with the most antichurch attitude.

Leaders whose churches are reaching the unchurched need no convincing of the primacy of preaching in their ministries. They were no less enthusiastic than their hearers.

What Type of Sermons?

Our surveys of the leaders of the churches that reach the unchurched provided fascinating insights into their types of preaching. We asked them to estimate the percentage of their sermons that reflect each of five styles:

Expository—Primarily an explanation or commentary on the biblical text; expounds the central idea of the text; often includes preaching through a book of the Bible.

Topical—Typically a sermon built around a topic with biblical application to the topic.

Thematic—Usually a series of sermons developed around a central theme or idea; does not typically involve preaching through a book of the Bible.

Narrative—Story form that, from the beginning to the end, develops the plot of the story as a theme; a biblical truth presented in parable form.

Doctrinal—A sermon or sermon series focused on a particular biblical teaching or doctrine.

We recognize that preaching styles are not always mutually exclusive. For example, an "expository" sermon on Ephesians 2 may sound very similar to a "doctrinal" sermon on soteriology or salvation using the same text. Nevertheless, the pastors were asked to identify the style that most closely represents their preaching.

The expository style of preaching was the dominant approach, but very few pastors limited themselves to one style. These results are similar to a previous study we conducted on Southern Baptists who were even more likely to preach expository sermons.[1]

Figure 11.4

Estimate the Percentage of Your Sermons That Reflect Each Preaching Style.

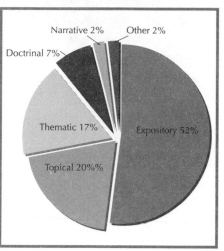

What pertinent comments from these leaders were related to their preaching styles? Among the more common statements were the following:

- The expository style was dominant because it was deemed to be the most faithful to the text and because it helped pastors avoid constantly choosing sermons based on their own present preferences.
- A majority of the leaders thought the power of the preached Word was underestimated in reaching the unchurched.
- Only one of the pastors preached one style of sermon all the time. The others saw wisdom in varying sermon approaches.
- Over 80 percent of the pastors never preach narrative sermons.
- Forty-four percent of the pastors preach at least two different sermons each week. These pastors were more likely to preach expository sermons than the leaders who preached only one sermon each week.

Can we therefore make any definitive conclusions about preaching style and effectiveness in reaching the unchurched? From a statistical perspective, it cannot be proven that one type of preaching, such as expository, is more effective in reaching the unchurched. One could argue, however, for a strong relationship or correlation between expository preaching and evangelistic effectiveness.

Yet we must also recognize that only 1 of the 101 pastors we interviewed preached exclusively expository sermons. All of the other pastors saw value in preaching topical, thematic, and doctrinal messages. And two of the leaders interviewed never preached expository sermons, yet their churches were still effective in reaching the unchurched. Thus, expository preaching is indeed the dominant preaching approach among these leaders but is not the only effective style.

Who Influenced Their Preaching?

We asked the leaders of those churches that reached the unchurched to share with us the key influences on their preaching and communicating effectively. They responded on a scale of 1 to 5 as follows:

1. Not an influence
2. A slight influence
3. An important influence
4. A very important influence
5. The most important influence

The leaders then rated eight different influences:

- Training in college or seminary
- Example of a mentor
- Participation in a conference or seminar
- Experience in church work
- Bible studies about effective preachers/communicators
- Books on effective preaching/communication

Figure 11.5 shows three key areas of influence: the example of a mentor, seminary or college training, and experience in church work.

Since we had already heard numerous times about the importance of a mentor in other areas, we were not surprised to discover the influence of a mentor in preaching. Nor were we surprised to find the value of experience in the preaching task. We were surprised, however, to hear that college and seminary training was almost as influential in preaching as a mentor or experiences. These results are significantly different than the results of the question that asked the importance of seminary or college

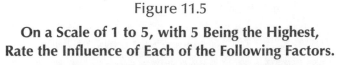

Figure 11.5

**On a Scale of 1 to 5, with 5 Being the Highest,
Rate the Influence of Each of the Following Factors.**

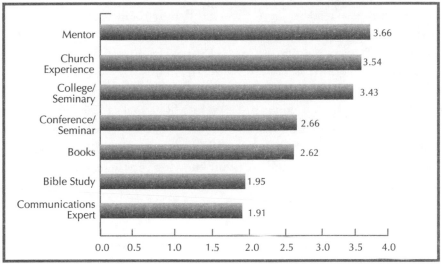

influence on leadership. According to the leaders of the effective churches, seminary and/or college made a significant contribution in training for the preaching task, but higher education woefully prepared these leaders for the day-to-day functions of leadership and the longer-term function of vision casting.

How Do These Preachers Connect?

We conducted follow-up interviews with these leaders after they completed the extensive survey we sent them. Since we already had data indicating the importance of preaching from the perspective of the formerly unchurched, we desired to hear from the pastors on one key issue: How do their sermons connect with the unchurched? Their responses could be categorized with five significant adjectives.

Biblical

More than any other factor, the leaders of the churches insisted that their sermons must first be biblical. This issue carries several possible connotations, but the leaders were clear on their meanings.

First, a biblical sermon means that the Bible's authority is sufficient. We have already heard from these pastors regarding their high view of Scripture. Almost all of the leaders' theology of Scripture could be described as conservative and evangelical.

Second, these leaders are determined that the biblical text must be the focus of the sermon. Even if the sermon is topical with several passages, "the biblical text is the authority," insists an Evangelical Free Church pastor.

Finally, a majority of the pastors told us in unsolicited comments that it is important to provide a good contextual understanding of the passages from which a sermon is preached. "I believe it's important," noted an Alabama Southern Baptist pastor, "that if you preach from one of Paul's letters, you must understand the times in which Paul lived. You cannot know the passage fully without knowing the times in which it was written."

Relevant

While the leaders of these effective churches would never compromise the biblical foundation of the sermons they preached, they also knew that the messages must connect with the hearers in their life situations. Indeed, "relevant" was an adjective used frequently by these pastors when speaking about preaching.

I personally interviewed a nondenominational pastor from North Carolina who spent hours each week collecting articles on current events and lifestyle issues. While he did not compromise the biblical integrity of the passages from which he preached, he was determined to make the ancient words relevant to the everyday lives of the listeners. "I get more comments about how I apply the texts to the people's lives than any other aspect of the sermon. I've also discovered that they remember the passages better when I make them relevant to where they are."

We asked some of the leaders if they felt any tension between biblical faithfulness to the text and relevancy to the listeners' lives. An Oklahoma pastor said forthrightly, "Absolutely not. I've heard some of the debate between biblical and relevant or expositional and relevant, but I've never felt like it was an either/or situation. It's ludicrous to say that you can't have relevant preaching if you're giving a good exposition of the text. That's stupid. We don't have to make the Bible relevant. If we're faithful to the text, it can't help but be relevant."

Transparent

"I don't use the pulpit as a place of personal confession," said a pastor whose church was near Seattle, "but I do let the people know that I'm like them, that I have struggles, that I'm human." We heard the formerly unchurched on several occasions say the pastors they heard did not have a "holier-than-thou" attitude.

A Kentucky pastor told us the story of how he used himself as an illustration to show lack of patience. "I moved the church to make some changes faster than they could handle. You could just sense the tension in the church. I realized I had made a mistake and needed to let the church catch its breath. So I told the people in my sermon on patience that I had been a poor example; I told them I needed to be more sensitive to them. Boy, was that well received!"

Many of the formerly unchurched shared with us about the transparency of the pastors of the churches where they eventually received Christ. This issue was critical to the formerly unchurched because many of them were "searching to see if anybody cared anymore, if anybody was real," Nancy A. of Virginia told us. Of course the high visibility of the pastor, particularly in the role of preaching, was a factor in the formerly unchurched becoming Christians.

"I realize that every time I preach," said Henry M., a Nazarene pastor, "there are probably several lost people listening to me. If I'm not authentic, then they may think Christ is not real either. It's an awesome responsibility."

Illustrative

Both the formerly unchurched and preachers of the effective churches agreed that the sermons they heard and preached make effective use of illustrations. But the preachers were often careful to point out that the illustrations were not the central thrust of the message. Noted Leonard T., an Assembly of God pastor: "Illustrations are important, but too many preachers build their sermons around them. The Bible passage must remain central."

Jarvis D. from Oregon says he spends a few hours each week finding good illustrations. "I've been told that my preaching really connects with the unchurched. I think one of the reasons is the illustrations I use. You can tell the congregation really understands the passage better when a good illustration is used. Jesus did it in his preaching, and he's a pretty good example."

Well-Prepared

If time is a good measure, the leaders of effective churches prepare well for the sermons they preach each week. Recall from chapter 9 the stark contrast between the pastors of the effective churches and pastors of the comparison churches.

Figure 11.6

Average Hours Per Week in Sermon Preparation

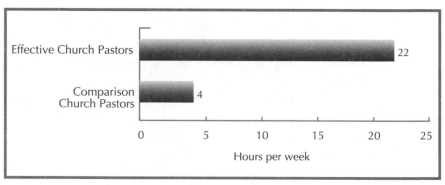

By a ratio of greater than 5 to 1, the leaders of the effective churches spent significantly more time in sermon preparation than the pastors of the comparison churches. What did the comparison church pastors do with the eighteen hours of "extra" time that was not spent in sermon preparation? For the most part, they were counseling church members; visiting hospitals, homes, and nursing homes; doing weddings and funerals; and spending several hours each week telephoning absentee and inactive church members. The pastors of the effective churches did not neglect these duties, but they did spread the work of ministry among the laity of the church.

As I was putting the final touches on this chapter, I spoke to a large gathering of church leaders in the Midwest. The issue of preaching and its correlation to reaching the unchurched was the topic of discussion and debate. And when I presented the average hours spent in sermon preparation by the effective pastors, a few of the attendees responded with skepticism. In fact, one person challenged my findings rather vigorously. He also gave me the names and addresses of four churches where he promised me the pastors spent no more than five hours each week in sermon preparation. All of the churches, he told me, were growing significantly.

My response was polite, but I really had little interest in taking up his challenge. We already had the data on hundreds of churches. Even if his four examples were exceptions to our averages, our study would not be countered by only four churches. I determined that I would not worry about his challenge. It is not unusual for me to encounter at least one person who has trouble accepting the data I present in speaking.

But for some reason I could not get this man's challenge out of my mind. Realizing that it would not resolve his questions, I nevertheless wrote the four churches and asked them for the past five years' statistics on conversions, attendance, and membership. Three of the four responded; the results were interesting.

First, in some respects, my conference antagonist was right. All three of the churches had at least doubled their attendance in the five years I studied. If he was right in asserting that the pastors only spent five hours each week in sermon preparation, they had done so while increasing their attendance.

But the data immediately revealed something the questioner had not obviously considered: none of the three churches met our criteria to be an "effective church" (see page 23). All three churches were indeed growing rapidly, but their source of growth was Christians moving from other churches to their churches. The leaders who spent an average of twenty-two hours per week in sermon preparation were in churches that reached the lost and unchurched.

An Addendum on the Preaching Issue

One issue still lingers. For preaching to be effective, it must be heard, and the unchurched by definition are not in church. So how can preaching reach the unchurched? The formerly unchurched and the leaders of the effective churches gave us three responses to the question.

First, "unchurched" does not mean "never in church." Review the information in chapter 1 that showed that even one million atheists and agnostics attended church on Easter Sunday 1999. It is highly likely that an unchurched person will "try" your church at some point. And, as we heard repeatedly from the formerly unchurched, their initial perception of the church is closely tied to the preaching.

Second, the effective preaching we have noted throughout this chapter is a great motivator to those attending the church. The members are both motivated and convicted to invite the unchurched and to witness to them.

Finally, while these leaders spend significant hours in sermon preparation each week, they also spend significant time dreaming, seeking God's vision, setting goals, and doing the work necessary to reach people for Christ. They are passionate about reaching the unchurched. It is this passion to reach people that often sets them apart from other leaders. But that is but one characteristic of churches that reach the unchurched. The next and concluding chapter put all of these pieces together. What does an unchurched-reaching church really look like? To that question we now turn.

To Become a Church for the Unchurched

Hey guys, I just became a Christian yesterday!
Know any good churches in St. Louis?

—"DealMe" in the Born Again 3
Internet Chat Room

Christina, at age thirty-four, is expecting her second child. Her husband, Tom, is one year older. Unlike many of the formerly unchurched we interviewed, the couple has never faced a major crisis in their lives or marriage. They obviously love each other deeply.

Christina and Tom had been Christians for only seven months at the time of this writing. When they moved to a mid-sized city in North Carolina, they decided to visit a Southern Baptist church. I asked them what prompted them to visit a church.

"I honestly don't know," Christina responded. "I can't even remember Tom and I having much discussion about it." Tom agreed, "Me either. Neither one of us had much of a church background. I guess we just decided it was the right thing to do."

Christina, Tom, and Amy, their three-year-old daughter, visited Cross Springs Baptist Church. "We thought we'd start there," Christina commented, "because the building and grounds looked real neat from the car."

"What was your first impression?" I asked.

"I was driving," Tom said, "and I was impressed by how well all the parking was marked. We went to a guest parking place. When we got out of the car, we were met by a man in a red coat, who identified himself as a greeter for the church. He asked if he could take us to the preschool area."

Christina and Tom both began to speak about the worship service, but Christina paused to allow Tom to speak. "The people were incredibly friendly. The music was great—a blend of traditional hymns and contemporary songs. The first time I heard Richard [the pastor] preach, I was hooked. He communicated extremely well, and I found myself learning a lot about the Bible in just thirty minutes. And remember, I was totally ignorant of the Bible."

The family returned every Sunday. They were invited to and got involved in a couples' Sunday school class. When a couple from the class visited them at home and shared how they could become Christians, both Tom and Christina were ready.

But the story does not end there. Tom, Christina, and Amy had moved to North Carolina so that Tom could join the family company. Tom and Christina's lives were radically changed when they became Christians. Then Tom's parents started visiting the Baptist church, if for no other reason, to see what had happened to the young couple. Within two months Tom's parents became Christians. Now Tom's older brother and his family are visiting the church.

I'd love to have that kind of story repeated thousands of times in years to come—to be repeated in your church as well. Therefore, in the following pages, I will summarize fifteen characteristics of churches that are effective in reaching the unchurched. See how your church measures up.

1. Major on Majors

Though I remain an obnoxious optimist about the future of the American church, I admit that I have my concerns. In my roles, past and present, as pastor, interim pastor, and church consultant, I have seen church members focus their energies on some of the most insignificant issues. Some members demand their brand of music; others get irritated when the order of worship is changed. Some members will complain when a minister does not make every telephone call he is expected to make; others fuss when the sermon goes five minutes too long. Some members seem to worship their buildings and location; others seem to have forgotten how to worship God. And in the meantime, tens of thousands die to face a Christless eternity, and so few church members seem to care.

The experience of listening to the formerly unchurched and of studying churches that reach the unchurched has been a joy, because these churches tend to major on majors. Other issues are treated, as they should be, as minor. Churches that reach the unchurched keep their priorities in order and their goals in clear view.

2. Be Biblical, Conservative, and Convictional

In my denomination we have been involved in a quarter-of-a-century "battle for the Bible." When Southern Baptists talk theology among themselves, the discussion is often perceived to be political. But it must be said without hesitation that churches that reach the unchurched are theologically conservative. They have a high view of Scripture. And their convictions about their beliefs are obvious.

> Churches that reach the unchurched are theologically conservative.

A church can attempt many good contextual efforts to reach the unchurched, but if it does not have the foundations of a high view of Scripture, the efforts are either futile or transient. I have yet to discover a church that consistently reaches the unchurched over a several-year period that is not conservative in its theology.

3. Give Evangelism Priority and Passion

To be honest, I thought only rarely of the need to tell others about Christ. Even though God had called me to ministry, and even though I had left my lofty successful position in the business world, I only had passing thoughts of the need to share Christ. But in 1983 my priorities were turned upside down.

One of the first courses I took as a seminary student was personal evangelism with Dr. Lewis Drummond. Two aspects of the course changed my life. First, Dr. Drummond had a passion for evangelism. We students were particularly mesmerized by his stories of M. L. Oneal, a layman of a church where Dr. Drummond had once served as pastor. "Oneal," as our professor called him, would not let a day pass without sharing Christ. Even as Oneal was being taken to surgery where he would die, he was telling the medical attendants about Jesus. What a passion Oneal and Dr. Drummond had for Christ!

Dr. Drummond did not limit our studies to his lectures. Every week he required us to share the gospel with a lost person. I wrote letters to lost

SURPRISING INSIGHTS FROM THE UNCHURCHED

family members. I witnessed on the streets of Louisville, Kentucky. I told my barber about Jesus. I intentionally developed relationships with unchurched persons. I developed a *priority* for evangelism that changed my life!

What do Saddleback Church (Lake Forest, California), Prestonwood Baptist Church (Dallas, Texas), Southeast Christian Church (Louisville, Kentucky), First Baptist Church (Jacksonville, Florida), Parkway Wesleyan Church (Roanoke, Virginia), and Willow Creek Community Church (South Barrington, Illinois) all have in common? They all make evangelism a priority. I have visited all of these churches. Though they all agree on the key doctrines of the Christian faith, they do have theological differences. Their worship styles range from traditional to blended to contemporary to seeker driven. Their common bonds, however, include a conviction of the authority of God's Word and a passion for evangelism.

Too many church leaders seek to copy the methodologies of churches without emulating their hearts. Never expect to be a church for the unchurched unless you have a passion for evangelism.

4. Provide Deep Biblical Teaching

Some readers may have been surprised by how vociferous the formerly unchurched were about their desires for strong biblical teaching. The evidence and data are clear. Both the formerly unchurched and the leaders of the churches that reached them verified the efficacy of "meaty" teaching and preaching to reach the unchurched and to strengthen the Christians. Strategies of recent years that sought to reach the unchurched through "lighter," less demanding teaching and preaching not only were ineffective, they were counterproductive as well.

5. Develop an Effective and Comprehensive Small-Group Ministry

The formerly unchurched told us they were attracted to small groups for two reasons: they desired further biblical teaching and training, and they sought to develop relationships with other Christians. As we have demonstrated statistically in this book, small groups dramatically impact the effectiveness of a church's outreach and assimilation. And in the churches we studied, Sunday school was the dominant expression of small groups.

226

What does this information say to churches that desire to reach the unchurched? It tells us that a comprehensive and effective small-group strategy is imperative. I regret that in the churches I pastored before becoming dean of a seminary I provided little leadership to the Sunday school organization. Because of my ignorance and immaturity, I allowed the Sunday school to exist without any aggressive leadership and input on my part.

Now, because of eight years of research, I see the utter stupidity of my failure. The work required to develop any kind of comprehensive small-group organization is massive. Such work demands senior pastor involvement and leadership. Without it the church will not be nearly as effective in reaching the unchurched.

6. Discern Patterns of Relationships in Your Own Church

One of the many surprises of our study was that one of the best connections to reach the unchurched was Christian wives reaching their unchurched husbands. We often think of the unchurched as people in totally pagan backgrounds who have no connection with the church. What our study told us was that many of the unchurched might be living in the same homes as our church members.

In a recent church consultation, I had a large proportion of the church members write the names of three unchurched people they knew well and then to note their relationships with these people. Again, the members were surprised to discover that a majority of their unchurched connections were in their own families. The church consequently developed new strategies to reach these people.

7. Check Your Facilities

The formerly unchurched spoke cogently of the necessity of having neat, clean, and updated facilities to reach people. "I saw a lot of things through unchurched eyes before I became a Christian a few months ago. What surprised me was how many churches let their facilities and their landscaping go to the dogs. It was as if they were advertising 'we don't care' by the way they looked. I sure didn't go back to those places."

Have an outsider (as I said earlier, a woman works best) look at your facilities honestly and objectively. Ask her to go to the rest rooms, kitchen, sanctuary, and offices. Let her look at classrooms and preschool space. Ask her opinion about the grounds and landscaping. In my consultation ministry, I have discovered that most eyesores can be remedied with a few donations and in-house, volunteer labor. And it is amazing to see how such projects can be tasks of church unity.

> Realize that one of the most critical areas for cleanliness, attractiveness, and modern equipment is the preschool.

Realize that one of the most critical areas for cleanliness, attractiveness, and modern equipment is the preschool. Dozens of formerly unchurched people told us that the quality of the preschool was one of the key issues that attracted them to a church.

Signage is important to the unchurched as well. A few thousand dollars invested in a quality outdoor sign and indoor directional signs is a wise expenditure. The unchurched are often terrified to come to a strange church. As unlikely as it may sound, good signage could make an eternal difference in someone's life.

8. Cultivate a User-Friendly Greeter Ministry

The formerly unchurched appreciated the presence of greeters. Listen to some of their specific recommendations and preferences:

- Greeters should be clearly identifiable, with coats, badges, or some other type of clear marking.
- Provide a welcome center with good and updated information on the church.
- Make certain your greeters represent a cross section of ages. Most churches tend to have mostly senior adults serve as greeters.
- Train greeters. "You won't believe some of the dumb comments I heard from greeters," Pat D. from Pennsylvania said. "The church would have been better off with no greeters." Greeters need training on how to greet, what to say, and what their primary functions are.
- Make certain the greeter ministry includes taking people to their ultimate destination in the church. Do not merely give them directions; give them an escort.

9. Keep the Friendliness Issue Before the Church

If we Christians on earth could attain sinless perfection, we would not need reminders to be happy and friendly. Meanwhile, church leaders must remind members to be friendly at all times. One smile, one kind word could make an eternal difference for an unbeliever.

As I said earlier, every church I have ever visited or consulted thinks it is friendly. These false perceptions are based on how members treat each other in the church. They do not see themselves from the perspective of an outsider. They do not realize that, while they speak to people they know and people they see each week, the outsider has no such connections. They need to be reminded each week to be friendly. Nearly four out of five formerly unchurched told us that the friendliness of the church was a factor in their becoming Christians and joining a particular church.

10. Seek Excellence

The fellowships of many churches have become havens for mediocrity. The formerly unchurched were completely turned off by poor music, unkempt facilities, poorly prepared sermons, and ill-equipped Sunday school teachers. The typical American unchurched person has come to expect excellence in the business world, in the marketplace, and in the entertainment industry. Often we heard the formerly unchurched voice surprise that God's church would accept anything that did not approach excellence. "I got to the point as I visited churches," Doug L. said, "that I began to believe that churches didn't give a rip about anything. It was a big letdown until I found Faith Community Church." Faith is the church that Doug eventually joined, the place where he accepted Christ. "Thank God for the people of Faith!" Doug exclaimed. "Their attitude of excellence may have been the difference between heaven or hell for me."

11. Provide an Inquirers'/New Members' Class

The formerly unchurched, for the most part, gladly attended an inquirers' class prior to their becoming Christians. By the time they were courageous enough to visit a church, they were eager to learn more about the church. Most of the effective churches in our study combined the inquirers' class with a new members' class. We need to remember that an unchurched person who visits our churches typically has an insatiable appetite to learn more. Such is the reason they desire strong biblical teaching and preaching. And such is the reason they eagerly attend an inquirers' class.

12. Expect Much/Receive Much

Churches that reach the unchurched are high-expectation churches. Their members are excited and fulfilled Christians. They belong to an organization that makes a difference. They gladly share their faith, invite friends and family members to church, and generally express excitement about their church. Leaders of these churches do not hesitate to ask members to get involved in ministry. They constantly urge them to develop a witnessing lifestyle.

High-expectation churches receive much because they expect much. The unchurched are in turn attracted to churches where the people are excited about their faith and the church where they serve.

13. Know Your Church's Purposes

Churches that reach the unchurched know the purposes for which the church exists better than comparison churches. We categorized the six major purposes of the church according to Acts 2:42–47:

- Worship
- Evangelism
- Ministry
- Prayer
- Fellowship
- Discipleship/equipping

A church that understands its purposes is more likely to evaluate itself according to those purposes. If the people of the church truly understand that evangelism is one of their major functions, they will ask questions if lost people are not being reached, and they will seek to be more effective in that area.

How do leaders help the people of the church learn the purposes of the church? They write mission statements. The pastors preach it, and the teachers teach it. They put it on publications. They repeat it. The purpose-driven church is more likely to be an unchurched-reaching church.

14. Foster Ministry Involvement

The formerly unchurched told us in many ways and many times, "We don't want to sit on the sidelines." These new Christians are incredibly eager to get involved, and their enthusiasm is contagious.

Unfortunately, some churches do a fair job of reaching the unchurched only to see them leave within a few months. Many of these churches have rigid and antiquated rules that prohibit ministry involvement of new members. I understand that new Christians should not be made Bible teachers immediately. But why not get them involved in a greeter ministry? I promise their smiles will not be forced. Why not get them involved in an evangelistic ministry? They probably know more unchurched people than anyone else in the church. A pastor in California said quite bluntly, "We try to get new Christians involved quickly before they get over Jesus!"

15. Never Forget the Power of Prayer

I do not put prayer near the end of this book as a postscript or an addendum to more pressing matters. Indeed, I feel as though I have not given adequate attention to the power of prayer in this discussion. But I say now without hesitation or reservation that prayer is key to reaching the unchurched. I rarely heard from an effective church that did not have a strong emphasis on prayer.

Evangelizing the unchurched is spiritual warfare. Satan and his demonic horde will do anything they can to hinder someone from becoming a believer. Only prayer can effectively break the bonds of complacency, tradition, and nit-picking that keep a church's focus off evangelism.

Most of the effective churches in our study not only had pervasive prayer ministries; they made certain these prayer ministries included a specific focus on lost and unchurched persons.

Lest we forget as well, the leaders of churches that reached the unchurched were people of prayer. And while an average of forty-five minutes per day in prayer may seem small, the effective church leaders' prayer lives were more time-consuming than the anemic level of most Christians.

Prayer is powerful. And prayer is a requisite to reach the unchurched.

For Pastors Only: You Must Lead

Lyle Schaller is probably the most widely read commentator on congregational life today. He is adamant that the key reason most churches do not grow or reach the unchurched is a failure of leadership. And while I do not put the same weight on the importance of the pastor as Schaller does, I nevertheless agree with his basic premise.

Schaller says pastors can be put into one of four categories.[1] The first category includes those "who fail to pay the rent on time or are not able to pay the rent on time or are not able to pay it in full every month."[2] Simply stated, these pastors, due to poor health, family problems, uncertainty of call, or poor work habits, do not carry out basic pastoral duties.

The second category is the "paying-the-rent pastor."[3] The "rent" includes preaching and worship, teaching and pastoral care, organization and administration. Schaller emphasizes that paying the rent is not a full-time job. These pastors use their discretionary time for activities that do not establish goals or a vision for the church.

Schaller's third group of pastors is called, "goal-driven pastors."[4] These leaders not only pay the rent, they help carry out projects and programs initiated by them or others in the congregation. If the goal is to reach younger families with children at home, the goal-driven pastor may seek to build a new preschool wing, to expand off-street parking, or to develop the latest "hot" program for young families. Goal-driven pastors use their discretionary time to enlist allies and to accomplish tasks necessary to reach their goals. These leaders tend to operate in a constant flurry of activity.

The pastor who does not pay the rent typically leads the church to decline. The pastor who does pay the rent, the task-driven pastor, cannot typically lead a church past 350 in attendance, according to Schaller. The goal-driven pastor, in contrast, can usually lead a church to about 700 in attendance. Schaller contends that we have few unchurched-reaching pastors because most church leaders fit into one of the three previous categories. Only a small number of pastors, says Schaller, are in a fourth group he calls vision driven. They are characterized as follows:[5]

- They see "paying the rent" as important, but they do not believe all the payments must be made by themselves personally. They seek to involve others in tasks.

- Instead of much activity and busywork, these leaders expect others to be involved; "they have high expectations of anyone who commits to being a disciple of Jesus Christ."[6]
- The vision-driven leader believes that the vision will be so compelling that enough key leaders cannot help but be drawn to it. The vision thus engenders alliances rather than the pastor creating them.
- For the vision-driven leader, a goal is not an end in itself. It is simply a building block to something greater and more exciting.
- The vision-driven leader sees few limitations. He truly believes anything is possible through Christ.

Perhaps Schaller's descriptions explain why our data indicates only four out of one hundred American churches could be described as effective churches. Very few pastors are actually vision driven.

I understand, however, why many pastors do not seek to be vision driven. They have been so abused, so criticized, so nitpicked by people who call themselves Christians that they no longer feel that the effort is worth the pain. I have been a pastor. I have dealt with some not-so-well-intentioned dragons. Sometimes it is just easier to pay the rent than to be verbally crucified.

Nevertheless, leaders must not quit the fight. Too much is at stake. Eternity is in the balance. Yes, too much pressure is placed on pastors. Certainly, unreasonable expectations abound. But this battle is part of a larger war. It is indeed spiritual warfare.

Pastors, be people of prayer. Seek God's face in hours of sermon preparation. Learn to communicate the best you can. Keep a sense of humor. Laugh at yourself at times. Be personally accountable to someone as you share your faith week by week. Seek excellence in all things. And lead your church to something so great that it will be a certain failure unless God is in it. Dream the big dream. Dream *God's* dream for your church.

To Storm the Gates of Hell

Thank you, reader, for taking time to read this book. Though the cover has my name as author, this work is truly the effort of 353 new Christians, 350 longer-term Christians, and more than 200 church leaders. Their insights have been invaluable, their contributions immeasurable.

And, yes, I am still an obnoxious optimist about the American church. I know, statistics show the church has plateaued. The number of conversions has not grown appreciably in two decades. And many, many churches still fight the demons of traditionalism, complacency, and spiritual apathy. But this research project has renewed my hope. I have heard from hundreds of persons whose lives have been transformed by the power of the living Christ. I have listened to many church leaders who have led their churches to reach a growing pagan population. I have entered the land of miracles, and I do not wish to return. Too much is at stake. Too many lives hang in eternity's balance.

It is my prayer for you, church leader, pastor, staff person, or layperson, that you will not grow weary. I am praying for you. Satan would love to see you discouraged, despondent, and defeated. But, in Christ's power, the victory is already ours. Let us enter the world of the unchurched not wishing for victory, but claiming victory. Let us not be defensive; instead, let us mount a powerful offense. Let us storm the gates of hell. And let us see, in God's power, more of the unchurched become the formerly unchurched. To God be the glory!

APPENDIX 1

Cluster Questions for the Formerly Unchurched

The following questions were asked of 353 formerly unchurched persons. We called them "cluster" questions, because each question often led to a series of other issues. We asked similar questions of the transfer churched to compare to the responses of the formerly unchurched.

Cluster Questions for the Formerly Unchurched

1. Discuss what level of activity, if any, you have had in any churches before coming to this church.
2. Discuss the factors involved in choosing this church. What was the single greatest factor?
3. Explain your initial thoughts when you first arrived on the church property. Where did you go first? What were your observations?
4. Did the name of the church influence your decision positively or negatively in becoming involved in this church?
5. How would you describe the worship style of your church? How did the style affect your decision to come to the church and return to the church?
6. Discuss the role the pastor and his preaching played in your coming to their church.
7. What factors caused you to return to the church?
8. Do you know the doctrinal or biblical beliefs of the church? How have they affected your decision to be a part of this church?
9. What relationships did you develop with church members prior to coming to the church? After coming to the church? What role did these relationships play in your decision to come or to stay?

10. When did you become a Christian? Describe the events that led to your decision.
11. Did someone from the church share with you how to become a Christian? Explain how this situation developed.
12. Are you presently involved in any small groups in the church or in Sunday school? Please describe.
13. Are you presently involved in any ministries in the church? Please describe.
14. What keeps you active in the church today?

APPENDIX 2

Leadership Survey

The following eleven-page survey was sent to 101 church leaders whose churches met our definition of an "effective church." The same survey was sent to 101 pastors whose churches did not meet the effective church criteria. These are the leaders of the "comparison" churches noted throughout the book.

FOR OFFICE USE ONLY:

Date Received _____/_____/_____   Survey Number _____

Leadership Survey

The Billy Graham School of Missions, Evangelism and Church Growth

Please provide the following information.

I. BASIC CHURCH INFORMATION

Church Name _____

Street Address _____

City _____ State _____ Zip _____

Phone: **Day** (____) _____ **Evening** (____) _____

Fax (if applicable) (____) _____

Age of the church (the number of years the church has been in existence as a constituted body): _____ years

A. Please use the most recent church information from your records or minutes to complete the following questions. If your church does not keep records for the following categories, please estimate to the best of your ability.

   1. Average Sunday school or Bible study attendance   _____

   2. Average worship attendance   _____

   3. Total additions by baptisms or conversions   _____

B. Please provide the following geographic and demographic information about the church.

   4. Church setting:

     _____ a. Open country/rural area

     _____ b. Town (500 to 2,499 people)

     _____ c. Small city (2,500 to 9,999 people)

     _____ d. Medium city/downtown (10,000 to 49,999 people)

     _____ e. Medium city/suburbs (10,000 to 49,999 people)

     _____ f. Large city/downtown (50,000+ people)

     _____ g. Large city/suburbs (50,000+ people)

   5. Congregational demographics of resident membership **(use your best estimates):**

Race		Age		Economic Levels	
Caucasian	____%	Under 18	____%	Upper class	____%
African-		19–35	____%	Middle class	____%
American	____%	36–50	____%	Lower class	____%
Hispanic	____%	51–65	____%		
Asian	____%	66+	____%		
Other	____%				
	100 %		100 %		100 %

II. Senior Pastor Information

   6. Your name _____

   7. Your highest education level:

     _____ a. High school   _____ d. Seminary (doctoral)

     _____ b. College   _____ e. Seminary studies (no degree)

     _____ c. Seminary (master's)

8. Are you full-time?   Yes _____ No _____

9. How long have you served
   at the church?   Years _____ Months _____

10. Which of the following tasks do you find most exciting and challenging? Least exciting and challenging? Please mark **three** tasks in each column.

	Most Exciting	*Least Exciting*
a. Pastoral care	_____	_____
b. Preaching	_____	_____
c. Administration	_____	_____
d. Discipleship/training members	_____	_____
e. Evangelism	_____	_____
f. Building campaigns	_____	_____
g. Visitation	_____	_____
h. Goal setting	_____	_____
i. Committee meetings	_____	_____
j. Budgeting	_____	_____
k. Future planning	_____	_____
l. Staff leadership	_____	_____
m. Other: _____	_____	_____
_____	_____	_____

III. Family Issues and Time Management

11. Are you married?   Yes _____ No _____

12. How many children do you have?   Boys _____ Girls _____

13. Estimate the amount of time that you spend on each of the following activities in a given week.

   a. Pastoral care*   _____
   b. Sermon preparation   _____
   c. Church administration   _____
   d. Discipleship/training members   _____
   e. Personal evangelism   _____
   f. Prospect visitation**   _____
   g. Custodial duties   _____
   h. Committee meetings   _____

(continued on next page)

i. Personal Bible study	_____
j. Prayer	_____
k. Goal setting	_____
l. Staff meetings	_____
m. Accountability group	_____
n. Worship	_____
o. Family time	_____
p. Sleep	_____
q. Meals	_____
r. Other: _____	_____
_____	_____
_____	_____
_____	_____

* Includes counseling, hospital visits, weddings, funerals, etc.
** Includes personal evangelism visits listed in 13(e).

IV. Preaching and Communication

14. In how many total services do you preach
    in a given week? _____

15. How many **different** sermons do you preach
    in a given week? _____

16. For each of the following preaching styles, estimate the percentage
    of your sermons that reflect that style:

    _____% a. *Expository*. Primarily explanation or commentary on
    the biblical text; expounds the central idea of the text;
    often includes preaching through a book of the Bible.

    _____% b. *Topical*. Typically, a sermon built around a topic,
    with biblical application to the topic.

    _____% c. *Thematic*. Usually a series of sermons developed
    around a central theme or idea; does not typically
    involve preaching through a book of the Bible.

    _____% d. *Narrative*. Story form that, from the beginning to
    the end, develops the plot of the story as a theme; a
    biblical truth presented in parable form.

    _____% e. *Doctrinal*. A sermon or sermon series focused on a
    particular biblical teaching or doctrine.

17. Using the following scale, please rate the level of influence of each of these factors on the senior pastor's development **as an effective communicator or preacher**.

1	2	3	4	5
Not an Influence	A Slight Influence	An Important Influence	A Very Important Influence	The Most Important Influence

_____ a. Training in college or seminary

_____ b. Example of a mentor

_____ c. Participation in a conference or seminar

_____ d. Experience in church work

_____ e. Bible studies about effective communicators/preachers

_____ f. Books on effective communication/preaching

_____ g. A communications expert

_____ h. Other: _____

V. Theology and Evangelism

18. Which of the following best expresses your belief about God?

_____ a. God is the creator of an orderly world but does not now guide it or intervene in its course of affairs or the lives of individuals.

_____ b. Although God has and can act in history and communicate with persons directly, it is not something that happens very often.

_____ c. God is constantly at work in the world directing people, nations, and events.

19. Which of the following best expresses your view of the Bible?

_____ a. The Bible is the record of many different people's responses to God, some of which may be inspired, some of which may not be inspired.

_____ b. The Bible is the inspired Word of God, and its basic moral and spiritual teachings are clear and true, even if it does contain some human error.

_____ c. The Bible is completely true and without error in any part and is the ultimate standard for truth and practice.

20. Which of the following best expresses your belief about sin and salvation?

_____ a. I believe all people are inherently good, and to the extent sin and salvation have meaning at all, it has to do with people realizing or not realizing their human potential for good.

_____ b. Although people are sinful, all people participate in God's salvation regardless of how they live their life, even if they do not believe in God.

_____ c. All people are sinful and must believe in and ask for God's forgiveness through Jesus Christ to be saved.

_____ d. All people are sinful and if they are to be saved, they must earn it through a good life devoted to God.

21. Which of the following best expresses your view of evangelism?

_____ a. Evangelism is being the presence of Christ which brings peace on earth to all humankind by meeting mental, emotional, physical, social, and spiritual needs.

_____ b. Evangelism is proclaiming the message of salvation through Jesus Christ in such a way that the unbelievers who hear it will clearly understand it.

_____ c. Evangelism involves proclaiming the message of salvation through Jesus Christ in such a way that the unbelievers who hear it will clearly understand it, and it involves persuading the unbeliever to become a disciple of Jesus Christ and a responsible member of a local church.

22. Briefly describe your understanding of the senior pastor's role and responsibility in the area of personal evangelism.

VI. Spiritual Disciplines and Personal Character

23. Using the scale below, please designate the importance of each of the following disciplines and characteristics as they relate to your leadership in the local church.

1	2	3	4	5
Not Important at All	Only Slightly Important	Important	Very Important, but Not Essential	Essential

_____ a. Credibility

_____ b. Financial openness

_____ c. Leadership by example

_____ d. Personal holiness

_____ e. Vibrant prayer life

_____ f. Fasting

_____ g. Personal Bible study

_____ h. Confession of sin

_____ i. Scripture memorization

_____ j. Biblical knowledge

_____ k. Ability to institute change

_____ l. Education

_____ m. Personal organization

_____ n. Management skills

_____ o. Good communication skills

_____ p. Courage

_____ q. Personal evangelism

_____ r. Kindness

_____ s. Gratitude

_____ t. Charismatic personality

_____ u. Ability to cast vision

_____ v. Heart for pastoral care

_____ w. Other: _____

_____ x. Other: _____

24. Briefly describe how a pastor's character affects his ability as a leader.

VII. Leadership Style

25. Define *leadership* as you understand the term.

26. Using the following scale, please rate the level of influence of each of these factors on your **development as an effective leader**.

1	2	3	4	5
Not an Influence	A Slight Influence	An Important Influence	A Very Important Influence	The Most Important Influence

_____ a. Training in college or seminary

_____ b. Example of a mentor

_____ c. Participation in a leadership conference or seminar

_____ d. Experiences of failure in church work

_____ e. Experiences of success in church work

_____ f. Bible studies about effective leaders

_____ g. Books on leadership

_____ h. A leadership expert, such as John Maxwell

_____ i. Other: _____

A. Styles

27. Using the following scale, please indicate the level to which each of the following leadership styles characterizes you.

1	2	3	4	5
Not Characteristic at All	Only Slightly Characteristic	Characteristic	Very Characteristic, but Not Completely Characteristic	Completely Characteristic

_____ a. Task oriented—high interest in production and getting things done

_____ b. Relationship oriented—high interest in people, feelings, and fellowship

_____ c. Goal oriented—high interest in setting goals and pushing for completion

_____ d. Dream oriented—a lot of time spent dreaming big dreams with little worry for completion

_____ e. Knowledge oriented—leads by superior knowledge and understanding rather than by example

_____ f. Organization oriented—organized above all else, every detail checked

_____ g. Loner oriented—rather work alone and risk accomplishing little

_____ h. Team player oriented—must work in a group and be part of a team effort; leads primarily by example

_____ i. Delegator oriented—leads by assigning tasks in nearly every situation

_____ j. Suggestion oriented—leads by making suggestions to others

28. What one book, other than the Bible, has most influenced you?

_____

B. Change

29. Using the following scale, *circle the number* that best signifies your leadership style related to change.

1	2	3	4	5	6	7	8

Sustaining: Tends to work to preserve the status quo; little willingness to change	**Reactionary**: Responds to needs, willing to change, but typically addresses needs only when they become apparent	**Visionary**: Often recognizes needs before they are apparent to others; leads in planning to meet the needs; encourages change when needed

30. Briefly describe your steps/principles/policies for leading the church through change.

31. How does your church typically respond to a challenge to change?

_____ a. Usually unwilling to change, regardless of the issue.

_____ b. Very reluctant to change; changes grudgingly only when forced by circumstances.

_____ c. Reluctant to change; but will do so when adequate study, prayer, and leadership support the need to change; change typically occurs slowly.

_____ d. Open to change as long as adequate study, prayer, and leadership support the need to change.

_____ e. Willing to change simply because leadership suggests the change is necessary.

_____ f. Other: _____

C. Criticism

32. When criticism arises, briefly describe your process for resolution.

33. How does criticism typically affect you? (check as many as apply)

_____ a. I am a very "thin skinned" person. I tend to take most criticism personally.

_____ b. I get angry and defensive.

_____ c. Criticism rarely affects me personally. I try to deal with the issues and not the personalities.

_____ d. I react defensively and emotionally at first, but later I tend to deal with the issues rationally and calmly.

_____ e. I have difficulty not having bad feelings about my critics for some time.

_____ f. I simply ignore criticism.

_____ g. I tend to be selective in how I respond to criticism. Different critics and criticisms engender different responses.

_____ h. Other: _____

34. List the people to whom you go for counsel and advice when problems arise. (Note: Titles and/or relationships are all that is needed—NO NAMES PLEASE.) (i.e., personal friend, accountability partner, chairman of the deacons, etc.)

VIII. Other

35. Using the following scale, how would you rate your overall effectiveness as a leader? (Please circle the number that applies.)

1	2	3	4	5
Not Effective at All	Only Slightly Effective	Effective	Very Effective, but Not Completely Effective	Completely Effective

36 What do you feel to be your greatest strengths in the area of pastoral leadership?

37. What do you feel to be your greatest weaknesses in the area of pastoral leadership?

38. Name some specific leadership decisions you have made in your church that had a **positive** impact and result.

39. Name some specific leadership decisions you have made in your church that had a **negative** impact and result.

40. Which of the following describes your decision-making process? (check as many as apply)

_____ a. I tend to make decisions on my own with little consultation with others.

_____ b. I make decisions quickly and with confidence.

_____ c. I make decisions quickly with some level of fear.

_____ d. I tend to make decisions only after significant consultation with others.

_____ e. I do not like to make independent decisions; I prefer to get a consensus.

_____ f. I prefer for others to make key decisions.

_____ g. I tend to have my decision in mind, but I like to develop a consensus before implementing the decision.

_____ h. Other: _____

41. Do you regularly mentor other Christians? If so, please briefly explain your involvement.

42. Please make any other comments regarding leadership or your personal leadership style.

Thank you for your time and openness in responding to our questionnaire. We at the Billy Graham School of Missions, Evangelism and Church Growth at the Southern Baptist Theological Seminary pray that this information will be used to benefit many leaders and churches. Remember, all of this information is **confidential**. None will be released without your permission.

Follow-up Cluster Questions for Leaders of Effective Churches

We interviewed over the telephone or in person 63 of the 101 effective church leaders who responded to the eleven-page survey in appendix 2. The cluster questions are so named because each question often led to other issues.

Follow-up Cluster Questions for Leaders of Effective Churches

1. What issues did you rethink when completing this survey?
2. What surprises did you discover about yourself when completing this survey?
3. If you were able to start over in your leadership role, what would you do differently?
4. If you are/were in a mentoring role with a young "Timothy," what do/would you emphasize to him?
5. Share in general terms an example of some of your most difficult leadership experiences.
6. What are some key factors in your church reaching the unchurched?
7. How have you assimilated these formerly unchurched people?
8. What other leadership issues or issues related to reaching the unchurched can you share with us?

APPENDIX 4

Unchurched-Reaching Readiness Inventory

Answer each of the 50 statements about your church by circling one number. See the end of the inventory to evaluate your church.

1 = strongly disagree
2 = disagree
3 = uncertain
4 = agree
5 = strongly agree

1. Our church has a strong desire to reach lost and unchurched people. 1 2 3 4 5

2. Our church is *not* stuck on unnecessary traditions. 1 2 3 4 5

3. Many people in our church share their faith regularly. 1 2 3 4 5

4. Many people in our church develop relationships with unchurched people. 1 2 3 4 5

5. The people in our church are friendly to outsiders. 1 2 3 4 5

6. Our pastor has a passion to reach lost and unchurched people. 1 2 3 4 5

7. People in our church are very unified; they do *not* tend to argue over minor issues. 1 2 3 4 5

8. An unchurched person would feel
   comfortable in our worship services.   1   2   3   4   5

9. We have a very effective greeters' ministry
   that makes visitors feel welcome.   1   2   3   4   5

10. Our pastor communicates very well publicly. 1   2   3   4   5

11. There is a lot of joy and laughter in
    our church.   1   2   3   4   5

12. Very few, if any, people get upset when the
    order of worship is changed.   1   2   3   4   5

13. People in our church do *not* argue over
    music and worship styles. We simply
    desire to reach people.   1   2   3   4   5

14. Our worship services are exciting and joyous. 1   2   3   4   5

15. Our pastor's sermons teach us much about
    the Bible.   1   2   3   4   5

16. Our pastor's sermons are relevant to our
    needs, hurts, and desires.   1   2   3   4   5

17. Personal evangelism is a priority in
    our church.   1   2   3   4   5

18. An unchurched person would feel
    comfortable in our worship services.   1   2   3   4   5

19. New members, including new Christians
    can get involved in our church immediately. 1   2   3   4   5

20. We pray for lost and unchurched people
    by name.   1   2   3   4   5

21. The people in our church know clearly
    what the major purposes of the
    church are.   1   2   3   4   5

22. Our facilities are neat, attractive,
    and clean.   1   2   3   4   5

23. Our rest rooms are always clean and
    well-supplied.   1   2   3   4   5

24. Our grounds and landscaping are very neat.   1   2   3   4   5

25. We keep our facilities in good repair.   1   2   3   4   5

26. Our preschool and children's area is neat, clean, modern-looking, with relatively new equipment, toys, and furniture.   1   2   3   4   5

27. Our sanctuary/worship center would be very attractive to an unchurched person.   1   2   3   4   5

28. Our music in the worship services would be attractive to an unchurched person.   1   2   3   4   5

29. We have a very good Sunday school/or small groups organization.   1   2   3   4   5

30. Over one-half of our regular attenders are in a small group or Sunday School class.   1   2   3   4   5

31. We create new small groups or Sunday school classes to reach new people.   1   2   3   4   5

32. An unchurched person would feel comfortable in a small group or Sunday school class in our church.   1   2   3   4   5

33. Our church's doctrine is clear to anyone who visits our church.   1   2   3   4   5

34. The leaders and the people in our church have a high view of the Bible.   1   2   3   4   5

35. You can easily tell by our pastor's preaching that he has conviction about his beliefs.   1   2   3   4   5

36. We have attempted many things to reach the unchurched.   1   2   3   4   5

37. Our pastor is a visionary.   1   2   3   4   5

38. The people in our church accept change readily.   1   2   3   4   5

39. Our church is uncompromising on biblical issues.   1   2   3   4   5

40. We have an effective new members'/
    inquirers' class in our church.   1   2   3   4   5

41. The leadership expects much of our
    members and the members expect
    much of themselves.   1   2   3   4   5

42. Our members are willing to get
    uncomfortable to reach the unchurched.   1   2   3   4   5

43. Our small groups or Sunday School
    classes provide great opportunities to
    learn the Bible.   1   2   3   4   5

44. Our pastor relates well to people.   1   2   3   4   5

45. We do not have any significant
    "sacred cows" in our church.   1   2   3   4   5

46. We see many unchurched reached
    for Christ in our church.   1   2   3   4   5

47. New Christians in our church are given
    immediate opportunities to be trained
    in evangelism.   1   2   3   4   5

48. The people in our church seek to be
    involved in ministry.   1   2   3   4   5

49. I would describe our church as a place
    where a person could come to be in a
    healing atmosphere.   1   2   3   4   5

50. A significant portion of our church's
    growth comes from reaching the
    unchurched.   1   2   3   4   5

Add the points from all of the statements to determine your church's UR (unchurched-reaching potential).

Point Total	Rating
225-250	UR 1
200-224	UR 2
175-199	UR 3
150-174	UR 4
125-149	UR 5
50-124	UR 6

UR 1   Excellent potential to reach the unchurched. Your church is probably one of the top 2 percent evangelistic churches in the nation.

UR 2   Very good potential to reach the unchurched. Certain improvements could be made, but your church is well above average.

UR 3   Above average potential to reach the unchurched. The church should make several changes, however, to reach more people.

UR 4   Average potential to reach the unchurched. "Average" is not great in America, because it takes 85 church members in America to reach one person for Christ. Many changes are needed.

UR 5   Below average potential to reach the unchurched. Your church has *very many* changes to make if it is ever to become a church obedient to the Great Commission.

UR 6   Poor potential to reach the unchurched. The church is inwardly focused and its very existence is in jeopardy. A new vision and a new way of thinking is necessary. It is not merely that changes must be made; rather the entire church must change.

APPENDIX 5

Church Health Survey

The following survey is used by the Rainer Group, a church and denominational consultation firm, to help discern the overall health of the church in six major areas: worship, evangelism, discipleship, ministry, prayer, and fellowship. The results are scored and interpreted by the Rainer Group. For more information contact www.rainergroup.com.

To the leader of the church administering this survey:

The enclosed surveys are to be distributed to adult members who attend your church at least once a month. The number of survey responses needed are:

Worship Attendance	Minimum Surveys Needed
Less than 100	30
101–200	35
201–300	45
301–400	60
Greater than 400	15% of worship attendance

We make no claims that the results of this Church Health Survey will give you a complete picture of the state of your church. It will, however, help you to see the perceptions and attitudes of your members, a major step in the diagnosis of church health.

You will receive an analysis of the survey divided into the six major functions of the church:

Worship Evangelism Discipleship Ministry Prayer Fellowship

If you request, we can also look at the following subcategories: unity/conflict, leadership, beliefs, church planting, missions, and worship services.

Thank you!

> This questionaire is designed to help us discern strengths, weaknesses, attitudes, and perceptions in your church. It is merely a tool and makes no claim to provide a complete diagnosis of church health.
>
> Please answer every question by marking the appropriate block. Do not skip any questions. If you have any doubts, mark the answer that best represents your thoughts.
>
> Do not put your name on this questionaire. This tool will be treated with complete confidentiality.
>
> Thank you for taking the time to help your church and God's work.

Church Health Survey

1. What is your gender?

   ❑ Male   ❑ Female

2. What is your age?

   ❑ Less than 20   ❑ 20–29   ❑ 30–39   ❑ 40–49
   ❑ 50–59   ❑ 60–69   ❑ 70 and above

3. How long have you been a member of this church?

   ❑ Less than one year   ❑ 1 to 5 years   ❑ 6 to 10 years
   ❑ More than 10 years

4. How long have you been a Christian?

   ❑ Less than one year   ❑ 1 to 5 years   ❑ 6 to 10 years
   ❑ More than 10 years

5. How many hours on the average do you spend in *all* church activities and ministries each week?

   ❑ Less than one hour   ❑ 1 to 5 hours   ❑ 6 to 10 hours
   ❑ More than 10 hours

	Strongly Agree	Agree	Uncertain/ Undecided	Disagree	Strongly Disagree
1. When I come to my church, I truly sense that I have worshiped God.	❑	❑	❑	❑	❑
2. I am involved in regular Bible study in my church.	❑	❑	❑	❑	❑
3. Our church has an intercessory prayer ministry in which many people participate.	❑	❑	❑	❑	❑
4. People in our church share their faith regularly.	❑	❑	❑	❑	❑
5. We have several cliques in our church.	❑	❑	❑	❑	❑
6. Our church has a good youth ministry.	❑	❑	❑	❑	❑
7. I learn a lot about the Bible through the pastor's sermons.	❑	❑	❑	❑	❑
8. I am growing in maturity as a Christian in my church.	❑	❑	❑	❑	❑
9. The leadership in my church regularly emphasizes the importance of prayer.	❑	❑	❑	❑	❑
10. Our church supports missionaries generously.	❑	❑	❑	❑	❑
11. It is difficult to become a part of existing groups in our church.	❑	❑	❑	❑	❑
12. Our church has a good music ministry.	❑	❑	❑	❑	❑
13. The music in our worship services leads me to worship.	❑	❑	❑	❑	❑
14. Most of those who attend our church are involved in regular Bible study.	❑	❑	❑	❑	❑
15. In today's busy world, it is understandable that Christians cannot set aside thirty to sixty minutes a day for prayer.	❑	❑	❑	❑	❑

	Strongly Agree	Agree	Uncertain/ Undecided	Disagree	Strongly Disagree
16. Our church seeks to find ways to reach people in our community.	❑	❑	❑	❑	❑
17. The priority focus of the church should be meeting the needs of the members.	❑	❑	❑	❑	❑
18. Our church has a good preschool and children's ministry.	❑	❑	❑	❑	❑
19. There is disagreement among the members at our church about the type of music and worship style.	❑	❑	❑	❑	❑
20. New Christians are discipled immediately after conversion in our church.	❑	❑	❑	❑	❑
21. Before we attempt any major effort in our church, we bathe it in prayer.	❑	❑	❑	❑	❑
22. Visitors feel welcome in our church.	❑	❑	❑	❑	❑
23. People in our church are willing to start new groups and classes.	❑	❑	❑	❑	❑
24. Our church does a good job of ministering to different ages of adults.	❑	❑	❑	❑	❑
25. The pastor's sermons are relevant to my needs and real life situations.	❑	❑	❑	❑	❑
26. Children in our church have opportunities to grow in maturity as Christians.	❑	❑	❑	❑	❑
27. Our church prays for non-Christians by name.	❑	❑	❑	❑	❑
28. Our Sunday school classes or small groups seek to reach people outside of our groups.	❑	❑	❑	❑	❑
29. Our church has been recently involved in conflict between members.	❑	❑	❑	❑	❑

	Strongly Agree	Agree	Uncertain/ Undecided	Disagree	Strongly Disagree
30. When there is a need in our church, many people respond.	❏	❏	❏	❏	❏
31. We have a good way of greeting guests in our worship services.	❏	❏	❏	❏	❏
32. I would rate the level of knowledge of the Bible as high in our church.	❏	❏	❏	❏	❏
33. Prayer is a central facet of our worship services.	❏	❏	❏	❏	❏
34. Our church emphasizes church planting as a means of reaching people.	❏	❏	❏	❏	❏
35. A number of the people in our church are angry at one another.	❏	❏	❏	❏	❏
36. I believe the pastor (and staff) should do most of the ministry.	❏	❏	❏	❏	❏
37. I like the blend of music and worship styles in our worship services.	❏	❏	❏	❏	❏
38. Our Sunday school/small groups are very strong in Bible study.	❏	❏	❏	❏	❏
39. We have special prayer emphases in our church.	❏	❏	❏	❏	❏
40. Our church has been involved recently in starting a new church.	❏	❏	❏	❏	❏
41. We have unresolved conflicts in our church.	❏	❏	❏	❏	❏
42. I am regularly involved in doing ministry in our church.	❏	❏	❏	❏	❏
43. The worship service time and length is just right.	❏	❏	❏	❏	❏
44. We tend to lose members within a few months after they have joined.	❏	❏	❏	❏	❏

	Strongly Agree	Agree	Uncertain/ Undecided	Disagree	Strongly Disagree
45. Our church makes available to everyone a list of prayer needs.	❏	❏	❏	❏	❏
46. Our church sends people regularly to do mission work around the world.	❏	❏	❏	❏	❏
47. The people in our church enjoy being together.	❏	❏	❏	❏	❏
48. Most members in our church know their spiritual gifts.	❏	❏	❏	❏	❏
49. The length of the sermons is just right.	❏	❏	❏	❏	❏
50. Our church seems to lose more people than we gain.	❏	❏	❏	❏	❏
51. Prayer is an integral part of our Sunday school classes or small groups.	❏	❏	❏	❏	❏
52. We have a known plan for regularly reaching out in our community.	❏	❏	❏	❏	❏
53. I have fellowship or social times with church members outside of church activities at least once a quarter.	❏	❏	❏	❏	❏
54. Most members in our church use their spiritual gifts in ministry.	❏	❏	❏	❏	❏
55. Our sanctuary/worship center is a good facility in which to worship.	❏	❏	❏	❏	❏
56. I would describe the commitment level of the majority of our members as low.	❏	❏	❏	❏	❏
57. We pray regularly for world missions in our church.	❏	❏	❏	❏	❏
58. A church should meet the needs of its own members before it reaches to others.	❏	❏	❏	❏	❏

	Strongly Agree	Agree	Uncertain/ Undecided	Disagree	Strongly Disagree
59. New members are quickly invited to different groups in the church.	❏	❏	❏	❏	❏
60. Whenever a job needs to get done, many people in our church volunteer.	❏	❏	❏	❏	❏
61. I have trouble finding a parking place when I come to church.	❏	❏	❏	❏	❏
62. The people in our church understand the church's doctrine, what we believe.	❏	❏	❏	❏	❏
63. Our church regularly prays for the ministries of the church.	❏	❏	❏	❏	❏
64. A church should not start a new church until it has adequate surplus in the budget.	❏	❏	❏	❏	❏
65. Our church is unified.	❏	❏	❏	❏	❏
66. It is difficult for me to get involved in ministry in my church.	❏	❏	❏	❏	❏
67. I like the order in which we go through worship.	❏	❏	❏	❏	❏
68. New members receive good training and information when they join our church.	❏	❏	❏	❏	❏
69. I believe that it is vitally important to have people praying during the worship services.	❏	❏	❏	❏	❏
70. People who share their faith should have the gift of evangelism.	❏	❏	❏	❏	❏
71. One of the reasons I come to church is because I enjoy the fellowship of other members.	❏	❏	❏	❏	❏
72. It is difficult for new members to get involved in ministry in our church.	❏	❏	❏	❏	❏

	Strongly Agree	Agree	Uncertain/ Undecided	Disagree	Strongly Disagree
73. Our worship services are prayerful experiences.	❏	❏	❏	❏	❏
74. Our church does a very good job at discipling members.	❏	❏	❏	❏	❏
75. I pray for my pastor, the pastor's family, and the staff of our church regularly.	❏	❏	❏	❏	❏
76. I regularly attempt to establish relationships with people who do not have a church home.	❏	❏	❏	❏	❏
77. I believe my voice is heard in this church.	❏	❏	❏	❏	❏
78. Most of the ministry in our church is done by a small number of people.	❏	❏	❏	❏	❏
79. We have good participation in singing in our worship services.	❏	❏	❏	❏	❏
80. We have many people involved in one-on-one discipling or mentoring.	❏	❏	❏	❏	❏
81. Prayer meetings in our church are boring.	❏	❏	❏	❏	❏
82. Our church provides regular opportunities for evangelism training.	❏	❏	❏	❏	❏
83. There is a healthy relationship between the pastor (and other staff of the church) and the people.	❏	❏	❏	❏	❏
84. Our church members have freedom to be creative in ministry.	❏	❏	❏	❏	❏
85. A non-Christian would be comfortable in our worship services.	❏	❏	❏	❏	❏
86. I have grown as a Christian since I have been at this church.	❏	❏	❏	❏	❏
87. Prayer meetings in church tend to be gossip times.	❏	❏	❏	❏	❏

	Strongly Agree	Agree	Uncertain/ Undecided	Disagree	Strongly Disagree
88. I have at least a few friendships/relationships with people who are not Christians.	❏	❏	❏	❏	❏
89. Our church deals quickly with open, flagrant, and unrepentant sin of church members.	❏	❏	❏	❏	❏
90. I receive fulfillment by doing ministry in our church.	❏	❏	❏	❏	❏
91. I like all the elements of our worship services.	❏	❏	❏	❏	❏
92. People in our church are given good training on how to develop a prayer life and quiet time.	❏	❏	❏	❏	❏
93. When we pray in our church, nothing happens.	❏	❏	❏	❏	❏
94. Our church sees people accept Christ on a regular basis.	❏	❏	❏	❏	❏
95. I am a part of a group or class that attempts to reach other people.	❏	❏	❏	❏	❏
96. The leadership of our church does a good job of equipping people to do ministry.	❏	❏	❏	❏	❏
97. There are too many distractions in our worship services.	❏	❏	❏	❏	❏
98. People in our church are given many opportunities to learn how to share and defend their faith.	❏	❏	❏	❏	❏
99. We have a place in our church where many people pray each week.	❏	❏	❏	❏	❏
100. I believe you have to be called to be a lifetime missionary to do international missions.	❏	❏	❏	❏	❏

	Strongly Agree	Agree	Uncertain/ Undecided	Disagree	Strongly Disagree
101. I am excited to be a part of this church.	❏	❏	❏	❏	❏
102. Our church is strong in benevolence ministry.	❏	❏	❏	❏	❏
103. I have been to other churches, and I think our worship services are among the best.	❏	❏	❏	❏	❏
104. The lifestyles of the members at our church are significantly different than the world's lifestyle.	❏	❏	❏	❏	❏
105. I believe the Bible teaches that prayer should be a daily part of every Christian's life.	❏	❏	❏	❏	❏
106. I believe that one of the purposes of Sunday school classes or small groups is evangelism.	❏	❏	❏	❏	❏
107. Coming to church on a regular basis is becoming increasingly difficult for me.	❏	❏	❏	❏	❏
108. We reach many people in our church by ministering to them.	❏	❏	❏	❏	❏
109. The Holy Spirit uses our worship services to lead people to make decisions for God.	❏	❏	❏	❏	❏
110. I know what I believe as a Christian and why I believe it.	❏	❏	❏	❏	❏
111. I pray regularly during the day.	❏	❏	❏	❏	❏
112. Our church has a portion of its budget allocated for mission work around the world.	❏	❏	❏	❏	❏
113. The community outside of our church sees us as a very unified church.	❏	❏	❏	❏	❏

	Strongly Agree	Agree	Uncertain/ Undecided	Disagree	Strongly Disagree
114. Our church is willing to minister to people regardless of ethnic background.	❏	❏	❏	❏	❏
115. There is the right emphasis on money and stewardship in our worship services.	❏	❏	❏	❏	❏
116. The more mature Christians in our church have a strong desire to help the less mature Christians in our church.	❏	❏	❏	❏	❏
117. Our church communicates prayers that are answered to the people of the church.	❏	❏	❏	❏	❏
118. When I see a new person in our church, I make every effort to introduce myself to him/her.	❏	❏	❏	❏	❏
119. Our church has a good reputation in the community.	❏	❏	❏	❏	❏
120. People in our church have someone to turn to when they need counseling.	❏	❏	❏	❏	❏
121. People of non-Christian faiths can worship God in the same way Christians do.	❏	❏	❏	❏	❏
122. The Bible is the word of God, perfect as it was originally written.	❏	❏	❏	❏	❏
123. God intervenes regularly in the lives of Christians.	❏	❏	❏	❏	❏
124. The only way to heaven is through Christ.	❏	❏	❏	❏	❏
125. Because everyone is a sinner, we can only have fellowship with God through the shed blood of Jesus Christ.	❏	❏	❏	❏	❏

	Strongly Agree	Agree	Uncertain/ Undecided	Disagree	Strongly Disagree
126. God is three persons: the Father, the Son, and the Holy Spirit.	❏	❏	❏	❏	❏
127. A good person of another faith other than Christianity may go to heaven.	❏	❏	❏	❏	❏
128. Hell is a literal place.	❏	❏	❏	❏	❏
129. God is in total control of our world.	❏	❏	❏	❏	❏
130. Jesus is the Son of God.	❏	❏	❏	❏	❏

APPENDIX 6

Research Design and Statistical Review

Methodology

This research design/project follows the criteria for qualitative design. The assumptions regarding this design are closely related to the structure and intent of the qualitative approach. This study is an excellent example of research assumptions that require a design that is concerned with process rather than outcomes or products. Thus, the primary research interest is meaning and interpretation—how people make sense out of their experiences.

This researcher uses primary instruments for data collection and interpretation, and this researcher is more than adequately equipped to function in that role, as these data are rich in descriptive analysis and inductive interpretation. The design has three sources of comparative data for clarification of the research assumptions. Also, the data are accurately documented and interpreted within the best characteristics of the qualitative approach. This study is representative of the qualitative research guidelines found in R. C. Bogdan and S. K. Biklen, *Qualitative Research for Educators: An Introduction to Theory and Methods* (Boston: Allyn & Bacon, 1992); and C. Marshall and G. B. Rossman, *Designing Qualitative Research* (Newburg Park, Calif.: Sage, 1989).

Population and Sample

The parameters of the data collection are identified, and the purposeful sample is specified. The number of subjects more than adequately provides for the content accuracy of the results. The amount of data available for analysis gives confidence in the summary of the findings. Sample size

271

is not critical for qualitative research design; however, the number of subjects used of three groups in this study is more than sufficient for the design requirements. The use of triangulation as data collection and a group comparison tactic improves the validity considerably (S. Mathison, "Why Triangulate?" *Educational Research* 17, 2 [1989]: 13–17).

Survey Instrument

The rationale for this study justifies the survey method. The only alternative for extracting data is the survey interview approach. At the time of this research no other research instrument existed. The comprehensive interview generated the data necessary to explore the research assumptions. The researcher describes carefully his survey process in hopes that the next design for this topic can move to a combined qualitative and quantitative approach. Obviously, no cause-and-effect conclusions are inferred from this study. No generalization is attempted or implied (A. Fink, *How to Ask Survey Questions* [Thousand Oaks, Calif.: Sage, 1995]; R. Sapsford, *Survey Research* [Thousand Oaks, Calif.: Sage, 1999]).

Statistics

The data collected from this type of study can only be interpreted with descriptive statistical analyses. There are those researchers who feel only inferential analyses are worth pursuing; contrary to that position, these descriptive results are rich with meaning and interpretation findings. These research assumptions can only be approached with the explanations rendered in this study. The foci of findings are accurately and thoroughly presented. The amount of material is exhaustive, and this researcher has selected the results and presented those which most directly relate to the reading audience. However, several additional paths of explanation remain to be explored from the data. Some researchers underrate the effective use of descriptive statistics, but study demonstrates this analysis at its best productivity. The main purpose of the analyses is to reduce the whole collection of data to simple and more understandable terms without distorting or losing too much of the valuable information collected. Dr. Rainer has done extremely well in this respect (H. M. Blalock Jr., *Social Statistics*, 2d ed. [New York: McGraw-Hill, 1979]).

Reviewer's Note:

The need for research in this area is critical, and those like Dr. Rainer who begin to explore topics such as the one in this study begin a process of discovery that will prove productive in future research. I lend my affirmation of the helpful work accomplished in this study.

— Jon Rainbow
Research and Statistics Consultant
    Associate Professor of Christian
    Education and Leadership
The Southern Baptist Theological Seminary
    Louisville, Kentucky

Notes

INTRODUCTION: Meet Donna and Joe

1. From research conducted for my *The Bridger Generation* (Nashville: Broadman & Holman, 1997).

2. "Church Attendance," *Barna Research Online*, www.barna.org, October 15, 1999.

3. See some of the results of these studies in Thom S. Rainer, *Effective Evangelistic Churches* (Nashville: Broadman & Holman, 1996), and Thom S. Rainer, *High Expectations* (Nashville: Broadman & Holman, 1999).

4. See appendix 6 for a research evaluation by Jon Rainbow.

CHAPTER 1: Shattering Myths about the Unchurched

1. "Church Attendance," *Barna Research Online*, www.barna.org, October 15, 1999.

2. Ibid.

3. See Thom S. Rainer, *The Bridger Generation* (Nashville: Broadman & Holman, 1997).

4. Brad Edmondson, "Unclaimed by God," *American Demographics*, www.demographics.com, August 1995.

5. Ibid.

6. "How Americans See Themselves," *Barna Research Online*, www.barna.org, May 27, 1998.

7. Ibid.

8. "Church Attendance."

9. "One Out of Three Adults Is Now Unchurched," *Barna Research Online*, www.barna.org, February 25, 1999.

10. See particularly Thom S. Rainer, *Effective Evangelistic Churches* (Nashville: Broadman & Holman, 1996).

11. Lee Strobel, *Inside the Mind of Unchurched Harry and Mary* (Grand Rapids: Zondervan, 1992).

12. "One Out of Three Adults Is Now Unchurched."

13. "Church Attendance."

14. See my book *High Expectations* (Nashville: Broadman & Holman, 1999), for the story of my paradigm shift in my attitude about Sunday school. See also Ken Hemphill, *Revitalizing the Sunday Morning Dinosaur* (Nashville: Broadman & Holman, 1997), for an excellent overview of the resurgence of Sunday school.

15. See Rainer, *Bridger Generation,* and George Barna, "Teens and Adults Have Little Chance of Accepting Christ as Their Savior," *The Barna Report,* October–December 1999.

CHAPTER 2: Pastors and Preaching Are Critical

1. See Thom S. Rainer, *Effective Evangelistic Churches* (Nashville: Broadman & Holman, 1997), especially chapter 3.

2. Rick Warren, *The Purpose-Driven Church* (Grand Rapids: Zondervan, 1995).

3. Thom S. Rainer, *High Expectations* (Nashville: Broadman & Holman, 1999), 6.

CHAPTER 3: Relationships That Click

1. George Barna, "What People Say They Want From a Church," *The Barna Report,* April–June 1999, 10–11.

2. Ibid.

3. Ibid.

4. Ibid.

5. Ibid.

6. Ibid.

7. W. Charles Arn, *How to Reach the Unchurched Families in Your Community* (Monrovia, Calif.: Church Growth, n.d.).

8. See Thom S. Rainer, *Effective Evangelistic Churches* (Nashville: Broadman & Holman, 1996), 25.

CHAPTER 4: Impressed by First Impressions

1. Lyle E. Schaller, *The Very Large Church* (Nashville: Abingdon, 2000), 79.

2. Ibid., 87.

3. Bob Russell with Rusty Russell, *When God Builds a Church* (West Monroe, La.: Howard, 2000), 113–14.

4. Ibid., 112.

5. Ibid., 113.

6. Cited in Stan Toler and Alan Nelson, *The Five Star Church* (Ventura, Calif.: Regal, 1999), 59.

CHAPTER 5: Why They Returned and Stayed

1. George Barna, *The Barna Report,* April–June 1999, 1.

2. Ibid., 2.

3. The research project on the churches is published in Thom S. Rainer, *High Expectations* (Nashville: Broadman & Holman, 1999).

4. Printed materials are readily available, announcements are made on a big screen, and the pastor's sermons consistently communicate high expectations.

5. The calculation of the retention ratio in a given year is as follows: worship attendance in year x minus worship attendance in year x–1 divided by total number of new members attending in year x.

6. George Barna, "More Than Twenty Million Churched Adults Actively Involved in Spiritual Growth Efforts," *Barna Research Online,* www.barna.org, May 9, 2000.

7. Barna, *The Barna Report,* 3.

8. Barna, *The Barna Report,* 1.

CHAPTER 6: Doctrine Really Matters

1. Billy Graham, *Just As I Am* (San Francisco and Grand Rapids: HarperSanFrancisco and Zondervan, 1997), 135–40.

2. Ibid., 135.

3. Ibid., 136.

4. Ibid., 138.

5. Ibid., 139.

6. Ibid. Italics in original.

7. Ibid.

8. George Barna, "What People Say They Want from a Church," *The Barna Report,* April–June 1999, 10–11.

CHAPTER 7: A Profile of the Unchurched-Reaching Leaders

1. Based on our surveys of 2,071 pastors in America representing fourteen denominations and nondenominational backgrounds.

2. This study was published in Thom S. Rainer, *Effective Evangelistic Churches* (Nashville: Broadman & Holman, 1996). The average tenure of pastors in this study was 10.2 years, and 7.3 years for pastors of effective Southern Baptist churches. See specifically page 44.

CHAPTER 8: What Makes These Leaders Tick?

1. *Southeast Outlook,* November 11, 1999, B-1.

2. The percentages cited in the second half of this chapter were derived from an open-ended question: "What have you learned the most about reaching the unchurched?" No objective instrument was used. The lead-

ers could respond to this question with few constraints; multiple responses were thus the norm.

3. See Thom S. Rainer, *The Bridger Generation* (Nashville: Broadman & Holman, 1997).

4. See Thom S. Rainer, *High Expectations* (Nashville: Broadman & Holman, 1999).

CHAPTER 9: Raising Leadership Issues

1. See "Top Ten Reasons to Attend a Church Service" in "Church Attendance," *Barna Research Online*, www.barna.org, October 13, 1999.

2. Ibid.

3. John Maxwell, *Developing the Leader within You* (Nashville: Thomas Nelson, 1993), 1.

4. See George Barna, *The Power of Vision* (Ventura, Calif.: Regal Books, 1992), 27.

CHAPTER 10: An Honest Look at Their Personal Strengths and Weaknesses

1. See Bob Russell, *When God Builds a Church* (West Monroe, La.: Howard, 2000), for further insights into Pastor Russell's leadership skills.

2. James C. Collins and Jerry I. Porras, *Built to Last* (New York: HarperBusiness, 1994), chap. 5.

3. Thom S. Rainer, *Eating the Elephant* (Nashville: Broadman & Holman, 1994).

CHAPTER 11: Preaching That Connects with the Unchurched

1. See Thom S. Rainer, *Effective Evangelistic Churches* (Nashville: Broadman & Holman, 1996), 1.

CONCLUSION: To Become a Church for the Unchurched

1. Lyle Schaller, *The Very Large Church* (Nashville: Abingdon, 2000). See chapters 4 and 5 for a great narrative on these categories of pastors.

2. Ibid., 117.

3. Ibid., 116.

4. Ibid., 118.

5. Ibid., see 121–124.

6. Ibid., 125.

Name and Subject Index

About the Author

Thom S. Rainer is the founding dean of the Billy Graham School of Missions, Evangelism and Church Growth at the Southern Baptist Theological Seminary in Louisville, Kentucky. He is also one of the leading church consultants in the nation and serves as president of the Rainer Group, a leading North American church and denominational consulting firm. Dr. Rainer has authored seven books and has coauthored or edited another five books. He is the proud father of three sons, Sam, Art, and Jess, and the grateful husband of Nellie Jo.

We want to hear from you. Please send your comments about this book to us in care of the address below. Thank you.

GRAND RAPIDS, MICHIGAN 49530

www.zondervan.com